THE JIGSAW PUZZLE

THE
JIGSAW
PUZZLE

Piecing Together a History

Anne D. Williams

BERKLEY BOOKS, NEW YORK

THE BERKLEY PUBLISHING GROUP
Published by the Penguin Group
Penguin Group (USA) Inc.
375 Hudson Street, New York, New York 10014, USA
Penguin Group (Canada), 10 Alcorn Avenue, Toronto, Ontario M4V 3B2, Canada
(a division of Pearson Penguin Canada Inc.)
Penguin Books Ltd., 80 Strand, London WC2R 0RL, England
Penguin Group Ireland, 25 St. Stephen's Green, Dublin 2, Ireland (a division of Penguin Books Ltd.)
Penguin Group (Australia), 250 Camberwell Road, Camberwell, Victoria 3124, Australia
(a division of Pearson Australia Group Pty. Ltd.)
Penguin Books India Pvt. Ltd., 11 Community Centre, Panchsheel Park, New Delhi—110 017, India
Penguin Group (NZ), Cnr. Airborne and Rosedale Roads, Albany, Auckland 1310, New Zealand
(a division of Pearson New Zealand Ltd.)
Penguin Books (South Africa) (Pty.) Ltd., 24 Sturdee Avenue, Rosebank, Johannesburg 2196,
South Africa

Penguin Books Ltd., Registered Offices: 80 Strand, London WC2R 0RL, England

This book is an original publication of The Berkley Publishing Group.

Earlier versions of some sections of this book have appeared in magazines (*Collector, Country Home, Early American Homes, Ephemera Journal, Game and Puzzle Collectors Quarterly*) and the author's exhibit catalogs (*Cutting A Fine Figure: The Art of the Jigsaw Puzzle*, 1996, and *The Art of the Puzzle: Astounding and Confounding*, 2000) and book (*Jigsaw Puzzles: An Illustrated History and Price Guide*, 1990).

First edition: November 2004

Library of Congress Cataloging-in-Publication Data

Williams, Anne D. (Anne Douglas), 1943–
    The jigsaw puzzle : piecing together a history / Anne D. Williams.—1st ed.
        p. cm.
    Includes bibliographical references and index.
    ISBN 0-425-19820-0
    1. Jigsaw puzzles—History.   I. Title.

GV1507.J5W554   2004
793.73—dc22

2004048995

PRINTED IN THE UNITED STATES OF AMERICA

10   9   8   7   6   5   4   3   2   1

For my father, Elwood Williams III
(1914–1982)
I am still trying to master the lessons he so lovingly taught.

Contents

Acknowledgments

This book is based on more than twenty years of research into the history of jigsaw puzzles. It would not have been possible without the help I have received from hundreds of individuals and organizations. I am very grateful to all of them. Here I name those who have made direct contributions to the present volume. Many more have helped along the way, but their stories did not fit in and must wait for the next book.

Scores of former jigsaw puzzle makers and their descendants have dug deep into their memories and files to help me fill in the pieces of the historical picture. Special thanks go to: the late Catherine L. Allen, Louise Barnard, Randolph Barton, Miles Bickelhaupt Jr., John Blythe, Bill Brewer, Ed Brewer, Marion Brooks, James L. Browning, Elizabeth Carlhian, Jim Carr, the late Ruth Clapp, Grace Cobb, Irene Cormier, the late Helen Fiss Corson, Helen Finnegan, the late Beatrice Dodge, the late Victoria Dodge, Jack Donahue, Irénée du Pont Jr., Bernard Einson, Patricia Eldredge, Angie Gagnon, the late Eva Gagnon, Margaret Gallagher, William Jefferys Jr., Herbert Kavet, the late Alice Kern, Katherine and Robert Lewin, John Madden, the late Harry Manning, Henry A. Martin Jr., Helen Mitchell, Mary-Lou Jones Palmer, Joan Piccolo, Madeleine B. Pritchard, Lorraine Riley, John Robrock, Nancy Rudman, David Russell, the late Eleanor Scherer, Don Scott, the late Roger Slattery, Ted Squires, Charlotte Stevens, the late Amy

Straus, the late Carroll A. Towne, the late Frank Ware, the late Towner K. Webster Jr., and the late Lora Willey.

I have also received valuable assistance from current jigsaw puzzle manufacturers. They have generously supplied catalogs and extensive information about the state of the industry. Notable contributions have come from: James C. Ayer, Ed Babski, Nancy Ballhagen, Mark Cappitella, George Ciesek, Eden Scott Detrick, Pat Duncan, Bob Fitting, Bob Gibson, Carol Glazer, Marcia Joslin, James Leith, Mary Ann Lombard, Michael Mandato, Mark Morris, Steve Richardson, Anne Ross, John Santanella, Margaret Schrumpf, Betsy Stuart, and Ronda Tidrick.

I have been extremely fortunate to teach at Bates College, which has supported my research in so many ways. The librarians have guided me to useful sources and located obscure references through a marvelous interlibrary loan system. The Bates College Museum of Art mounted the first major exhibition of jigsaw puzzles in the United States in 1988. In conjunction with that exhibition, I had the privilege of teaching an Elderhostel course devoted to jigsaw puzzles. Bates has awarded me several grants (including ones funded by Roger C. Schmutz, Kathleen Curry Akers, and the Mellon Foundation) to cover travel to major libraries across the country and some other expenses of preparing this book. Dozens of my colleagues at Bates have provided gracious, patient, and expert assistance as I have sought to understand the relationship of puzzles to history, culture, technology, and more. Scholars elsewhere have helped as well. I am particularly grateful to Marlene Barron, Betty A. Ford, John J. Fox, Nancy Maldonado, and Jerome Singer.

I have developed enormous respect, admiration, and gratitude for the librarians and archivists who work so hard and so well to preserve the past and make it accessible to researchers. They have provided dedicated service and invaluable resources wherever I have gone, from the great Library of Congress to the smallest local historical societies that must rely entirely on volunteers. I have also benefited from the foresight of companies such as Parker Brothers, which maintained detailed historical records through the decades, even though the company's archives had no apparent relevance to the current balance sheet.

Museums have been another vital resource. Curators of many institutional collections have welcomed my visits and taken the time to bring puzzles out of storage so I could study them. I greatly appreciate the initiative and expertise of the National Heritage Museum in Lexington, Massachusetts, and the Katonah Museum of Art in Katonah, New York, in organizing comprehensive exhibitions of puzzles in 1996 and 2000 respectively. They have helped to increase awareness of jigsaw puzzle history and brought me contacts from people that I would never have met otherwise.

I am grateful to the numerous dealers who have found homes for old jigsaw puzzles so that they are preserved. Also to the individuals, from close relatives to total strangers, who have generously donated puzzles and other research materials that have added to my knowledge of puzzle history.

Fellow collectors have shared their puzzles and their knowledge generously. I have learned much from members of the Association of Game and Puzzle Collectors and the Benevolent Confraternity of Dissectologists, as well as from eBay sellers and other users who were willing to share their treasures after they outbid me. My thanks for specific information that aided this book go to: Bob Armstrong, Betty and Bill Barnard, David and Patsy Beffa-Negrini, Geert Bekkering, John Blythe, the late Anna Boardman, Bob Cole, Verl Cook, Paul Davis, the late Lee Dennis, Pinney Deupree, Pagey Elliott, Ron Fink, Robert L. Fisher, Don Friedman, Steve Guardino, Judy Gehman, Mark Geis, Geraldine Goodwin, Jerry Guiles, Gordon Hayter, Rosemary Howbrigg, Dave and Nanny Howland, Grace Linscott, Joyce Magee, Lynn Mankin, Chris McCann, Jim McWhorter, Penny Melling, Peggy Mithoefer, Dave Oglesby, Steve Olin, Philip Orbanes, Sharon and Todd Pattison, Jim Phelan, Jo Ann Reister, Harry Rinker, Jim Rohacs, John Seymour, Joe Seymour, Melinda Shebell, Will Shortz, the late Herbert Siegel, Jerry Slocum, Charles and Sharon Small, Mildred and John Spear, Susan Stock, Annabelle Thompson, Jay Thompson, Gus and Marty Trowbridge, Harry and Jean Walker, Bruce Whitehill, Liz and Dick Wilmes, and Wayne Wolf.

I owe special thanks to Senior Editors Kim Lionetti and Allison McCabe, and to the others at The Berkley Publishing Group who have transformed my manuscript into final form. Before that, Helen Andrews, Sally McGinty, and Bryce Wolf read the draft and did much to improve it. They and other close friends have aided and abetted my passion for jigsaws and accompanied me on many puzzling journeys and discoveries.

My most steadfast and enthusiastic supporters have been my family. Various aunts and uncles have tracked down the answers to puzzle questions for me and provided accommodations when I was researching nearby. My siblings, Libby and James, tuned into jigsaws years ago. They are always delighting me by finding puzzling items that I have never seen before. Most important, my late parents always gave me love, encouragement, and support for whatever I wished to attempt.

Finally, the history of jigsaw puzzles is a work in progress. Many pieces still elude me. Some have yet to find their proper place in the overall image. And surely a few are in the wrong places. I welcome additions and corrections from readers who can help complete the picture.

Anne D. Williams
Lewiston, Maine
May 2004

Foreword

BY WILL SHORTZ

Someday I'd like to read a really well-researched study on why people do puzzles—and why some of us are more obsessed with them than others.

As a professional crossword editor and puzzlemaker, who spends part of his spare time solving others' puzzles for fun, obviously my obsession runs deeper than most. I don't limit myself to words either. Almost any puzzle will do—jigsaw, mathematical, logical, mystery, mechanical, etc. Put a teasing challenge in front of me and I'm happy.

I've always suspected there's a genetic predisposition to puzzling. This is the only explanation for my interest, since no one ever taught me. My maternal grandmother, whom I never met, was addicted to crosswords in the mid-1920s, I'm told, during the great crossword craze. The puzzle gene skipped a generation (my mother) and completely bypassed my brother and sister, but manifested itself full-blown in me.

Like almost every family in America, when I was growing up we occasionally solved jigsaw puzzles together. To be precise, we'd lay out the five hundred or so pieces together on a card table. We'd complete the border and part of the design. Around 10 P.M. everyone but me would get tired and go to bed, while I'd stay up to put in "just a few more pieces." Bothered by the incompleteness of the picture, and unable to stop, I'd keep working until 3 or 5 A.M., or however long it would take me to finish. When the others would arise before me in the morning, the puzzle would be done.

Puzzles aren't just a way to kill time, as many think. In my experience, the most avid puzzlers are often people with the least amount of discretionary time. Somehow busy people feel compelled to break their usual busyness with a different kind of busyness. This is their definition of "rest." Bill Clinton, the epitome of busyness, is said to solve six to eight crosswords a week, and his assistants pack his "beloved" puzzles for him to take on every trip.

In my case, I like the satisfaction that comes from seeing a difficult challenge through from beginning to end. This is a feeling we don't experience much in everyday life, because a) most of life's challenges don't have definitive solutions, and b) as individuals we're usually not completely responsible for anything anyway.

I also like the soothing mental process of puzzle solving, the creativity necessary to finding a clever answer, the sense that I'm matching wits with another human being, and the knowledge and insights I gain along the way. These pleasures apply to puzzles of all varieties.

Anne D. Williams, whom I've known for more than fifteen years, and who is the world's foremost expert on jigsaw puzzles, has her own theories on puzzle solving, which she discusses in this book. She also traces the history of jigsaw puzzles here and describes their culture in greater depth than has ever been done before.

Anne probably has the largest collection of antique jigsaw puzzles in the world, which she draws on for her work. Without doubt she has spent more time researching jigsaw puzzle history than anyone else, reading obscure articles on the subject at many libraries, seeking out and interviewing noted puzzle cutters from the 1920s to the present, and compiling a gigantic index of every American jigsaw puzzle manufacturer she can find a record of.

Then she organizes this information by topic and writes entertainingly about her discoveries. Her historical articles on jigsaw puzzles appear in almost every issue of *Game Times,* the publication of the Association of Game and Puzzle Collectors, to which Anne and I both belong.

This book is the synthesis of years of Anne's collecting and study. If you like puzzles at least a tenth as much as I do, you're in for a treat.

—Will Shortz

Preface

I do not remember exactly when I put my first jigsaw puzzle together, but it must have been when I was very young. My mother loved puzzles. During World War II, when I was a toddler and my father was a naval lieutenant in the Pacific, she regularly rented jigsaws from Womrath's bookstore on the upper east side of Manhattan.

As I grew up, puzzles were an integral part of our family life. On rainy weekends or vacation days, my mother would get us kids out of her hair and at the same time keep us entertained by sending us off to do puzzles. At holiday gatherings, we invariably put together a large jigsaw. I remember vividly my mix of pleasure and impatience during the seemingly interminable ritual that preceded the puzzling. We had to set up the card tables, place the floor lamps around them just so, and, at my mother's insistence, turn all the pieces face up before we could start joining them together.

As a special treat, once every six years or so, my mother would bring out "Alice in Wonderland," an awesome 1,000-piecer that her parents had owned. The lovely Alice with a flock of rabbits, made from a print by Fred Morgan, inspired both fear and excitement. She was much too difficult for any of us to tackle alone. But the joint family effort was always worth it, as Alice and her companions gradually took shape against the soft green forest background.

Our family had a decided preference for wooden puzzles. The pieces had a heft to them, and they made a satisfying thwack when pressed into place. They were harder to ruin than flimsy cardboard ones. They did not bend or break, and the clatter they made when falling on the floor kept them from getting lost. Our favorite puzzles contained enchanting figure pieces shaped like birds, boats, butterflies, ballerinas, and the like. And even in the contours of ordinary puzzle pieces, our imaginations concocted outlines of ducks, dogs or other creatures.

My mother was the quickest puzzler, while my father mostly kibitzed. My two siblings and I would plug away at fitting in the pieces, sidetracked by periodic squabbles about who got to do the red pieces, or who had to work where the glare from the lamp was worst, and, of course, who got to put in the last piece.

The disappearance of wooden jigsaws from most department stores in the late 1960s forced us to settle for cardboard puzzles. But they were not really the same. Ten years later, after a few false starts, I learned how to cut a passable wooden jigsaw puzzle from scratch. I found that cutting pieces was just as satisfying, though in a different way, as putting them together. For a while, I even toyed with the idea of ending my career as an educator and becoming a commercial jigsaw puzzle manufacturer.

Then, in 1980, I discovered that old wooden puzzles still lurked in flea markets, often selling at ridiculously low prices. On my first foray to one of the largest, Renninger's Spring Extravaganza in Kutztown, Pennsylvania, I struck gold at a furniture dealer's booth. For $10 I bought three complete wooden puzzles that he had found in a bureau drawer. This find convinced me that hunting for puzzles would be both easier and more fun than slaving away for hours over a hot scroll saw to cut them.

When the family puzzles passed to me a few years later, I realized that what my mother had always viewed as an accumulation was actually a full-blown collection. It numbered almost one hundred wooden puzzles, even though she had given away dozens of puzzles over the years and had thrown out most of the ones with missing pieces. So with such a fine collection, why did I feel the need to add to it, to the point where I now own an embarrassingly large number of puzzles? (If I were to stop buying them today, it would take *at least* a year to finish putting together all the recent acquisitions in the backlog pile.)

One reason is that the puzzle images, which reflect the interests and pre-occupations of their times, fascinate me. They offer glimpses of the past that tease me into digging deeper. I have learned an eclectic assortment of tid-bits: titles and casts of the most popular movies of 1933, names of Civil War generals, and brand names of long-forgotten patent medicines and other consumer products. Who would have guessed that "Chicken Dinner" was the name of a popular candy bar in the 1930s? My colleagues at Bates College regularly help me sort out historical puzzles: how shifting political boundaries can date dissected maps, the symbolism of a puzzle made from a cartoon of the Spanish-American War, and the identity of David Levine caricatures on a *New York Review of Books* puzzle. I am grateful to them and to friends and scholars elsewhere for teaching me so much about popular culture, technology, and art of the past.

I am also entranced by the variety of old jigsaw puzzles: the creativity and intricacy of them. Early puzzle makers did not limit themselves to the grid-like patterns that typify today's puzzles. As I admired the craft and artistry of the early puzzles, I realized that each individual cutter had brought both skill and imagination to the task. When I first encountered a puzzle with an irregular edge and pieces cut on the color lines, I remember it had me stumped for hours. After finally finishing it, I wanted to know more about Marjorie Bouvé, the cutter who had played all those tricks on me.

The tales behind the puzzles are much more elusive than the puzzles themselves. A few stories have fallen into my lap when sellers, friends, and other aficionados have supplied contacts or clues. But most require long hours of detective work. Starting with the name and address on the box, I search old city directories, current phone books, microfilmed newspapers, and the Internet. On dozens of occasions I have been able to locate and in-terview people who had made jigsaw puzzles, or their surviving relatives.

The stories are fascinating and have been generously shared. Harry Manning, at the age of 96, related his clear memories of Parker Brothers in 1908. His first job there as a teenager was to sand "Pastime" puzzles and do personal errands for founder George S. Parker. Helen Fiss Corson filled me in about a noncommercial puzzle maker of that period. She had carefully saved her grandfather Fiss's puzzles and the notebook where he recorded when various friends and relatives borrowed them. Cal Towne told me how his wife had fended off the tax collector as he struggled to supplement his income by cutting jigsaw puzzles in the 1930s. And Mary-Lou Jones Palmer recalled her parents' selling their "Falls" puzzles to English royalty.[1]

Related stories are those of the puzzle owners, how they used and cherished their puzzles. Fragments can appear on the boxes. Many bear inscriptions that recount the puzzle's history: who assembled it, how long it took, comments about its quality and difficulty, condition reports about lost pieces, the date, and sometimes even a weather report for that day. The best puzzles progressed through the hands of many family members and friends.

One particularly intriguing tale came with a 1908 Milton Bradley "Perfection" puzzle, 400 noninterlocking and color-line-cut pieces of a river scene at dusk. Someone had turned the puzzle over and written a number on the back of each piece, going consecutively across the rows, from 1 to 400. A handwritten note in the box reads:

> This belonged to father. In his memory Bennie and I put it together each New Year's.

I have always wondered about the writer. Was it a son or a daughter? Did this child inherit father's enthusiasm for dark, difficult puzzles? Was the annual remembrance of father so tedious that, in desperation, he or she (or Bennie) numbered the pieces to speed up their New Year's ritual? Or had they numbered the pieces to assist a new generation of puzzlers, still too young to assemble this jigsaw, yet eager to help out? The answer to this particular puzzle continues to tease and elude me.

As I morphed into a collector of stories, as well as puzzles, I realized that I was accumulating a treasure trove of social, cultural, and economic history. I needed to preserve these tales of American jigsaw puzzles and the craftspeople who created them. At first I thought this would be a straightforward task. Surely there could be only a few dozen puzzle makers at most, right?

I could not have been more wrong. After twenty-five years of research, I have identified more than 5,500 brands of jigsaw puzzles made by American craftspeople and companies before 1971. Additional makers, who were pre-

In her youth the author favored jigsaw puzzles, a blue teddy bear, and books as companions between bath and bedtime.
Photo by Jessie P. Williams

viously unknown, are continually surfacing. Sometimes a puzzle is the only evidence that remains of a company's existence. I am now convinced that I will never find out about all the manufacturers. Thus, the quest to document the history of the American jigsaw puzzle has become my metapuzzle.

This book presents some of that history to a broad audience of puzzle aficionados. Although I discuss the origins of the jigsaw puzzle in Europe and some worldwide trends in puzzling today, the focus is on the American jigsaw puzzle. The chapters cover every dimension of jigsaw puzzles in the United States, from their introduction in the eighteenth century to the present day.

A note to readers who also enjoy word, math, logic, and mechanical puzzles: In the chapters that follow, "puzzle" refers to jigsaw puzzle, unless otherwise specified. I hope that you, as well as the many puzzlers who concentrate on jigsaws, will find much to interest you in this book.

Happy puzzling!

Anne D. Williams
Lewiston, Maine
May 2004

1

Bringing Order
out of Chaos

OOH, THAT WAS TRICKY!

© John Springer Collection/Corbis

In this scene from Citizen Kane, the immense unfinished jigsaw puzzle symbolizes the boring, shallow, and lonely life of Kane's showgirl wife.

Queen Elizabeth, Bill Gates, Stephen King, Albert Einstein, Barbara Bush, virtually every preschooler in America, and millions more—how can they all fit naturally into the same sentence? They all love jigsaw puzzles.

Despite competition from today's glitzy electronic and multimedia entertainment, the jigsaw puzzle is still going strong as it approaches the 250th anniversary of its birth. It originated in the mid-1700s as an educational device. The "dissected map" taught geography to children as they pieced countries together. From those origins the puzzle went forward to cut-up pictures, first for children, and later for grown-ups.

Today the world of jigsaw puzzles encompasses everything from two-piecers for infants to 18,000-piece monsters for adults with a spare year or two on their hands. They come in cardboard, wood, plastic, rubber, and foam, as well as exotic materials such as silver and chocolate. Puzzle subjects include cartoon characters, photographs, fine art, and advertising messages. Three-dimensional jigsaws have joined traditional flat ones. Novelty puzzles serve as postcards, games, detective stories, candy, and music makers. There are even electronic ones—not very tactile, but at least the computer never loses any pieces.

How has the jigsaw puzzle evolved over the last two and a half centuries, in the face of changing culture and technology? What does the history of puzzling reveal about society, both today and in the past? And why are so many people smitten with jigsaw puzzles?

The Allure of the Puzzle

On the face of it, a jigsaw puzzle is a ridiculous exercise in make-work and wasted time. The manufacturer takes a perfectly good picture, glues it to a backing, chops it into small bits, and tosses them into a box. The puzzler then spends hours sorting and joining the pieces back together, risking backache and eyestrain. To compound the absurdity, the box top shows the picture. Assembly is totally unnecessary unless, of course, the puzzler wants to glue the bits back together and preserve the picture. But then why not just buy the picture in the first place and skip the mutilation and the other intermediate steps?[1]

One answer comes from a *New York Times* feature written at the peak of America's greatest puzzle craze, during the Great Depression of the 1930s:

> The jig-saw appeals to the creative sense. Here is a mass of material, in itself meaning nothing. A man starts placing it together, and soon finds that he is building something, that something is growing under his eyes by the labor of his hands. If he is a real fan, and has not looked at the picture of the completed puzzle, he knows not what he is making; he is venturing into uncharted seas, seeking the known from the unknown.[2]

The visual and pictorial elements are crucial to the jigsaw puzzle. A piece's colors, patterns, and shape give clues to where it might fit. Joining the pieces that make a face is a small triumph that spurs the puzzler on to find the rest of the figure. As sections emerge, the puzzler savors those parts of the picture. Finally, the end result is a completed picture to admire and enjoy.

Handling the individual pieces reveals intriguing details that escape notice when viewing the picture as a whole, and thus yields insight into the mind of the artist.[3] Furthermore, many puzzles contain miniature treasures. Figure pieces shaped like birds, animals, and other recognizable silhouettes attest to the creativity and craftsmanship of the puzzle designer. Picking up the pieces, turning them around to attempt a fit, and hearing the satisfying sound of two pieces locking together all add more sensory dimensions to the experience.

But there is much more than just the visual and the tactile. Jigsaw puzzles mix challenge with play. Puzzlers are testing themselves, proving that they have the cleverness and persistence to find the solution. They relish matching wits with a puzzle creator who has used devious cutting designs or unusual images to lead the assembler down blind alleys. "Ooh, that was tricky!" they exclaim with approval, when the piece that ultimately fills a gap turns out to have an entirely different color and shape from what was anticipated. And if the last dozen pieces take just as long to place as the first, it is a challenging puzzle indeed.

A jigsaw puzzle can produce total absorption, allowing the puzzler to shut out all distractions and worries. The sequence of pieces falling into place soothes and relaxes in stressful times.

Or it can seduce and entrance. How many have said, "Just one more piece . . ." yet remained to place a hundred more? The thrill of the emerging picture, like a siren, beckons and leads the puzzler on so that time stands still. Some addicts even measure out their puzzles carefully, limiting themselves to 30 minutes per day, for fear that the pieces would otherwise take over their lives.

Puzzling is not always solitary. In fact, it lends itself to social occasions. Thoughts of holidays and vacations evoke a jigsaw puzzle as a focal point in many families. All ages can sit around the table and work at different paces. They can enjoy a companionable silence or share thoughts, experiences, and philosophies, along with comments about the puzzle. A puzzler from Kennebunkport, Maine, identified only as "B. P. B.," wrote to one contemporary manufacturer:

The puzzle table is where a mother can hear lots of secrets! After Stave [puzzles] came into my life I began learning lots more about our sons. There's something about sitting around a puzzle table, working together for long periods of time.[4]

Naturally, elements of competition and game playing then come into it too. Who is the fastest puzzler? Who gets the thrill of putting in the last piece? And who is the family tease, the one who pockets a piece and finally produces it triumphantly after a search of the floor on hands and knees proves fruitless?

Bringing order out of chaos is one of the great satisfactions of the puzzler. Unlike a real-world problem that may have no satisfactory answer, a jigsaw puzzle holds the promise of an attractive solution. There is also an element of control. It is important to know that the solution is both achievable *and* fun. Thus, while a few will tackle a large puzzle that is all one color as the ultimate test, most people select puzzles that will give them pleasure, not ones that become endless chores. And if a jigsaw turns out to be impossibly difficult or boring, the solution is simple—just put it back in the box!

Who Does Jigsaw Puzzles?

Puzzlers can choose from among many kinds of challenges—jigsaws, crosswords, cryptograms, mazes, logic, mechanical, problems in recreational mathematics, and even video games. All are specially contrived problems that require ingenuity and skill to find an elegant solution. Each calls for a different combination of visual, analytical, verbal, quantitative, logical, and manipulative abilities. So each appeals to different individuals.[5]

Who does jigsaw puzzles? The *New York Times* made this stark assessment seven decades ago:

> Lovers of jig-saw puzzles fall into two principal classes: lonely people who have nothing to do and very busy and brilliant people who find it soothing to work puzzles in the midst of brain activity.[6]

The cliché of the lonely and bored puzzler is epitomized in the 1941 film *Citizen Kane*. Kane's showgirl wife sits alone at an enormous table in the magnate's castle and plucks listlessly at a few of the hundreds of puzzle pieces spread out before her. The unfinished puzzle symbolizes her shallow and meaningless life.

The rest of us are busy and brilliant, of course! We join captains of industry such as Bill Gates, J. P. Morgan, Henry Luce, Charles Schwab, and various Fords, du Ponts, Rockefellers, and Vanderbilts, and heads of state such as Queen Elizabeth, Theodore Roosevelt, Calvin Coolidge, Herbert Hoover, Dwight D. Eisenhower, and George W. Bush. People in the entertainment and creative fields—Bing Crosby, Jean Harlow, Stephen King, and Stephen Sondheim, for example—constitute another group of famous puzzlers.

But these two stereotypes do not do justice to the full range of puzzlers. Almost everyone does jigsaw puzzles in childhood. Substantial numbers continue on into adulthood. Today, as in the past, they come from all educational and social backgrounds and occupations. An avid puzzler might be a waitress just as well as a computer analyst, writer, or homemaker.

The other side of the story is that some people avoid jigsaws, either because they are too difficult or because they are not challenging enough. A few even fear jigsaws, feeling that they have little aptitude or patience for joining bits together. Mechanical puzzlers, on the other hand, often look down on jigsaws, seeing them as banal and overly formulaic. They search instead for a variety of challenges, each with its own unknown process and exciting twist. Jigsaw puzzlers typically fall between these two extremes.

People on vacations often do jigsaw puzzles, so some hotels and inns keep puzzles on hand for their guests. Enforced idleness similarly leads many to cope by doing jigsaw puzzles. When Tupac Amaru revolutionaries seized the Japanese ambassador's residence in Lima, Peru, the seventy-two hostages asked the International Red Cross for a large shipment of jigsaws. The pastime provided an absorbing distraction from their predicament.[7] Puzzles turn up for the same reason in prisons, sickrooms, hospitals, and nursing homes.

There are some demographic distinctions. Young adults are the least likely to do puzzles. They are too busy getting settled in their careers and searching for mates. When they reach their thirties, they come back to puzzles as a family activity with young children, and later with not so young children and friends. Retirees, who have more time available and fond recollections of nonelectronic entertainment, are among the most likely to turn to jigsaws as a leisure activity.

Although preschool boys and girls seem to do jigsaw puzzles with the same frequency, a difference emerges as they grow older. Among adults, well over half of all puzzlers are female, according to puzzle manufacturers.[8] The percentage is even higher for competitive puzzlers. At the National Jigsaw Puzzle Championships in Athens, Ohio, three-quarters of the entrants and all of the winners have been women. Whether the gender differences are due to visual spatial abilities, fine motor skills, the incidence of color blindness (higher in males), socialization, practice, or some unknown factor remains unclear.

Some special situations are associated with the visual spatial skills that make a good puzzler. The great scientist Albert Einstein learned to talk very late, at age three, and had poor verbal and social skills throughout his school years. But his childhood preoccupation with jigsaw puzzles and building blocks was a forerunner of his later ability to create, play, and mentally puzzle with visual images and ideas.[9] Recent research on late-talking children reveals that they especially enjoy puzzles, music, mathematics, and computers, and are predominantly male. They are often diagnosed as developmentally delayed, sometimes even as autistic.[10]

The connection of puzzles to mental abilities is also showing up in research on Alzheimer's disease. Mental calisthenics such as game playing, puzzling, reading, and other intellectual activities seem to ward off brain drain and dementia.[11]

Jigsaws also offer some therapy for those who are already afflicted. President Ronald Reagan, who used to help his daughter Maureen do jigsaw puzzles when she was young, found solace during the early stages of Alzheimer's when they again did simple puzzles together. Only now it was the father who said, "I want to do the horse," and the daughter who filled in the harder parts.[12]

Puzzling Styles

How do people approach jigsaw puzzles? Unlike games, jigsaw puzzles have no fixed rules. As long as all the pieces come together in the end, just about anything goes. Anything, that is, except for Ann-Margret's approach in her role as Karl Malden's girlfriend in *The Cincinnati Kid*. When she couldn't find the piece she was looking for, she used her nail file and scissors to trim another one to fit the gap, then hammered it in with her fist.

Most puzzlers develop strategies that help them do a jigsaw puzzle. Those with good memories for shapes often start by looking for the pieces with straight edges and assembling the outer border of the puzzle. Others look first for a group of pieces that all have the same distinctive color or pattern, then work out from the color blocks. The best puzzlers tailor their strategies to the puzzle, since irregular edges can defeat the first approach, and the second fails with images in muted colors.

It is not uncommon for jigsaw puzzlers to impose more formal rules on themselves and on fellow puzzlers in order to organize and facilitate assembly: Turn all the pieces right side up before joining any together; do not stack pieces on top of each; the youngest gets to put in the last piece.

Some puzzlers set rules that intensify the challenge: No peeking at the picture on the box; if two pieces come out of the box joined together, separate them. And for the real masochist, there are these strictures: Do not touch a piece until you know exactly where it fits; deduct points for trying a piece that does not fit; and, most extreme, as each individual piece is removed from the box, it must be placed in the correct position.

Many puzzlers are quite casual. They can leave a puzzle out for weeks, even months, coming back to it from time to time until it is finished. Others are very serious indeed, attacking the puzzle like an enemy to be conquered. They systematically marshal its pieces into regiments of similar colors or specific shapes. These are the people who "work" a jigsaw puzzle. When a distinctively shaped piece eludes their grasp, they search doggedly, with rising panic that it might be missing. But (almost) everyone eventually discovers that "all work and no play" can be counterproductive. Somehow pieces just seem to fly into place when the puzzler returns to a puzzle with a fresh perspective after even a short break.

More than a few feel impelled to give names to the pieces, in order to get a better handle on them. They find it easier to search for the "running man" or the "turtle-shaped" piece than for some unnamed shape.

Despite a few attempts at a comprehensive classification of piece shapes and cutting designs, there still is no generally accepted nomenclature. Manufacturers use a variety of terms, as do puzzlers. Puzzle pieces can have "loops" and "sockets," "knobs" and "holes," "tabs" and "slots," "keys" and "locks," or any of several other alternative designations. Special designs are known as shapes, silhouettes, figurals, whimsies, and just figure or character pieces. Take your pick.[13]

Competitive Puzzling

The Supreme Court ruled unanimously in 1937 that jigsaw puzzles were not games. This odd decision came about when a puzzle company sued for a tax refund. Viking Manufacturing claimed its products should have been exempt from an excise tax that had been imposed on games and sporting goods in 1932. The Court's support for Viking hinged in part on the definition of a jigsaw puzzle as a solitary pursuit, "a contrivance designed for testing ingenuity," in contrast with a game in which two or more people compete to win according to some set rules. The decision also noted that the toy "trade recognized a definite distinction between puzzles and games," and if Congress had wanted to tax jigsaw puzzles, it should have said so explicitly.[14]

The Supreme Court ruling, however, has had no impact on how people actually use puzzles. Competitive puzzling was around in the 1930s and continues to the present day. While most people view jigsaw puzzles as leisurely pursuits to be done alone or with family and friends, a few seek greater challenges.

Who can assemble a given puzzle the fastest? Speed contests probably go back to the earliest days of the jigsaw puzzle when siblings raced each other to finish dissected maps. By the 1930s formal tournaments took place in

At the National Jigsaw Puzzle Championships in Athens, Ohio, in 1984, hundreds of doubles teams competed to assemble a 1000-piece puzzle.
Courtesy of The Dairy Barn Arts Center, Athens, Ohio

several cities. Each entrant had to complete the same puzzle, a new one that none of the contestants had ever seen before.

The best-known tournament was the National Jigsaw Puzzle Championships, held in Athens, Ohio, seven times between 1982 and 1990. Hundreds of devotees flocked to Athens from all over the country, and from as far away as New Zealand. One year, a fanatic from Texas arrived in a limousine filled with puzzles that she used for practicing her assembly technique before the contest began. Her custom-made cowboy boots with a hand-tooled puzzle piece design awed the crowd, many of whom had come in family groups just to enjoy the company of other puzzlers.

The top puzzlers used all the available clues: shape, color, pattern, and the picture on the box. (Contest rules prohibited them from doing the puzzle with the picture side down!) Interestingly, most did not start with the border and corner pieces. Instead they began by matching distinctive colors and patterns within the image. The finalists all demonstrated superb memory, intense concentration, and exceptional peripheral vision. While apparently looking at the center of the puzzle, they could pluck a piece from the edge of the table and unerringly fit it into its proper place in the middle.[15]

Joellen Beifuss, a student at Duke University, set the singles record in 1983. Using an ambidextrous technique, she assembled a 500-piece puzzle in 59 minutes and 43 seconds. Beifuss did even better the next year. She fit in one piece every 6.5 seconds in the semifinals, making a total time of 54 minutes and 10 seconds. Sisters Lisa Heiser and Lori Reeves set the record in the doubles division in 1985 by completing a 1,000-piece puzzle in 68 minutes and 13 seconds.

The National Jigsaw Puzzle Championships collapsed after the 1990 contest for several reasons, not least of which was that the two founding organizers moved away from Athens. Without their enthusiasm and energy, the whole operation ran out of steam.

Since 1990, only a few jigsaw puzzle tournaments have taken place in the United States and abroad, and no reports of any faster speeds in competition have surfaced. We are a long way from the scene depicted in Antoine Bello's mystery novel *The Missing Piece*.[16] He envisions a time when competitive jigsaw puzzling is the world's most popular sport and the "JP Tour" attracts contestants from dozens of countries.

A second dimension of puzzle competition is the quest for the world's most difficult puzzle. In part, this is a question of size—the bigger the puzzle, the longer it takes to assemble. The *Guinness Book of World Records* has tracked jigsaw puzzles for decades, publishing the record holders for both the number of pieces and the dimensions. A 50,000-piece puzzle made in Philadelphia in 1933 has been surpassed several times, most recently in 1998 by a 209,250-piece jigsaw covering 505 square feet in Taiwan. Jointly sponsored by Disney and the Hotai Motor Company, the puzzle depicted characters from the Disney film *Mulan*.[17]

The biggest puzzle in terms of surface area covered 51,484 square feet when it was put together in a stadium in Marseilles, France, in 1992. Thirty people spent a week assembling the 43,924 pieces to form an image of a sardine, the city's mascot. An even bigger effort is currently in progress in northern Mexico, where several civic groups are jointly planning a million-piece puzzle in an effort to promote tourism in Durango state.[18]

Puzzle difficulty is not just a matter of size. It depends too on the picture and how the pieces are cut, since puzzlers use both color and shape as clues when they are doing a puzzle. A monochromatic image, or one with random and unconnected bits of color, is much harder to assemble than a bright picture with distinct areas of color. Pieces that are all very similar in shape and noninterlocking can increase the difficulty of a puzzle markedly.

Manufacturers have competed for bragging rights as they have tried to produce jigsaw puzzles that would stump everyone who attempted them. Springbok Editions set off the race in the 1960s with its version of "The world's most difficult puzzle," showing an abstract Jackson Pollock painting. Today, Buffalo Games uses the same sobriquet for its puzzles with the same image on both sides. Several different companies have made puzzles with identically shaped pieces, so only the picture gives clues to assembly.

Only a few puzzle makers have dared to put their money where their mouths are. Steve Richardson of Stave Puzzles in Norwich, Vermont, threw down the gauntlet in a June 1995 contest. He offered a $10,000 prize to the first person to assemble his 225-piece puzzle of an octopus within 10,000 seconds (2 hours, 47 minutes). No ordinary cephalopod, "Olivia" featured many interchangeable pieces with thousands of incorrect configurations and only one correct solution. The challengers all failed.

A few years later in England Christopher Monckton designed the fiendish "Eternity," a puzzle that offered a £1 million prize if it was assembled within four years. It was a nonpictorial puzzle, consisting of 209 geometric-shaped pieces, all with the same solid color on both sides. The task was to figure out which of the staggering number of permutations allowed all the pieces to fit within the puzzle's frame.

Monckton, the son of a viscount and a former advisor to Margaret Thatcher, had underestimated the power and speed of computers. Two young Cambridge mathematicians, Alex Selby and Oliver Riordan, programmed two personal computers to check every possible arrangement. Six months of full-time calculating gave them the prize. Although Monckton had to sell his 67-room ancestral mansion in Scotland to make good on the £1 million, he was undaunted and began work on "Eternity II," with the promise of help from one of the winners.[19]

What Is a Jigsaw Puzzle?

What exactly qualifies as a jigsaw puzzle? (By 1900 this term had largely replaced the earlier "dissected picture" and "picture puzzle." It refers to the jig saws that manufacturers were using then to cut out puzzles.) *Webster's Third Unabridged Dictionary* provides this definition:

> A puzzle made by cutting or sawing a picture into small pieces, also called a picture puzzle.

The definition, and this book, exclude rearrangement puzzles, whose pieces are blank. One such puzzle, the Stomachion, dates back at least to the third century B.C., when Archimedes wrote about it. The most familiar one is the tangram, whose goal is to use the seven geometrical pieces to form a square, or some other predetermined shape.[20]

Interestingly, *Webster's* says nothing about whether the pieces interlock or even whether all the pieces have unique shapes (although some other dictionaries specify irregular pieces and a rigid backing to the picture). A picture cut into small triangles is thus a jigsaw puzzle, albeit more difficult than if each piece had a unique shape. Cube puzzles (blocks with pictures on all six sides) and metamorphic puzzles (whose pieces can be rearranged to form more than one picture) are also subclasses of jigsaws.

Despite the simplicity of the dictionary definition, jigsaw puzzles have taken many forms over the years. People have thought up an enormous number of ways to make them and play with them. Their appeal throughout time is undeniable.

Now, onward to their history.

2

From Schoolroom to Playroom

LEARN TO PUT THE HEADS TOGETHER
IN SUCCESSION . . .

The British Sovereigns, made by William Darton & Son circa 1830, made history lessons come alive, as children tried to put all the kings and queens in their proper order.

Virtually every American school child has played with a puzzle map of the United States. It is easy to put Florida, Texas, and California into place on the edges. But making sense out of all the rectangular states in the middle is a challenge, even for some adults. Solving the puzzle involves real concentration and learning about geography.

The "dissected map" exemplifies the initial educational mission of the earliest jigsaw puzzles, which were first created in the mid-1700s. The years since have witnessed huge transformations in puzzles for children. The educational puzzle is still around, not just in map form, but to teach a variety of lessons. Students, preschoolers, and even adults can learn from jigsaw puzzles.

The lesson puzzle is only one part of a large market for children's puzzles in the twenty-first century. The subject matter has expanded dramatically over time, to encompass entertainment as well as didactic topics. Licensed properties, which first appeared on jigsaw puzzles at the end of the 1800s, have grown in importance. Popular culture themes from the entertainment world—television, movies, comic books, and video games—now dominate jigsaw puzzles for children.

Origins of the Jigsaw Puzzle

The eighteenth century brought urbanization and industrialization, along with the view that children were distinct beings, not just miniature adults.[1] Wealthy parents of this period, eager to give their offspring every advantage, paid close attention to the new theories on education.

The philosopher John Locke became one of the leading authorities on this topic in 1693 with the publication of his book, *Some Thoughts Concerning Education*.[2] He advocated the use of educational toys, such as dice with letters of the alphabet on the sides. Locke's idea that play could both engage the reluctant student and reinforce traditional lessons quickly gained acceptance in eighteenth-century homes and schools.

The development of the jigsaw puzzle was a natural outgrowth of Locke's ideas, although its precise origins remain uncertain. Linda Hannas, an English scholar, has documented the central role played by John Spilsbury, a London mapmaker.[3] Recent scholars, however, have challenged the view that he invented the jigsaw puzzle in 1760.

English documents show that a French educator, Madame Marie-Jeanne Le Prince de Beaumont, was using "wooden maps" to teach young ladies in London in 1759.[4] While the wooden maps most likely were jigsaw puzzles, none remain to reveal whether Madame Beaumont or someone else manufactured them. Still earlier contenders for the title of inventor include Covens & Mortier, an Amsterdam mapmaking firm, and Martin Engelbrecht, a publisher in Augsburg, Germany. There are surviving puzzles made with both companies' prints. But while the prints date from the 1740s, it is quite possible that the firms actually made the puzzles several decades later.[5]

Whoever the inventor of the jigsaw puzzle, it is clear that the early subject matter was geography. By the 1760s the children of England's King George III were playing with jigsaws, known then as "dissected maps." As a youth, George IV perhaps even drew and dissected his own puzzles under the guidance of the royal governess, Lady Charlotte Finch.[6] It was an era when the sun never set on the British Empire. Knowledge of the world and its political boundaries would have been vital to the future king.

The children of England's King George III learned geography in the 1760s from the dissected maps housed in this specially made cabinet.

Courtesy of David Miles, Canterbury, England
Photos © Cotsen Family Foundation

The royal puzzle cabinet, containing sixteen dissected maps of assorted continents and countries, was preserved by Lady Finch and her descendants.[7] When the family consigned it to Christie's London auction in 2000, it fetched an astounding £56,400 (just over $85,000 at the prevailing exchange rate). Two of the royal cabinet's puzzles, Ireland and Scotland, are the work of the above-mentioned John Spilsbury. He is the most prolific and best documented of the pioneer puzzle makers and deserves credit for making dissected maps into a commercial success. The 1763 London city directory includes Spilsbury in its "List of the Masters and Professors of the Polite and Liberal Arts and Sciences" as an "Engraver and Map Dissector in Wood, in order to facilitate the Teaching of Geography."[8]

Spilsbury's trade card advertised more than two dozen dissected maps, including the world, five different continents, and a variety of individual countries, mostly European. He engraved and printed his own maps, carefully tinting the black-and-white prints with watercolors to distinguish individual countries or provinces.

Making the maps into puzzles was simply a matter of pasting them

onto thin mahogany boards and cutting them along the political boundaries, using a handheld fretsaw with a very fine blade. He packaged them
in wooden boxes, with plain printed labels. Although there was no picture
of the complete puzzle on the lid, the box contained an uncolored guide
map to help the youngster who was assembling the puzzle for the first
time.

Spilsbury catered to the affluent. His best puzzles, rectangular maps in
dovetailed hardwood boxes with sliding lids, sold for as much as 1 guinea
(21 shillings). He also offered less expensive versions "without the sea." By
omitting the oceans and packaging these puzzles in simple chipboard boxes,
he could market them for 7 shillings and sixpence.[9] But most English families
could not afford even these cheaper editions. The typical worker earned only
1 or 2 shillings per day.[10]

Dissected maps quickly reached not only the homes of the British royal
family and peerage, but also the elite boarding schools for boys. In 1765
young Thomas Grimstone, who was studying at Cheam in Surrey, wrote
home:

> Dear Papa, I lost one of the Countis of my wooden map the name of it is
> flintshire do you think I can get another.[11]

Spilsbury's premature death at age 29 in 1769 left other publishers to capitalize on his success. They soon extended the idea of puzzle lessons from
geography to other subjects.

William Darton, a prominent London publisher of children's books,
teamed up with Charles Dilly in 1787 to adapt the jigsaw to teaching history. Their *Engravings for Teaching the Elements of English History and Chronol-
ogy* depicted the sequence of thirty-two kings and queens from William the
Conqueror to George II together with facts about their reigns, each monarch
on a separate rectangular piece. The pieces were so nearly identical in size
and shape that a child had to study the dates and facts on each piece to assemble them in the correct order. The publishers printed a detailed lesson
plan on the interlocking border pieces:

Directions. 1. Learn to put the heads together in succession. 2. Get the dates of the inner ovals and the houses of the respective kings. 3. Learn the names of the principal personages of each reign separately. 4. Get by heart the historical and chronological facts of the respective reigns, with the dates of battles, treaties etc.[12]

Religious and moral teachings in puzzle form soon followed. The books of the Bible, lives of the saints, and stories such as *Pilgrim's Progress* all made their way onto jigsaw puzzles by the end of the eighteenth century. These were especially suitable for use on Sundays, when devout parents typically forbade active or secular play. Other dissected lessons included the alphabet, arithmetic, government, natural history, and science.

Once introduced, jigsaw puzzles could not be limited to educational subjects alone. Puzzles for amusement, with no explicit didactic purpose, appeared as early as 1785 in England. Publisher John Wallis was the first of many who adapted William Cowper's popular poem "John Gilpin" to the jigsaw puzzle.

The lighter subjects, though relatively rare in the eighteenth century, grew steadily in importance after 1800. Puzzles based on nursery rhymes, fairy tales, and books intrigued children more than the overtly educational subjects. *Robinson Crusoe, Gulliver's Travels, William Tell,* and *Uncle Tom's Cabin* and other stories all appeared in jigsaw form. There was also a ready market for puzzles that celebrated memorable events, such as the coronation of Queen Victoria in 1838, the great fire at the Tower of London in 1841, and the Crystal Palace Exhibition of 1851.

The packaging became more attractive. The earliest puzzles for children usually had a guide picture tucked into the box. By the mid-nineteenth century, the manufacturers realized that pasting the guide picture onto the lid made it less likely to be damaged or lost. More important, the showier box commanded attention and helped buyers decide which puzzles to purchase.

The shift to more appealing topics coincided with a reduction in production costs, so puzzles became accessible to the rising middle class. Advances in printing during the nineteenth century meant that engravings and woodcuts gave way to less costly lithographs. Some publishers began to employ children who used stencils to color the prints; the crudeness of the coloring reflects their low skills and the correspondingly low wages. Woodworking also advanced, with fast power scroll saws replacing the less efficient handheld ones. The substitution of cheap softwoods for mahogany helped bring costs down still further.

Developments in European puzzle production paralleled those in Britain with a few exceptions. The packaging was one major difference. British puzzles came jumbled up in a box that was too small to hold the puzzle assembled. In contrast, European puzzles were usually sold flat in wide boxes, often in sets of three or more. Another difference was the cutting style. British puzzles had interlocking pieces only on the edges, whereas European puzzles typically interlocked throughout.

Early American Jigsaw Puzzles

Puzzle lessons arrived in the newly established United States in the late 1700s, by way of imports from England and Europe. Some affluent Americans brought them home from travels abroad. Others, who kept up with the latest trends in England and on the Continent, purchased them in major eastern port cities.

In 1811 Mason Brown, who was visiting in New York City, sent gifts to his nine-year-old brother Orlando, at home in Frankfort, Kentucky. Orlando wrote in return:

> I thank you for the things sent by Mr. Coleman. The Penknife was a very good one but it has absconded. The dissected Map is thought to be a great curiosity by the boys in this place. I put it together the first trial.[13]

Another example of an early import is "Riley's Biographical & Chronological Dissected Tablets of English History Composed for the Amusement of Her Royal Highness, the Princess Amelia." It came to Anne Arundel County, Maryland, around 1795 and is now in the Smithsonian Institution's collection.

Shopkeepers advertised new arrivals, especially at holiday times. The Boston *Daily Advertiser,* for example, printed this notice on December 23, 1818:

> M. Newman, No. 82, Court Street has just received by the Ann Alexander from London an elegant assortment of . . . Dissected Maps and Puzzles . . . and Toys, with a great variety of other articles too numerous to mention.[14]

The earliest confirmed American manufacturer is Andrew T. Goodrich of New York City. (James and Joseph Crukshank, stationers and publishers in Philadelphia, advertised dissected maps in 1804 but probably were importers only.) Goodrich was a publisher who operated a bookstore and circulating library for three decades, beginning in 1813. He proclaimed his entry into the puzzle industry in the *New York Evening Post* on January 7, 1818:

> A. T. Goodrich & Co. No. 124 Broadway, corner of Cedar-street, have the pleasure of announcing to their friends and the public that they have just completed a new and elegant Dissected Map of the United States, which has long been a desideratum in this country for domestic instruction and juvenile improvement. A. T. G. & Co. intend to complete a series of useful and correct dissected maps, to which they will respectfully solicit the public attention.[15]

Later Goodrich catalogs itemize a full line of map puzzles, both continents and individual countries, for sale from $1.50 to $2.50.[16] These were very high prices, more than a day's earnings for most workers. In the United States, as in England, only the upper classes could afford puzzles initially.

Dissected maps grew in popularity and distribution before the Civil War. There is even a legend that Abraham Lincoln was a puzzler in the early 1830s. Years later, a Pennsylvania puzzle manufacturer invoked the famous president's name to stimulate sales of his "Lincoln's Lessons in Graphic Geography":

> An old farmer in Illinois used to tell how, when a young man, Mr. Lincoln learned the Geography of the United States by cutting up a map into states and territories and making himself familiar with their forms and relative

sizes, their population, products, and other facts of interest and value. He was just the man to get clear ideas from a device so simple as the sectional map.[17]

In 1850 Samuel McCleary and John Pierce of Hoosick, New York, made several innovations with their "Geographical Analysis of the State of New York." They included a detailed table of the canals, rivers, and railroads in each county, along with instructions for several educational games that children could play with the pieces. Emma Willard, pioneering educator and founder of the Troy Female Academy, devised one of the games. Her testimonial appeared on the label, along with those of New York Governor Hamilton Fish, the Union College president, and other prominent educators of the day.

Following the European practice, McCleary and Pierce designed the puzzle to lie flat within the frame of the shallow wooden box, making it easier for children to contain the pieces and study the assembled map. They also invented an intriguing and novel die-cutting method, which they patented in 1849. Because the technique required a separate die for each piece, it was too impractical to catch on with other manufacturers.

Other domestic producers of dissected maps before the Civil War included Kelly & Levin in Boston, J. H. Colton in New York, and in Philadelphia both Thomas T. Ash and S. Augustus Mitchell.

As with map puzzles, production of picture puzzles for amusement started in the United States more than fifty years after it did in Britain and Europe. By the early 1850s, companies in at least two eastern cities were making picture puzzles. W. & S. B. Ives, a game publisher in Salem, Massachusetts, and V. S. W. Parkhurst of Providence, Rhode Island, made simple hand-colored cardboard puzzles, sliced into a few pieces.

Farther south in Philadelphia, four firms were dissecting pictures in the 1850s and 1860s. Thomas S. Wagner, Jacob Shaffer, M. H. Traubel, and Davis, Porter & Co. may well have had some business connections, since the same pictures show up on more than one company's puzzles. Joining them in the early 1860s were Charles Magnus of New York and Mark Salom of Boston, who used hand-colored lithographs of Civil War scenes for some of their dissections.

Domestic production of jigsaw puzzles really took off after the Civil War,

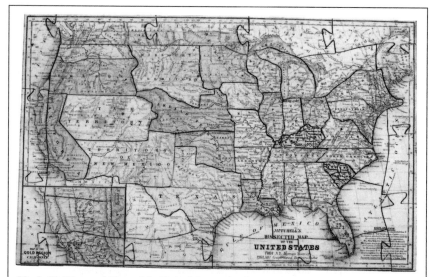

Mitchell's Dissected Map of the United States, made in 1854, shows the location of major Indian tribes and the newly discovered gold mines of California, but few other states west of the Mississippi.

when the industrial revolution was in full swing in the United States. Puzzles gained wider distribution during this period. Rising incomes, rapidly increasing urban populations, and expanding railroad networks meant that more families had access to all kinds of manufactured goods. Two giants of children's publishing, Milton Bradley of Springfield, Massachusetts, and McLoughlin Brothers of New York City, rose to prominence at this time. By the 1876 celebration of the United States centennial, both companies were turning out puzzles and games in huge volumes, competing very effectively with imports from Europe.

Milton Bradley had set up shop in the 1850s as the first lithographer in Springfield, Massachusetts. He designed and published "The Checkered Game of Life" in 1860. Although it was quite successful, he viewed games as only a sideline. In fact, the company might still be just dabbling in games if Abraham Lincoln had not grown a beard.

At the time of the 1860 election, Bradley had produced a lithograph of

Milton Bradley's *Smashed Up Locomotive, A Mechanical Puzzle for Boys*, although only 56 pieces, was a challenge to youngsters of the 1870s and 1880s.

the next president, based on a photograph showing a clean shaven Lincoln. The pictures sold well initially, so Bradley ran off vast quantities of the print in anticipation of still greater demand when the new president took office. But shortly thereafter, Lincoln grew a beard. No one wanted the out-of-date pictures. With a now worthless inventory, Bradley decided to return to the game business. His small travel kit of "Games for Soldiers" was a great success during the Civil War, and the company never looked back.[18]

Bradley added dissected maps and picture puzzles to his catalog in the late 1860s. An early best seller was "The Smashed Up Locomotive, A Mechanical Puzzle for Boys," which showed an engine and tender and identified all the parts.

Milton Bradley took a strong interest in education, beginning in 1869 when he edited and published *The Paradise of Childhood*.[19] This book by Edward Wiebé described the theories and methods of Friedrich Froebel, a German educator who studied child development and advocated directed play in kindergartens. Bradley took on the mission of producing not only games and puzzles, but also Froebel toys, books, art materials, activity sets, blackboards, and many other school supplies.

McLoughlin Brothers was Bradley's biggest rival in the game and puzzle business for decades, until Bradley finally acquired the company in 1920. The firm began in 1828 as a publisher of children's books, and expanded into the areas of jigsaw puzzles, blocks, games, paper dolls, and valentines during the 1850s and 1860s.

Both companies used chromolithography, a new method of color printing that supplanted hand coloring for children's puzzles by the 1870s. McLoughlin Brothers in particular made the most of the new techniques, producing puzzles with rich, brilliant colors. The company chose dramatic and appealing subjects that glorified the industrial spirit of the United States as it entered its second century. Puzzles showing locomotives, steamships, the Brooklyn Bridge, and airships took their place alongside the maps and the more traditional scenes of animals and children's stories.

McLoughlin Brothers opened a modern color printing factory in Brooklyn in 1870, and by the 1890s employed seventy-five artists, including Thomas Nast, the renowned editorial cartoonist.[20] Much of the McLoughlin artwork did double or triple duty, as the company's products complemented each other. The color plates in their children's books often appeared both on jigsaw puzzles and on cube puzzles (blocks with pictures on each side that could form six different scenes from one book).

Selchow & Righter Company was the third major puzzle and game manufacturer to rise to prominence in the 1870s. The company is most remembered as the longtime maker of Scrabble, Trivial Pursuit, and Parcheesi. It also had an important part in developing puzzles targeted at children who were learning how to read.[21]

Elisha G. Selchow began as a box maker in New York City in the 1860s. Among his customers was Albert Swift, a game manufacturer. When Swift fell on hard times and could not pay his bills, Selchow took over the game business. He kept on John Righter, Swift's talented clerk, and made him a full partner in 1880.

The company's 1875–76 catalog announced a new item, "Sliced Animals or Spelling Made Easy." The box held fourteen simple puzzles of animals, each cut into one-inch-wide strips with letters on the left sides. Three-year-olds could easily assemble the three-piece cow, the four-piece bear, and the five-piece horse puzzles, based only on the pictures, even before they could read the name spelled vertically on the edge.

The sliced puzzles were so popular that the company added "Sliced

Selchow & Righter made *Sliced Nations* and other simple spelling puzzles from the 1870s through the 1930s. This colorful set introduced American children to the stereotypes of foreigners that prevailed in 1881.

Birds," "Sliced Objects," and "Sliced Nations" to its line over the next few years. Other companies copied the concept shamelessly with minor variations in titles: "Sectional Animals" by Milton Bradley, "Criss Cross Spelling Slips" by McLoughlin Brothers, "Cut-up Animals" by Parker Brothers, "Animal Slips" by Peter G. Thomson, and many more. Selchow & Righter's lawsuit against one of the copiers in 1895 was ironic, since its own "Sliced Birds" had blatantly plagiarized some of John James Audubon's drawings. At any rate, even though Selchow & Righter won its case, it still had little success in stemming the flow of knockoffs.

Although the earliest American puzzles were made of wood, by the 1880s the industry had shifted to less expensive fiberboard or thinner cardboard. Still another cost-saving measure was to make boxes from cardboard instead of wood. More efficient production techniques also helped companies cut costs.

American firms in the late nineteenth century used power scroll saws or band saws, rather than the handheld fretsaws employed to cut the first

English puzzles. Many also saved labor costs by stacking the uncut puzzles, then cutting two or more at a time. Nail holes in the corners and a loose fit are telltale signs of stack cutting, which required a very thick blade to cut through the entire stack. Companies that made thin cardboard puzzles, such as the sliced animals, sometimes employed dies and knifelike guillotines for cutting, but most such mechanisms were not strong enough to cut wood or fiberboard.

As American manufacturing grew, the role of imported puzzles diminished. Nevertheless, Germany and other countries continued to send puzzles to the United States. Many of these were small puzzles for very young children or six-sided cube puzzles. European puzzles usually did not identify the manufacturer on the box. Beginning in 1893, however, United States law required a label specifying the country of origin on all imported goods.

Preschool Puzzles

During the early 1900s puzzles began to play a bigger role in the education not just of school-age children, but of younger children as well. Playing is the business of childhood. Even before formal education begins, puzzles offer alluring opportunities for a child to develop fundamental skills that are the building blocks for later schoolwork. Preschool puzzles seek to stimulate and foster this development, rather than to teach specific school subjects.

Assembling puzzles develops hand-eye coordination and the fine motor skills that a child will need later to hold and guide a pencil. Successful puzzle assembly also requires visual and spatial skills: the ability to recognize patterns, sizes, angles, shapes, and colors, and to see that pieces will fit if they are rotated or turned over. These skills too are critical precursors to learning the alphabet and numbers.

Puzzling involves logical problem-solving and conceptual thinking. Through a process of trial and error, and perhaps with some help from an adult, a child doing a clown puzzle discovers that it makes sense to place the hat on top of the clown's face, not over the socks. Strategies such as turning all the pieces face up, making sure that no pieces overlap, and sorting out the edge pieces come easily to an adult, but must be learned by a child.

The child who is having fun putting a puzzle together is also developing patience and concentration. Indeed, small children derive so much satisfaction from completing a puzzle that they often solve the same one over and over again.

Children bring a great deal of imagination to their puzzles. For example, a child might use the six different vehicles in a simple transportation theme puzzle as the elements for creating a make-believe street. Professor Jerome Singer, a psychologist at Yale University, notes that this type of play gives a child both a feeling of accomplishment and a sense of control.

> Seeing a real fire engine or airplane is overwhelming. But the child can hold a puzzle piece, make stories that go with it, and move it. The creation of a miniature world is the forerunner of the adult's skills at changing the world.[22]

There is a clear progression in the puzzles that preschoolers use today. A shape sorter for a one-year-old is the most basic type of puzzle, where the idea is to fit a piece of a certain shape into the matching hole. The next step is the form board puzzle, a board with recesses for a few separate pieces, perhaps eight different animals or four different things that fly.

By age three, children can solve more complex puzzles of 10 to 20 pieces. But most still do best with puzzles in frame trays that are cut on the color lines, so each piece represents a distinct object such as a head, arm, torso, or leg. At slightly older ages, children gain dexterity and can move up to interlocking puzzles with smaller pieces, and that are not contained within a frame tray. Many preschoolers can even do puzzles with 150 or more pieces. In the process they learn to persist and make sense of a large jumble of visual and spatial information, where every piece is different. A four-year-old who can complete such a project attains a well-justified pride of accomplishment.[23]

These elements of child development, which seem so obvious today, were not generally understood one hundred years ago. In 1900 few children attended nursery school or organized daycare, but their numbers grew steadily over time. Educators thus intensified their study of preschoolers, focusing specifically on how they use playthings and learn from them.[24]

In Italy during the first decade of the century, Dr. Maria Montessori developed new teaching methods and materials for children, including those as young as age two. Her theories about unstructured classrooms and how children learn better through discovery than through instruction seemed radical then. Montessori's ideas gained only a tiny foothold in the United States at the time, and did not win broader acceptance here until the 1960s.[25]

Montessori had studied the methods of earlier educators who specialized in teaching mentally deficient children. Drawing on their work, she prescribed inset puzzles, now commonly known as form boards, as one type of learning material. The boards contained distinct geometrically shaped pieces—circles, squares, triangles, and so forth. A knob attached to each piece made it easy for a toddler to grasp and manipulate it. She encouraged children both to fit pieces into the boards and to trace around the edges to develop their skills with writing implements.[26]

Similar pictorial form boards soon became important tools for assessment, along with simple puzzles where the idea was to assemble half a dozen pieces that made up a stylized human figure or a profile of a face. Physicians on Ellis Island used form boards to test adult immigrants before World War I. Most adults, even those who could not speak English or who were illiterate, could solve the form board puzzle in less than three minutes. Those who gave up or took much longer were deemed mentally incompetent and were subject to deportation.[27]

Charlotte Gano Garrison of Columbia University's Teachers College played a major role in extending the idea of the form board to the frame tray puzzle in the United States. Garrison served as principal of the Horace Mann Kindergarten, a demonstration school operated by Teachers College, from 1910 to 1937. She taught a course at Teachers College on play materials for preschool children, and wrote a book on the same topic.[28] Because few suitable toys were commercially available, she and her colleagues at first designed their own play materials and had them fabricated by the college's carpenter.

During the 1910s psychologists began to use simple form board puzzles, such as this one made by the Stoelting Company in Chicago, to measure the intelligence of both children and adults.

By the early 1930s Garrison and Rita Berman, the mother of one of the kindergarten students, had opened a retail store on Madison Avenue to fill the void in the availability of educational toys. Garrison was the advisor, and Berman did the "spade work." Garrison later described the beginnings of their Educational Playthings shop:

> It was very very difficult to get the kind of play materials that we wanted then. The old kind of formal kindergarten material was out so far as we were concerned. . . . We developed all sorts of things. We bought what we could that was good, but what we couldn't, we made.[29]

Educational Playthings sold the "Modern Playway Nursery Toy" brand of frame tray puzzles, each with fewer than a dozen plywood pieces.

Their success encouraged others to design and produce frame tray puzzles. Many manufacturers consulted with educators or, like Hymie and Ruth Berman in Minneapolis, used their own backgrounds in psychology and social work. The Bermans concluded that commercially available toys and puzzles were much inferior to what Hymie could make in his home workshop. They started the Judy Company, named after their daughter, in 1937. Judy became a leader in the development of multicultural puzzles during the early 1950s.[30]

Charlotte Garrison, who taught at Columbia University's Teachers College, was a leader in designing toys for young children, including this 8-piece sailboat tray puzzle, circa 1930.

Playskool, now a giant in the industry and a subsidiary of Hasbro, began making wood kindergarten materials in Chicago in the late 1920s. The company added "puzzle plaques" to its line in 1941. Sifo in St. Paul, Minnesota, and Holgate Toys in Kane, Pennsylvania, entered the puzzle business just after World War II. The latter hired Jarvis Rockwell, brother of artist Norman Rockwell, to design their toys.

An innovation came to the U.S. in 1952 when Creative Playthings of Princeton, New Jersey, marketed its "See Inside" brand of frame tray puzzles. Removing the pieces of a circus tent puzzle, for example, revealed a picture of acts performing inside the big top.[31] Later companies took the concept even further with multilayer frame tray puzzles. One example, designed by Helen Seymour of Plainsboro, New Jersey, in the early 1980s, featured a hen in the top layer, chicks in the middle layer, and eggs at the bottom.

By the 1970s, Fisher-Price of East Aurora, New York, and many of its competitors had made the knobs on each piece a standard feature, some sixty years after Montessori had developed them.

Floor puzzles that are too large to fit on a table also made a comeback at this time. Milton Bradley had sold an eight-foot-long "Sectional Railroad

Puzzle" in the 1880s, followed by its "Twilight Locomotive Puzzle Box" between the two world wars. The latter consisted of six eighteen-inch-wide puzzles, each showing a railroad car. When fully assembled, they combined to make an impressive train that stretched nine feet from engine to boxcar.

Floor puzzles of the last few decades have featured larger pieces (four to five inches square) and much more varied subjects than their predecessors. But as in the past, they offer opportunities for several children to play with the same puzzle at once and take advantage of the child's comfort with playing on the floor.

Frame tray and floor puzzles are still standard fare for preschoolers.[32] Hundreds of companies make them in thousands of variations today. In fact, preschool puzzles account for two-thirds of all children's puzzles that are sold.[33]

Other Twentieth-Century Subjects

Beyond the focus on preschool puzzles, other big changes in the subject matter of jigsaw puzzles occurred after 1900 in the United States.

Of course, there were still plenty of educational puzzles for school-age children, teaching standard lessons of history, religion, science, spelling, and arithmetic. Puzzles continued their centuries-old mission of geographical instruction, as children still pored over cut-up maps. The world's fast-changing political divisions meant that world map puzzles soon became outdated. Multiconcept Designs of Hamilton, Ontario, addressed this challenge in the 1990s by promising to send updated pieces to buyers of its magnetic puzzle globe whenever country names and boundaries changed.

New lessons, such as learning how to tell time, joined the traditional ones. The familiar clock puzzles with movable hands go back a century. A puzzle of flat blocks with a clock face on one side and a calendar on the other appeared in 1905, patented by Jefferson H. Fitch of Jeffersonville, Indiana, and produced by Strauss Manufacturing Company of New York City. Thirteen years later, Myron Gilman of Westfield, Massachusetts, patented and sold an interlocking jigsaw puzzle version, the "Gilman Little Clock

Builder." Despite children's growing reliance on digital timepieces,
manufacturers still issue clock puzzles with new designs each year.

Environmental education took
off in the 1960s after the publication of Rachel Carson's book
Silent Spring.[34] A flood of puzzles
showing endangered species, rain
forests, and other natural history
subjects followed. Annie Power and
Steve Schumaker of Malvern, Pennsylvania, created a particularly ingenious puzzle in the mid-1990s. It
consists of 34 large wood pieces,
each picturing a tropical fish or
other reef dweller, which fit together into the shape of a giant colorful fish. The back of each piece
gives the name and facts about that
particular creature. Their "Pieceful
Solutions" series also included puzzles devoted to butterflies, frogs, snakes,
and other animals.

Rainbow Crafts, the developer of Play-
Doh, made this puzzle clock around
1970. It features movable hands to help
children learn to tell time.
Courtesy of Hasbro

But twentieth-century puzzles were not all didactic. In fact, the vast majority of puzzles for school-age children are now designed for entertainment
rather than education.

Illustrated books are still a rich source of puzzle images. Puzzle makers of
the 1930s and 1940s gave old tales a fresh look by using pictures by contemporary artists such as Fern Bisel Peat, Jessie Willcox Smith, Maria L. Kirk,
Ethel Hayes, and Ruth Newton. New stories about Raggedy Ann and Andy
by Johnny Gruelle, and Harrison Cady's illustration of the characters from
children's books by Thornton Burgess, also appeared on puzzles at this time.

At first, puzzle companies could simply buy extra prints of some illustrations at cost from book publishers. But soon the publishers (and others)

realized that the characters and the artwork had enormous money-making potential. The concept of licensed properties owned by media giants took off.

The licensing trend in puzzles actually originated in the 1890s with R. F. Outcault's "Yellow Kid" comic strip. The Kid first appeared on a McLoughlin Brothers jigsaw in 1896. He also stimulated a major fight over intellectual property when publisher William Randolph Hearst outbid rival Joseph Pulitzer for the popular strip. Pulitzer's response and the ensuing lengthy legal battle gave rise to the epithet "yellow journalism."[35]

The twentieth century brought new entertainment media that were scarcely dreamed of in 1900. Movies, animated cartoons, comic books, radio, television, computer games, and the Internet contributed to a novel and modern popular culture that riveted and delighted children (and adults too). The entertainment industry was quick to seize on the additional profit opportunities generated by tying puzzles and other toys to copyrighted productions. The puzzle companies happily signed on, knowing that the mammoth promotional campaigns mounted for the other media would stimulate demand for their products too.

Mickey Mouse and his friends, who made their film debut in 1928, appeared just five years later on jigsaw puzzles made by the Saalfield Company of Akron, Ohio. Mickey, Minnie, Donald Duck, Pluto, and Goofy have been available in puzzle form ever since. Saalfield also scored big with its other licensed puzzles, featuring characters such as Popeye, Our Gang, Tarzan, and the Katzenjammer Kids.

Many of the children's puzzles of the 1930s were advertising premiums, touted on radio shows by the sponsors and given away with toothpaste, soap, cereals, and other products. They featured Amos 'n' Andy, The Goldbergs, Radio Orphan Annie, and other favorites. Licensing became even more important in the 1950s, when television entered most American living rooms. The baby boom generation grew up on a steady diet of Westerns, superhero dramas, Saturday morning cartoons, variety shows, and situation comedies. Howdy Doody, Hopalong Cassidy, Superman, Huckleberry Hound, Yogi Bear, and the Beverly Hillbillies were just a few of the television characters with puzzle spinoffs. Virtually every Disney movie and television series had puzzles associated with it, from *Sleeping Beauty* to *101 Dalmatians* to *Mary Poppins* and the *Mickey Mouse Club.*

By the start of the twenty-first century, the licensing phenomenon had captured the bulk of the action in children's puzzles. The cast of characters has changed a bit, but the Disney empire still licenses puzzles tied to new blockbuster animated films such as *Monsters, Inc., Toy Story,* and *The Lion King* and regular revivals of old favorites. Sales of Mickey Mouse items worldwide totaled $4.7 billion in 2002.[36]

Other entertainment giants include Steven Spielberg (*E. T., Shrek, Men in Black,* and more) and Public Broadcasting. The latter has jumped on the licensing bandwagon with perennials such as *Sesame Street* and newer brands such as *Arthur* and *Clifford the Big Red Dog.* Today it is hard to find a child's toy that does *not* feature some licensed property.

Bells and Whistles

Using licensed properties is only one strategy that puzzle manufacturers employ to compete with the high-tech media that provide so many leisure-time options for today's children. Gimmicks and "enhancements" are another technique that manufacturers have used for years, so that their puzzles attract children by entertaining on several levels.

One common device is the puzzle whose pieces can yield more than one picture. Double-sided puzzles, to make two different pictures, and cube puzzles, which make six different pictures, both date back to the early nineteenth century in England and Europe, and came to the United States shortly thereafter.

Puzzles with mix-and-match pieces are even older.[37] Rudolph Ackermann made the first "Changeable Ladies" and "Changeable Gentlemen" puzzles in London in 1819. They spawned generations of metamorphic puzzles, including "Changeable Charlie" blocks. Charlie's more than four million possible expressions delighted children from the late 1940s through the 1970s. A modern variant is the "dress up" puzzle that helps children express moods by changing the character's clothing or face.

These 1948 *Changeable Charlie* blocks by Gaston Manufacturing Company, with pictures on four sides of each piece, could make millions of different facial expressions.
Courtesy of Hasbro

Sometimes the novelty is in the packaging. In the 1880s the Bliss Manufacturing Company of Pawtucket, Rhode Island, sold lithographed wooden train sets that contained puzzle blocks inside the cars. Today several companies make toy wagons that carry a load of puzzle blocks. Ceaco of Watertown, Massachusetts, has made a "Big Rig" puzzle whose cardboard box is shaped like a vehicle and can be played with.

Puzzle and book combinations are another old idea that have come back into vogue today. As early as 1867 *Demorest's Young America,* a children's magazine, included a page printed with a map of the eastern United States. A cutting design printed on the back of the page guided children to make their own dissected map with scissors. Four decades later, Frederick A. Stokes of New York City was one of several firms to publish books with puzzle pieces printed on some pages, and outlines of the pieces on others. Children could cut out the pieces and paste them in the proper spots to form the complete pictures.

Around 1920, Ideal Book Builders of Chicago published books that contained simple die-cut puzzles. The Tractor Training Service aimed at an older audience with a series of educational puzzles in the 1950s. These depicted engineering diagrams of various tractor engines, and were accompanied by a large textbook for aspiring mechanics in vocational and technical schools. Dozens of publishers have followed their lead over the years, and puzzle books are very popular today.

Puzzle games are perennial favorites. Some lotto games in the nineteenth century were really form boards in which the pieces completed a picture. Many English game makers at that time cut their playing boards into jigsaw puzzles; once the puzzle was assembled, the game could begin. The jigsaw puzzle image could also incorporate other types of puzzles such as rebuses, hidden objects, and mazes. The last few decades in the United States have also brought a revival of puzzle games with all kinds of rules. Some play like "Go Fish," in which players first draw random pieces, then compete to finish a puzzle. Others are more complex.

Another popular twist is the puzzle with sound. Selchow & Righter put out a "Picto Toons" set in 1958; each box contained a record and four puzzles that showed scenes from the lyrics. During the 1960s several music companies put out children's records with frame tray puzzles built into the album covers.

Western Publishing Company of Racine, Wisconsin, and Mattel of Hawthorne, California, both designed talking puzzles in 1968. Mattel's required batteries, but Western's "Sound A Round" set included a tone arm on which a child could play the disk with the puzzle in the center. In the 1980s Connor Toys of Wausau, Wisconsin, manufactured a "Melody Puzzle" that played a tune after all the pieces were correctly placed in the frame tray. Talking and singing puzzle sets are widely available now because microchips are so inexpensive.

Other novelties include puzzles with unusual visual effects. They sport holographic or glow-in-the-dark images, or need to be viewed with 3-D glasses. Birthday cards with small jigsaw puzzles enclosed, magnetic puzzles, and edible puzzles made of candy can also be found on the market today.

The Children's Puzzle Industry After 1900

Not only did the subjects of jigsaw puzzles change during the twentieth century, but there were also big changes in the industry, both in production methods and in the lineup of firms.

Wood was the most common material for jigsaw puzzles before 1900. In the years since, most makers of children's puzzles have shifted to materials that cost less and require technologies with lower labor costs.

Die-cutting puzzles from cardboard largely replaced cutting wooden puzzles with saws. Because a steel rule die stamps out an entire puzzle at once, a few workers with one press can turn out hundreds of puzzles per day. Although some puzzles were cut with dies during the 1800s, they had only simple noninterlocking pieces. Advances in strengthening and bending steel rule in the 1910s and 1920s opened up new possibilities. Dies could produce interlocking pieces and other complex configurations. The new technology meant that a cardboard puzzle cost just a fraction of what its wooden counterpart did.

Since toddlers have a tendency to tear or chew cardboard pieces, there is still a place for puzzles of more durable materials. Today's preschool puzzles often are made of plywood, because it resists warping more than the solid woods used for earlier puzzles. Even cheaper than plywood are composites made from sawdust and wood chips. While brands such as Upson Board, Tekwood, and Masonite were all popular during the middle of the twentieth century, medium-density fiberboard became the common choice in the last few decades.

Plastics came into widespread use in the toy industry after World War II and have found a place in preschool puzzles as well. Injection molds can produce lightweight, three-dimensional plastic pieces in bright colors.

Lauri Puzzles of Phillips-Avon, Maine, made a brilliant innovation in the 1960s when it began stamping preschool puzzles out of crepe rubber, a material often used for the soles of shoes. Like plastic, it is durable, lightweight, and washable, and the colors are slow to fade. Lauri also endeared itself to parents by guaranteeing to supply replacements for lost pieces for a nominal charge. In 2003 Lauri became a subsidiary of Smethport Specialty Co. of Smethport, Pennsylvania.

Newer but similar materials for puzzles have emerged in the last two decades. EVA (ethylene vinyl acetate) foam has gained a large following, since large interlocking squares make great floor mats for playrooms. Smaller EVA squares with inset pictures or letters can serve as both puzzles and building toys. A few manufacturers have even made puzzles out of sponges so they can double as bath toys.

The changes in technology and materials, along with world events, encouraged the growth of American puzzle companies during the 1900s. The outbreak of World War I in 1914 brought a temporary halt to most imports from Europe and provided a great stimulus to domestic manufacturing, especially in the toy industry. Germany, which had dominated the toy industry until then, was unable to regain its place in the chaotic decades that followed.

Milton Bradley and Selchow & Righter continued to thrive as major players in children's puzzles after World War I. Parker Brothers of Salem, Massachusetts, which had been founded in 1883, made some puzzles in addition to its bigger line of games. These three were joined around 1915 by Madmar Quality Company of Utica, New York, and later by the Judy Company, Playskool, Holgate, and other makers of preschool puzzles.

Three other companies that were founded before 1945 also rose to prominence in children's puzzles just after World War II, including Jaymar Specialty Company and the Joseph K. Straus Company, both located in Brooklyn, New York, and Tuco Workshops of Lockport, New York.

Some important companies came to the puzzle industry by indirect, although logical routes. Several

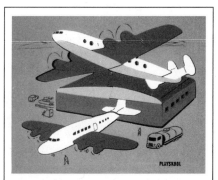

Playskool's 20-piece *Airport* tray puzzle, circa 1945, helped preschoolers distinguish colors and shapes.

Courtesy of Hasbro

established publishers of children's books began making jigsaw puzzles. They already had presses and a ready source of illustrations, and it was easy to add die-cutting equipment. Whitman Publishing Company of Racine, Wisconsin, Platt and Munk of New York City, Samuel Gabriel and Sons of New York City, and Saalfield Publishing of Akron, Ohio, were some of the most important companies in this category.

Another breeding ground for puzzle companies has been the paper box industry. The technology of die-cutting puzzles is very similar to that of stamping out cardboard boxes—and it is more profitable to ship boxes with puzzles in them than empty boxes containing only air. Warren Paper Products Company of Lafayette, Indiana, E. E. Fairchild of Rochester, New York, and the Consolidated Paper Box Company of Somerville, Massachusetts, all joined the puzzle industry in the first half of the century and continued to make children's puzzles for decades.

After World War II, foreign countries began to export more toys to the United States. In jigsaw puzzles there were two extremes during the 1950s and 1960s. G. J. Hayter of Bournemouth, England, and Simplex of Holland exported high-quality wooden puzzles, while a number of Japanese manufactures sent flimsy cardboard puzzles to be sold on racks in five-and-dime stores. In the 1970s Ravensburger in Germany and Galt in England became important exporters of quality children's puzzles, and they remain so to this day.

With the easing of trade restrictions in the last quarter of the twentieth century, a flood of children's puzzles now comes to the United States each year, primarily from China and other Asian countries with low manufacturing costs. Furthermore, some American companies, such as the innovative Lights, Camera, Interaction! (maker of the Melissa and Doug brand) of Westport, Connecticut, have either moved their factories overseas, or outsourced puzzle manufacturing to foreign subcontractors.

Nevertheless, new puzzle companies with domestic manufacturing facilities continued to spring up. Every Buddies Puzzles! of Corvallis, Oregon, is one of several makers of high-end wooden puzzles that came on the scene in the 1980s and 1990s. In die-cut puzzles, the Great American Puzzle Factory of South Norwalk, Connecticut, and Ceaco have emerged since 1985 as two leading producers of attractive and creative children's puzzles.

The second half of the twentieth century was also a time of consolidation, as the economics of distribution and advertising favored large firms. Milton Bradley acquired Playskool in 1962. Selchow & Righter bought out Fairchild. Through a series of purchases, Hasbro of Pawtucket, Rhode Island, then acquired Milton Bradley, Parker Brothers, Selchow & Righter, Whitman, and the remnants of several other puzzle companies. It still uses the venerated brand names of Playskool, Milton Bradley, and Parker Brothers, but has discontinued most of the others.

Mattel, the other contemporary toy giant, bought out Fisher-Price and an English company, Spear's Games. Spear's had earlier acquired G. J. Hayter, which had exported many wood children's puzzles to the U.S. from 1950 on. School Specialty Inc. acquired the Judy Company and several other makers of preschool puzzles in 2004.

Today's children's puzzles have come a long way from John Spilsbury's first dissected maps. Yet puzzles retain their educational mission to some extent even today. Puzzle maps encourage youngsters to learn the countries, their states, and their capitals, just as they did over two hundred years ago. Preschool puzzles continue to help young children develop the basic skills of coordination, color and pattern recognition, and spatial relationships. And of course, children love jigsaw puzzles because they are just plain fun.

3

Grown-Ups Turn to Cut-Ups

BRIDGE AND WHIST FELL BY THE WAYSIDE AS THE
PUZZLE TOOK THE UNITED STATES BY STORM.

NEW PUZZLE MENACES THE CITY'S SANITY

Young and Old, Rich and Poor,
All Hard at Work Fitting Cut-
Up Pictures Together.

SOLITAIRE IS FORGOTTEN

Two Clergymen, a Supreme Court Justice, and a Noted Financier Among
the Latest Converts to the Craze.

The picture-puzzle craze has come to
town, and those who are not staying
awake nights to fit the puzzles together
are using them as a sedative to put them

NEW PUZZLE MENACES
THE CITY'S SANITY
Young and Old, Rich and Poor,
All Hard at Work Fitting Cut-Up Pictures Together.

With this dramatic headline in May 1908, the *New York Times* marked the onset of a full-blown craze for jigsaw puzzles in the United States.[1] The article cited notables who had already succumbed to the mania, including a Supreme Court justice, clergymen, college professors, and military men. The child's plaything had taken new form as the adult's passion.

Adults had done jigsaws before, of course. Parents in earlier centuries had helped their children learn to assemble their dissected maps and pictorial puzzles. A few exceptional children's puzzles even had both the images and the complexity to intrigue a parent. It is easy to envision a father and son working together on McLoughlin's 1893 "Mammoth Naval Scroll Puzzle." This 110-piece puzzle of the White Squadron, more than three feet wide, showed the battleship *Massachusetts* flanked by six cruisers. The great blue expanses of sea and sky and the cluster of white hulls would have challenged an adult as well as a ten-year-old.

Virtually all the other puzzles available in the nineteenth century had juvenile pictures, contained fewer than 75 pieces, and were too simple to hold an adult's interest for more than a few minutes. One exception comes from the firm of F. P. Henke in the Netherlands, who made large, difficult puzzles—200 pieces and up—as early as 1830.[2] Judging from the fact that only a handful have survived, they failed to catch on with adults in Europe. Nor is there any evidence that they ever crossed the Atlantic to reach North America.

What caused the reincarnation of the jigsaw puzzle as an adult entertainment in the United States at the turn of the century? While the mania was sudden, the transformation was a bit more gradual. It emerged out of two movements that came together in the 1870s: women's handicrafts and fretwork.

During the last three decades of the Victorian era, middle- and upper-class women were actively pursuing arts and crafts in their growing leisure time. They went beyond the traditional needlework and decorative art to explore new fields. Magazines, and books such as *Pretty Arts for the Employment of Leisure Hours: A Book for Ladies,* provided both encouragement and instruction for women to use handheld fretsaws.[3] (Light woodworking with fretsaws, which resemble coping saws, had hitherto been the exclusive province of men.) Specialized books on fretwork appeared in great numbers at the same time.[4]

John W. Penney of Mechanic Falls, Maine, operates the treadle powered "Dirigo" scroll saw that his company made in the 1870s.

Maine State Museum, Augusta, Maine

The introduction of the foot-powered fretsaw, also known as a jig or scroll saw, spurred these endeavors to greater heights. Demonstrations of its use at the 1876 Centennial Exposition in Philadelphia motivated thousands of Americans to take up fretwork as a hobby.[5] The treadle saw was a lightweight portable model for home use that sold for $3, unlike heavy and expensive industrial predecessors that were permanently installed in factories. It looked like a sewing machine, with a thin saw blade in place of a needle, and was just as easy to operate.

Women joined men in making

wooden fretwork items for the home, using commercially available patterns for shelves, frames, bookends, clocks and the like. Some women brought in modest incomes by selling their handiwork through the Women's Exchanges that sprang up after 1880. Others donated their crafts to charities, to be sold at fund-raising bazaars.[6]

From fretwork, it was a natural extension to make jigsaw puzzles. In 1873 the Reverend Joseph Matthews in England wrote a book for boys on how to cut children's puzzles with a handheld fretsaw.[7] Whether that book reached the United States or whether Americans independently took up amateur puzzle making is not known. But in 1898 the Reverend Charles P. B. Jefferys (1862–1900) of Philadelphia cut puzzles with a treadle saw for family and friends while recovering from an illness at his family's summer home in East Hampton, New York. Some, made from political cartoons of the day, had more than 150 pieces and were clearly intended for adults. While his puzzles and history have survived, there were undoubtedly more late nineteenth-century puzzles for adults that have been lost.

Within ten years of Jefferys' work, the jigsaw puzzle for adults had become a commercial sensation. It was an era when radio broadcasting was two decades in the future, television was not even imagined, and few homes had electricity. Card games had been the most popular after-dinner pastime for adults. But bridge and whist fell by the wayside as the puzzle took the United States by storm and completely transformed entertainment in affluent American homes.

The Start of the Craze

The first commercial manufacturer was a young woman in eastern Massachusetts, whose name unfortunately has been lost.[8] In 1907 she was looking for a way to raise money for charity. Using colorful magazine covers that would appeal to adults, she made jigsaws of 100 to 200 small pieces. Her puzzles were extremely difficult, by virtue of their noninterlocking pieces, all shaped vaguely like squares, triangles, or oblongs. Color-line cutting exacerbated the assembler's confusion. Cutting straight along the line where a roof met the sky in the picture, for example, produced pieces that were either brown or blue, with nothing to indicate that they fit next to each other. Indeed, inexperienced puzzlers were fooled into thinking they were edge pieces.

When the puzzles appeared for sale at a fair to benefit a children's hospital, they created a furor and a huge demand for more of the novel amusements. The young entrepreneur cut more to sell through Women's Exchanges, and she made $600 during the winter months of 1907–08. As department stores sought to carry stocks of puzzles, other entrepreneurs turned to making puzzles too. According to one contemporary report:

> Hundreds of women and girls are now engaged in this curious home industry. Magazines have been stripped of covers, colored pictorials have been robbed of every suitable picture, and all sorts of wood have been used for the background.[9]

Part of the initial appeal of the puzzles for adults had to do with a poor economy. Puzzle maker Isabel Ayer of Boston later explained:

> The puzzle craze started at the time of the business depression in 1907. It was before the movies were developed and the business men were so wrought up, so mentally tired, that they took to solving them for mental relaxation. They saved many a man from suicide because of his worries. They took his mind off his troubles, and rested it. They proved to be fascinating. . . . It is essentially a man's game, but it is interesting to the whole family.[10]

After sweeping through Boston the novelty spread farther afield, even though the economy was by then recovering. Puzzles were the talk of the town in New York and other major American cities during the spring of 1908. The craze continued at a fever pitch in the United States for the next two years, while also spreading overseas. It reached London in March 1909 and Paris a year later.

Who were the puzzlers who continually demanded more and more puzzles to keep them busy? President Theodore Roosevelt, Czar Nicholas II of Russia, and financier J. P. Morgan were among them.[11] One writer reported that "Morgan, when he was putting over a big deal, would shut himself into a room and solve picture puzzles to rest his mind."[12] Another described a Boston physician who owned more than one hundred puzzles:

> This doctor finds his puzzles a valuable part of his pharmacopoeia. He prescribes them for wealthy patients living in hotel apartments or going South for the winter; and no Boston traveling trunk may be said to be complete nowadays without one of them, at least, tucked into it.[13]

High society embraced the jigsaw, so much so that several puzzle companies incorporated the word "Society" into their brand names. Puzzles became *de rigeur* at house parties in Long Island, Newport, and other posh resorts:

> So general has their use become at these affairs that on Saturdays the shops selling the puzzles and the factories themselves are besieged by customers about to take week-end trips to the country, who clamor for puzzles to take with them in order to add to the gayety at their destinations.[14]

Hostesses set up card tables with a different puzzle on each one, and awarded prizes to the teams that finished their puzzles the fastest. On Fifth Avenue, Mrs. Gouverneur Morris, "one of the most prominent society

The label on this 1908 puzzle box shows how adults became immersed in the new pastime.

women in New York," opened the Mrs. Vanity Fair shop, stocked almost exclusively with puzzles.[15]

What made the puzzles such a success? Unlike children's jigsaws or those for today's adults, the ones of the 1907–10 craze were truly mysteries. There was no picture on the box to guide the puzzler. Only a title, often enigmatic in itself, gave any guidance as to what the finished picture might look like.

The artwork, either magazine prints or commercially available lithographs, represented the popular taste of the day and had broad appeal. Images from Japan and Europe, Gibson girls, courtship scenes, and other human interest pictures all decorated jigsaw puzzles. The artists of the golden age of illustration—Maxfield Parrish, the Leyendeckers, and Howard Chandler Christy, among others—appear frequently.

The psychological element was important. Adults who were familiar only with simple children's puzzles became immersed, indeed addicted, through a regular progression.[16] On first exposure to the new toy, men typically dismissed it as trivial and childish and ridiculed those who found it so fascinating. But those who scoffed joined in, when they concluded that the puzzlers were clearly incompetent and needed a demonstration of how to solve the puzzle. Then, surprised to find the puzzle such hard going, they got their backs up, refusing to be defeated by such a silly thing. Soon they too were totally absorbed, ignoring meals while chanting "just one more piece" and staying up till the wee hours of the morning in a fierce effort to put the last piece into place. Once finished, they immediately sought out a bigger and more difficult puzzle.

The obsession was so great that there was a rush to find ways to make puzzles ever more challenging. Irregular borders deceived puzzlers whose strategy was to start with the edge pieces. Puzzles with images on both sides of the wood more than doubled the difficulty. Pictures with subdued coloring and even black-and-white drawings by Charles Gibson failed to satisfy the most fanatical puzzlers. The extremists demanded jigsaw puzzles with no pictures and only the grain of the wood to give clues to the proper assembly. Silver puzzles with pictures engraved on both sides gave these diehards a run for their money—in this case a hefty $35 for a 100-piece jigsaw.[17]

Jigsaws were a hit, not just with weary businessmen, but with professional men in all fields, as well as with women and teenagers. But, contrary to the *New York Times* headline, the poor were *not* doing puzzles in 1908. The average American worker earned only $12 per week at the time, while the puzzles cost 1 cent per piece, or $4 for a 400-piece puzzle. Working-class families could not afford them. The prices were even a stretch for the middle class, given that puzzlers rarely wanted to assemble a given picture more than once. They yearned for new images to enjoy and conquer.

The obvious answer to the problem of cost was to circulate individual puzzles among many devotees. Several mechanisms arose to facilitate the recycling process. Major cities offered rental libraries. Just as today people rent movies for an evening's entertainment, a century ago they rented jigsaw puzzles, for 5 to 10 cents per day.

Another solution was the puzzle exchange, such as the one at Fifth Avenue and Forty-fourth Street in New York City. Once finished with a puzzle, the owner could pay a 50-cent charge and trade it in for another puzzle of the same size. The Exchange's labels reassuringly proclaimed, "All puzzles sterilized by the Sanitation and Supply Co., 320 Fifth Avenue." This claim is dubious, since it is not clear how it was possible to sterilize something made of wood and paper in those days. In several other cities, individuals joined together to form puzzle clubs. Each member purchased one puzzle, then traded with others in the club, often in a fixed rotation every two weeks.

The U.S. Patent and Trademark Office received a flurry of patent applications for special puzzles. Nellie Olinger of Mount Pleasant, Pennsylvania, applied for a patent on her puzzle postal card at the end of 1908. Raphael Tuck of England produced similar postcard puzzles a few months later, before Olinger's patent had been approved. In 1909 Mary A. Houghton of Boston designed a raised puzzle for the blind, with pieces of the central figures thicker than those of the background. Theodore G. Strater of West Tisbury, Massachusetts, received a patent in 1909 on a tray with an adjustable frame to contain puzzles of different sizes and prevent the pieces from scattering.[18]

The jigsaw puzzle inspired its share of fiction. Short stories in magazines portrayed both the obsessions and the frustrations.[19] In *The Emerald City of Oz* L. Frank Baum's imaginary land grew to include the perplexing town of

Fuddlecumjig, whose inhabitants fell apart into small pieces and scattered themselves whenever strangers approached. Dorothy used her experience with the picture puzzle craze in Kansas to reassemble the cook and enough of the Fuddles to host a luncheon party.[20]

The Puzzle Manufacturers

For the first year of the craze, women who operated home workshops or very small factories constituted the majority of puzzle cutters. Most were upper class, even "society" women. More than a few set up puzzle businesses as an entertainment, with the income being distinctly secondary.

Countess Ella Festetics established a small workshop at the home of her millionaire father on Madison Avenue and donated the profits of her puzzle sales to charity. She declared:

> I first took up the puzzles this winter because the work amused me. It is true that my puzzles have been sold. I do the work only for the amusement.[21]

Many progressed from amusement to serious enterprise. Marjorie Bouvé (1879–1970), who was listed in the Brookline, Massachusetts, social directory, was among the best of the cutters who turned puzzles into a home business. She made thousands of mahogany "Ye Squirlijig Puzzles," including some with unusually tricky irregular borders, during the years of the puzzle craze. An energetic woman of many interests, she went on to found the Boston-Bouvé School of Physical Education, now a part of Northeastern University.

Isabel Ayer was another talented entrepreneur in Boston. In 1904 she opened the Fountain Pen Store in the Old South Building on Washington Street. She enjoyed working with her hands, so it was natural for her to buy a treadle scroll saw and start cutting when the puzzle craze struck in 1907. A newspaper feature on "Successful Women" credited her with establishing the first rental library for jigsaw puzzles.[22] She renamed her business the

Picture Puzzle Exchange, and made puzzles her career for another thirty-five years, shipping them throughout the United States and abroad. In addition to cutting and renting puzzles, she sold supplies (pictures, wood, blades, boxes, and so forth), thus helping many noncommercial puzzle makers get started.

Margaret Richardson (1876–1948) operated her "Perplexity" puzzle business on an even bigger scale in New York City. She claimed the credit for bringing the puzzle craze from Boston to New York in early 1908:

> A relative of my husband's suggested that I take advantage of the cut-puzzle craze, then starting in Boston. This appealed to me, as making the puzzles seemed rather good fun, and selling them would mean more good fun, and extra money to spend. With no more serious purpose than filling spare time and gaining a little pocket money, I bought a jig saw.[23]

She began selling her puzzles to families and friends by word of mouth. A few months later her sales had soared so much that she hired more than forty employees to cut, sand, and package the puzzles and set up a small factory near her Washington Square apartment. She took on complex business dealings, arranging an exclusive marketing agreement with Brentano's bookstore and pursuing successful trademark litigation against imitators. Her husband, the son of the prominent architect H. H. Richardson, eventually had to quit his job with the telephone company to help manage the puzzle business.

Perplexity puzzles went to buyers as far away as San Francisco, London and Paris. They could be as large and complex as the buyer desired, with prices up to $30. Richardson proudly related:

> Among our many schemes to be original, we conceived one that added zest for addicts and incidentally saved our time and boxes. We put three or four puzzles into one box, and for this heartbreaking mixture charged a good fat extra price. Our crowning effort was a puzzle cut for the Duchess of Marlborough, having 2700 pieces.[24]

The business was quite rewarding, since it took only about two hours to manufacture a 200-piece puzzle that sold for $2. By 1910, when the craze ended, the Richardsons had amassed enough profits to retire to Cape Cod. She continued to cut puzzles in modest numbers for years to come, as did at least two of her employees, William Lord and his son Edgar.

Ayer, Richardson, and Bouvé were among the biggest producers of jigsaw puzzles during the three years of the craze. Several hundred other small-scale cutters were hard at work at scroll saws, producing puzzles with names such as "Whatisit," "Putmeright," "Bewildering Bits," "Puzzleitis," "Phunnicut," "Vexation," "Puzzles for Never-Go-Outs," and "Puzzles for Grown-Ups and Shut-Ins." Some brands were of lesser quality, hastily and randomly cut out of lithographs with muddy colors; these generally sold for ½ cent per piece.

A substantial number of men supplied puzzles, including Earl Smith, who made the "Boston Puzzle" as far away as Lisbon, Iowa. An enterprising young Harvard student paid for his college education by selling his "Whatami" puzzles.[25] The most prolific was Frank M. Goss of Melrose, Massachusetts. After forty years of working for a textbook publisher, he made "Leisure Hour" puzzles during the 1910s and 1920s.

Histories have survived of several amateur puzzle makers of the period. Godfrey Pyle, son of artist Howard Pyle, spent some time at the scroll saw as a young teenager in Wilmington, Delaware. The elder Pyle wrote short stories to go with each puzzle produced by Godfrey Pyle & Co., as the young "captain of industry" styled himself.[26]

At the other end of the age spectrum, George W. Fiss (1835–1925) of Philadelphia cut puzzles after he retired from the wool business. He and his nephew, G. W. Fiss Jr., together made over one hundred puzzles using fine European lithographs, then loaned them out over many years to family and friends.[27]

In Newton, Massachusetts, three schoolteachers took up puzzle making as an avocation. Caroline Lowe, Ellen Tewksbury, and Madeleine Thurston all made puzzles for family and friends during their working years, and later too in their retirement in New Ipswich, New Hampshire.[28]

The craze also brought some adult puzzles made out of cardboard, although these were much less successful than the wooden ones. Manufacturers had to use very thin cardboard and very simple cutting designs with relatively few pieces, because die-cutting technology was quite primitive at the time. Nevertheless, a number of consumer products companies used them as advertising premiums.

Parker Brothers' Pastime Puzzles

While the small-scale manufacturers predominated from 1907 to 1910, it was a large game company that played a major role in keeping the adult puzzle going.

The established manufacturers of games and children's puzzles were slow in catching up with the puzzle craze. Milton Bradley, Parker Brothers (later famous for the game of Monopoly), Selchow & Righter, and E. I. Horsman had been big names with bestselling products in the toy departments for decades. But they did not begin making puzzles for adults until late in 1908.

Once started, they added more brand names to the hundreds of choices then on the market. Milton Bradley and Selchow & Righter sold good numbers of their "Perfection" and "Pictura" puzzles. Horsman got off to a rough start, with a legal challenge to its "Perplexyu" name (most likely from Margaret Richardson and her "Perplexity" brand), after which it adopted the "Confuseyu" name instead. All three makers bowed out of the adult puzzle market within a few years after the end of the craze.

Parker Brothers, however, produced a product that was immediately and immensely successful. The company actually stopped making its main line of games for a full year in 1909. In addition to devoting all its existing resources to jigsaws, the firm rented a special building and hired one hundred fifty new workers.[29] A total of two hundred twenty-five puzzle cutters turned out more than fifteen thousand puzzles per week.[30] Parker's "Pastime" puzzles were bestsellers for fifty years. They were innovative and creative, and set new standards of excellence.

George S. Parker had founded the Salem, Massachusetts, game company as a sixteen-year-old in 1883. An avid game player, he had the knack for inventing and marketing interesting games. For the company's first twenty-five years, it made games and only a few puzzles for children. Like other game companies, Parker Brothers rounded out its product line with dissected maps, sliced puzzles, and other simple puzzles.

Parker first advertised its Pastime puzzles in trade magazines in July 1908. The earliest Pastimes were small, rather crude, and relatively easy to assemble, since they did not use color-line cutting. But over the next three years Parker employees developed a cutting style that enlivened the jigsaw puzzle in new ways.

First, they adopted the prevailing style of color-line cutting. As noted above, this made it much more difficult for puzzlers to recognize when two pieces of different colors actually fit next to each other. Pastime cutters, however, used color-line cutting only along the major color divisions within a puzzle.

After separating the main colors, they cut each large section into interlocking pieces. The loops and locks were distinctive enough that they supplied many clues as to which pieces fit together. The interlocks also helped stabilize the assembled pieces. A careless move or a sneeze did not scatter the pieces and force the puzzler to start all over again, as with a noninterlocking (or "push-fit") puzzle.

Parker increased quality by using sturdy three-ply basswood, which made it possible to cut interlocking pieces with loops that had narrow necks. The earliest puzzles, both Parker's and those of other makers, had been made of solid wood, sometimes even from recycled cigar boxes. But the solid wood was susceptible to breakage along the grain at the narrow necks of the interlocks, as well as to warping.

The company's most important innovation was that each Pastime puzzle incorporated numerous pieces shaped like recognizable objects. Silhouettes of birds and butterflies in the skies, fish in the lakes, and animals and autos in the yards graced their puzzles. Letters and numerals, as well as geometric shapes, fleurs-de-lis, and other symmetrical curlicue designs appeared throughout each Pastime.

The figure pieces, usually 12 percent of the pieces, made it easier to assemble a puzzle. The piece that fit between the horns on the bull-shaped piece, for example, was more recognizable than a nondescript rounded loop. Yet figure pieces added so much interest to the puzzles, especially in the blander background areas, that most puzzlers much preferred them to any other cutting style.

Figure pieces were not a new idea. Matthews's 1873 book mentions them, and they had appeared in a few children's puzzles in the nineteenth century.[31] So it is really a mystery how Parker succeeded in patenting the idea in 1917. As it turns out, there is no evidence that Parker ever enforced the patent. By the time it expired in 1934, many other puzzle makers had been using figure pieces regularly for several years.

While Pastimes were the main product in Parker's adult puzzle line, the company also offered a few others. They developed "Contest Sets," large boxes containing up to twelve individually boxed small puzzles, for use at puzzle parties. A special "Saint Valentine Pastime" brand had all the figure pieces shaped like hearts and arrows. Parker also experimented with more simply cut puzzles such as the "Climax" and "Jig-A-Jig" labels, and, during World War I, "For Soldiers in Cantonment and at the Front." The last three brands sold for less than the prevailing 1-cent-per-piece rate of the Pastimes.

Parker, like most other companies at the time, accepted special orders from individual customers. A puzzler could send a favorite print to the company to be cut up, or request special figure pieces to spell out names and dates. In the 1920s the company made a 10,000-piece puzzle from a five-foot-by-seven-foot poster of West Point for puzzle enthusiasts Pierrepont and Ray Noyes, leaders of New York's Oneida Colony. The puzzle took six months to assemble and is still on display at the Mansion House in Oneida, New York.

Parker Brothers hired only women to cut puzzles. A commonly cited rationale was that men lacked the manual dexterity needed to cut the small, intricate pieces. Furthermore, since most women of the time already knew how to use sewing machines, it was easy for them to master the use of a treadle saw. But this explanation is contradicted by the experience of competitors. In Margaret Richardson's factory in New York, all the cutters were men.

Parker Brothers of Salem, Massachusetts, hired only women to cut its "Pastime" puzzles. Employees had to cut at least 1,400 pieces per day.
Courtesy of Philip Orbanes

Parker probably favored female workers because their wages were so much lower than men's in Salem at that time. One cutter later reported that she earned less, after thirty-five years of skilled work in Parker's puzzle department, than her husband earned as a factory custodian.[32]

The "Pastime girls," as the cutters were known, were working-class women, primarily in their teens and twenties. Most had left high school before graduating, so they could contribute to their families' incomes. Despite their low levels of formal education, many were very talented and creative artists with the saw.

Parker supplied its employees with patterns for standard figure pieces, but the best cutters, encouraged by their supervisors, would spend time at home in the evening drawing their own special designs. They cut out these patterns for angels, Easter baskets, and other complex shapes with scissors. Eva Gagnon recalled:

> If I'd go some place, and I'd see a pretty design, I'd make one when I'd come home. I made a story out of these things in my mind all the time when I worked. The forelady was afraid of a mouse. And when she saw a mouse on the floor, she'd jump up on her desk, on the chair. So I made a table, and I made a woman sitting on the table, and the mouse in the bottom. And that night I put it in the puzzle.[33]

The most skilled Pastime girls did the cutting on the custom orders that came to the company.

The most skilled puzzle cutters at Parker Brothers designed their own patterns for figure pieces, instead of using those supplied by the company. Eva Audet Gagnon created these designs in the 1930s.

In addition to being artistic, the puzzle cutters worked very quickly. Each was expected to cut at least 1,400 pieces per day.[34] This was a fast and furious pace, especially since the 1,400 had to include 168 figure pieces. Workers who fell behind earned less, since they were paid piece rates (of course!) until the minimum wage was imposed in 1937. In fact, Parker Brothers ran the Pastime department more like a craft atelier, in which each worker had autonomy and control, than like the standard factory operations in the rest of the company.

Parker distributed its Pastime puzzles nationwide, both by mail order directly to consumers and through department and stationery stores. Its branches in London and Paris helped the company obtain fine European prints for puzzles, and also to sell puzzles when the craze spread overseas.

The End of the Craze

The puzzle mania ran its course after two years. Sales tapered off in 1910 in the United States, though they subsided a bit later in Europe. Most of the manufacturers who were active during the craze stopped making puzzles

During the 1930s Madmar Quality Company of Utica, New York, marketed this set of four 50-piece puzzles in a small trunk, for use at parties, in contests, or while traveling.

when it ended. Parker Brothers resumed production of games, although it remained the biggest producer of jigsaws. The company's annual catalogs listed hundreds of available puzzle titles in sizes from 65 to 1,200 pieces.

Joining Parker Brothers during World War I was Madmar Quality Company of Utica, New York. Miles H. Bickelhaupt founded the company to make wooden games and toys in 1915 and named it after his infant daughter Madeleine Mary.[35] He added dissected maps and picture puzzles to the line by 1917, and within a few years puzzles for both children and adults had become the company's principal product. Madmar puzzles were less intricate than those of Parker Brothers, and only rarely had figure pieces. But they also were less expensive and of good quality. They successfully filled a market niche and pleased puzzle aficionados until 1966, when the company ceased production.

During the 1910s and 1920s, jigsaw puzzles continued to sell slowly but steadily as amusements for adults. By the 1930s, a generation after the first craze, the time was ripe for a new mania to strike.

4

The Great Depression Mania

WE WILL GO DOWN IN HISTORY AS
THE NATION WHO WORKED JIG SAW PUZZLES WHILE
OUR COUNTRY WAS FALLING IN RUINS.

Universal-International News

Puzzle madness was in full swing in early 1933. Universal Newsreel almost certainly staged this scene of people who suspended trays from their necks so they could continue to do puzzles while crossing the street.

"Now I can finish my jig-saw puzzle," declared the inmate on death row in Pennsylvania, when his sentence was reduced to life imprisonment. Firefighters had to force a man doing a jig-saw puzzle to leave his burning Toronto apartment in midwinter. Undaunted, he continued to assemble it outside on the sidewalk.[1]

Entertainers crooned the latest songs, "You Made a Jig-Saw Puzzle out of My Heart" and "I'm the Jig-Saw Man." Moviegoers roared with laughter as comedian Stan Laurel's gift of a puzzle ruined Oliver Hardy's wedding in *Me and My Pal*. In arcades, players tilted pinball machines, trying to construct pictures of the Chicago World's Fair with puzzle pieces controlled by rolling balls.

The year was 1933, the peak of the continent's obsession with jigsaw puzzles. They were everywhere: in stores, at newsstands, in films, in newspapers, and, most important, on card tables in living rooms throughout the country. In one week alone, ten million newly minted puzzles went into American homes. After several months at that frantic pace, pieces of chopped-up pictures had inundated the nation's thirty-one million households.[2]

Not everyone was happy. At least one marriage fell into ruins because of excessive spending on jigsaw puzzles. And a prominent Detroit minister preached:

Ancient history tells us that Nero fiddled while Rome was burning. We will go down in history as the nation who worked jig saw puzzles while our country was falling in ruins.[3]

This second big jigsaw puzzle craze flourished during the early 1930s, bringing some welcome relief to the suffering in the depths of the Great Depression. The addiction hit virtually all levels of society, unlike the craze of 1907–10, which had been confined to the upper classes. With unemployment so widespread, people had plenty of time, both to cut up pictures and to reassemble them. The fad built up slowly, beginning with a revival of wood puzzles in 1930. Free advertising puzzles appeared in mid-1932 and were followed by cheap weekly cardboard puzzles in the fall. Together, they ignited nine months of true mania and induced even low-income families to join in the fun.

The Crash and Its Puzzling Outcome

The Roaring Twenties came to a halt with the stock market crash on "Black Thursday," October 24, 1929. Financial panic sent the country into an economic tailspin, followed by a sustained depression that lasted throughout the 1930s. It was the worst economic collapse that the United States has ever known. Unemployment climbed to 25 percent by 1933, with much deeper job cuts in major urban manufacturing centers. In Detroit and Harlem, for example, unemployment soared to 50 percent.[4] The dire economic situation, combined with persistent drought in the Midwest, resulted in massive numbers of farm foreclosures and displaced persons in rural areas.

Of those who still had jobs, most lost income because of both cutbacks in the average work week (from forty-eight to thirty-five hours in four years) and a 20 percent reduction in average hourly wages. (The consumer price index fell too, but not enough to offset the lower earnings.)[5] Even families who had escaped these immediate financial setbacks had lost their economic security—no one knew what would come next. Herbert Hoover's Republican administration was helpless to turn the economy around.

With a shortage of funds and a surplus of time, people looked for inexpensive amusements to fill their new unexpected leisure. The depression years brought a succession of fads, from miniature golf in 1930, to jigsaw puzzles, and then on to Monopoly in 1935–36. One trade magazine noted a boom in the sales of board and card games:

> People are being forced to curtail expenses. In place of the usual theatres, picture shows, dining and dancing, adult games are being substituted, for people must have their amusement and when they haven't the money to spend for expensive forms you will find them more interested in the inexpensive.[6]

There was a big psychological element too. Puzzles and games diverted people from their problems. Even better, these pastimes allowed for success in a dismal and dreary time when economic failure was the rule. Finishing a jigsaw puzzle or winning a game gave the player a sense of mastery and achievement that was hard to come by in other facets of daily life. Puzzling and game playing within the family or among friends also provided a comforting network of support when economic troubles were tearing at the social fabric.

Finally, an entire generation had grown up in the twenty years since the first jigsaw puzzle craze. The cyclical nature of such fads made the revival almost inevitable.

Wood Puzzles Set the Craze in Motion

Interest in jigsaws began to swell again in 1930, as the depression's grip tightened. The media reported on prominent heads of state who were doing puzzles: former President Calvin Coolidge, King George V of England (who regularly purchased 1,500-piece puzzles from Parker Brothers), and Benito Mussolini. President Hoover kept them at his summer retreat in Virginia, where visitors such as Charles and Anne Lindbergh enjoyed them. The First Lady was so accomplished that she often did her puzzles with the picture side down, relying only on the shapes of the pieces and the wood grain for clues to the solution.[7]

Hollywood stars got into the act too. Jean Harlow, Clark Gable, and Eddie Cantor were among those who developed a taste for puzzles.[8] Jigsaws were the most popular party pastime at the Beverly Hills mansion of screen star Harold Lloyd:

> The Lloyds have sent to New York and abroad for the most difficult and unique of puzzles and most any Sunday finds movie celebrities exclaiming like children over the intricacies of the cut-outs.[9]

The average citizen, however, had trouble affording hand-cut wood puzzles, which then sold for 1½ cents per piece. For example, a 500-piece puzzle cost $7.50, a formidable expense compared with 3 cents a pound for flour, 10 cents a pound for pork chops, and 12 cents a pound for prime rib roast in grocery stores at the time.

The lending library once again came to the rescue and became a key to the surging popularity of jigsaw puzzles. Although some puzzle exchanges had existed in the past, during the 1930s they blossomed as never before. Puzzles rented for 3 to 10 cents a day, depending on their size, or 15 cents and up for a week. Some private rental libraries simply added puzzles to their shelves, next to the books. Other outlets included drugstores, department stores, and the workshops of individual puzzle producers. In Newport, Rhode Island, and other cities, individuals organized puzzle clubs that bought puzzles, then rotated them among the members. Milkmen in Maine would carry puzzles along with dairy products for delivery on their routes.

Lost pieces were the bane of the rental establishments, as no one wanted to borrow a puzzle that was not complete. Proprietors adopted various devices to deal with the problem. Some threatened dire penalties if patrons lost pieces. Others cajoled. In New Haven, Connecticut, the Brick Row Book Shop decorated the lid of each puzzle box with this poem:

> *Please Don't Lose a Piece of Puzzle*
> *So Just Keep the Dog in Muzzle*
> *Trouser-Cuff and Morris Chair*
> *Are a Menace—Please Use Care.*

Many libraries counted the pieces of each puzzle when it was returned, to check that the total matched the number specified on the label. Some libraries even assembled each puzzle in between loans, to ascertain its condition. A few avoided this time-consuming practice by supplying borrowers with trays and insisting that they bring back each puzzle assembled. Some libraries refused to rent to people who had small children or dogs that chewed the pieces.

Cutting replacement pieces and coloring them so that they blended into the original puzzle picture required much time and skill. Therefore, libraries charged fees for lost pieces. The ultimate sanction was to force the borrower to buy any puzzle that was returned with a piece missing.

Missing pieces often turned up much later, tossed in with other puzzles, making it hard to return these orphans to their proper boxes. One remedy, adopted by a Minneapolis company among others, was to give each puzzle a serial number, then mark that number on the back of each of its pieces with a rubber stamp. Surprises turned up too. In Portland, Maine, one of Alice Kern's rental puzzles came back with several false teeth sprinkled among the pieces![10]

One of the premier rental libraries was Josephine Flood's Picture Puzzle Mart, established in 1929 in New York City. Flood sent specially selected posters and prints to the Parker Brothers factory and insisted that the company assign only the best Pastime workers to cut them into puzzles for her. She favored very large and difficult puzzles. Since her library charged by the day, the longer it took to complete the puzzle, the more money came in. The Picture Puzzle Mart label was designed to assuage any guilt that borrowers felt about frittering away their hours on frivolous amusements. It assured puzzlers that all proceeds went to support summer outings for carefully selected poor but deserving girls from congested districts of the city.

Wood Puzzle Manufacturing

In response to the growing demand, the big puzzle manufacturers stepped up production. Parker Brothers doubled the number of women cutting its Pastime puzzles between 1928 and 1931, to more than one hundred workers. Madmar Quality Company increased its advertising substantially in 1930 and 1931.

In this age of gloom and flurry
Which is rife with strife and worry
We should all relax and rest
Claims Oscar Guzzle.
So I let collectors wait
In the hall or at the gate
While I work upon my nifty
Madmar Puzzle.

madmar quality company
UTICA· NEW YORK

A March 1932 advertisement by Madmar touted jigsaw puzzles as an antidote to the gloom and worry of the Great Depression.

By 1932 most of the other major game companies, such as Milton Bradley and Selchow & Righter, had returned to making wood puzzles for adults. In addition to selling puzzles through its regular retail outlets, Bradley offered a $48 package for rental libraries, including two dozen of its "Premier" puzzles in assorted sizes, a mahogany storage cabinet, cards with the library's imprint, advertising material, and "complete instructions for launching immediately into this profitable business."[11]

Several new puzzle companies started up. In Brooklyn, New York, Joseph K. Straus (1879–1957) founded a business that produced jigsaws for the next four decades. At the age of sixteen, Straus began a sixty-year career in the toy industry by working for the Ullman Manufacturing Company, a maker of prints, picture frames, and children's items. He became a sales representative for the firm in 1906, just before it spent several years making "Society" jigsaw puzzles during the first craze. So it was logical for Straus to decide to make jigsaw puzzles in the 1930s. He sold them nationwide to the many toy industry buyers whom he already knew.[12]

Straus started his own operation in a corner of the Ullman factory and made an immediate hit with a puzzle showing the newly elected President Franklin D. Roosevelt. He reached retail customers with a puzzle of the month club. The firm reduced costs by stacking four puzzles together and cutting them simultaneously in standard strip patterns. This technique resulted in a no-frills but still attractive wood puzzle.

Straus also made children's puzzles and developed some more elaborate items for adults. "Sculptured" puzzles, cut in two layers, gave a three-dimensional effect. Special-edition puzzles, done in the company's later years for FAO Schwarz, Henri Bendel, and other retailers, often featured simple figure pieces.

Other firms were less long-lived and depended more on local markets. An example was the Barnard-Clogston Company, which started up in Melrose, Massachusetts, in the fall of 1932. A dozen or so women cut puzzles that the company sold in the Boston area for a few years. Barnard-Clogston also operated the Spectator Puzzle Library as an outlet for its wares. In Winsted, Connecticut, Gail Borden Munsill (died 1934), the wealthy great grandson and namesake of the inventor of condensed milk, started the Leisure Moment Puzzle Company. The factory helped the town survive the depression by employing forty men during the winter of 1932–33.

Companies in other industries turned to making jigsaw puzzles. S. S. Adams, a novelty manufacturer in Asbury Park, New Jersey, made its "Superfine Jig-Saw Puzzles" for several years. Employees in Western Electric's Hawthorne Works in Cicero, Illinois, made puzzles at the factory when there was not enough regular work to keep them employed full time. In Scotia, New York, hit hard by layoffs at the nearby General Electric plant, the Veteran's Emergency Association made and rented puzzles.

Their puzzle labels stated that they also supplied "experienced men for automobile repairing, building, razing, painting," and dozens of other types of jobs.

The Shut-In Society, a sheltered workshop in Philadelphia, capitalized on the puzzle craze and sold its "Jigger" puzzles through stores and Women's Exchanges. Strawbridge & Clothier, a large Philadelphia department store, bought hundreds of their puzzles in December 1932, causing the Society to bring in extra workers from their homes and from hospitals to fill the order. Huge crowds gathered at the puzzle display in the store's book department, where stacks of puzzles surrounded a scroll saw operated by one of the boys from the Society. The result was a windfall to the Society, with three thousand puzzles selling in the three weeks before Christmas, at prices of $1 to $10.[13]

Demonstrations of puzzle cutting in stores both large and small became very common in 1932. In Brookline, Massachusetts, one shop in the central shopping district offered customized designs:

> A jig saw puzzle cutting machine is kept in operation in the window, cutting puzzles to order. A sign in the window reads: "Bring in your own picture and we will cut it at the rate of one cent per cut. For a small additional charge you may have the name or initials of a friend cut into the puzzle—which makes a nice Christmas present." Every time the jig saw is started going, the sidewalk outside the shop becomes so crowded that it is almost impossible to pass, and one has to join the group of neck-stretchers in front of the window.[14]

Kodak's retail stores and other companies also offered personalized puzzles to customers who wanted a snapshot enlarged and cut up. Some of the customized puzzles raised eyebrows:

> [One woman] had a map drawn, charting her somewhat stormy matrimonial career. Her former husbands were represented symbolically as reefs and shoals threatening her frail galleon of love. "Here is my life in pieces," she blithely tells guests. "See whether you can put it together again." This is a very difficult puzzle. Nobody has yet succeeded in fitting husband No. 1 into his proper place.[15]

The Home Workshops

The big companies were not the only manufacturers of wood puzzles during the depression. Indeed, the real proliferation of wood puzzles came not from the large and medium-sized manufacturers with national distribution networks, but at the local level. The craftsperson producing on a small scale for a single city played a major role in the depression years, even more so than during the pre-World War I craze.

The rising incomes of the 1920s had brought changes in American society. Electrification had come to homes in towns and cities. The average work week had fallen to the six-day, forty-eight-hour norm, from much higher levels at the turn of the century. With the increased leisure had come a new movement to promote arts, crafts, collecting, and other hobbies as a way to spend that time enjoyably and productively.[16]

All these trends meant that when puzzles once again became popular in the depression years, a cottage industry of home workshops was ready to make them. It was fueled by several magazines that promoted all kinds of workshop activities.

Popular Science Monthly's instructions on how to cut wooden puzzles in March 1932 initiated a spate of articles devoted to this topic. In July 1932 *The Home Craftsman* announced a contest with $50 in prizes to be awarded for the best jigsaw puzzle cutting pattern. *Popular Homecraft*'s series of articles by Towner K. Webster Jr. was especially influential and became the core of a 36-page booklet *Jigsaw Puzzles—And How to Make 'Em*.[17] The articles in the hobby and workshop press supplied not only technical information on making puzzles, but also advice on how to sell them.

The timely tips, plus the overall economic situation, convinced hundreds, if not thousands, to go into the puzzle business. For many men who had lost their jobs working with machinery or wood, it was an easy transition. Carpenters, cabinetmakers, machinists, and architects were typical of the skilled craftspeople who were laid off because houses were no longer being built or furnished. Others, especially women and teenage boys, discovered that a jigsaw was no more complicated to operate than

This 1933 booklet contains instructions on how to make and sell jigsaw puzzles, plus many advertisements from manfacturers of saws, plywood, prints, glues and other supplies.

a sewing machine, and that they could start a puzzle business with very little capital.

The "Picture Puzzle Maker: Get the Thrill of Making Your Own Puzzles" by Baumgarten & Co. of Baltimore was one of the starter kits available for novice cutters. It contained several pictures, plywood, and everything else needed to convert the materials into puzzles, including a handheld fretsaw.

More experienced crafters patronized their local hardware stores or ordered supplies from mail order catalogs. H. L. Wild and Lazard Frères in New York City, Goes Lithographing in Chicago, and dozens of other specialized firms filled the home workshop magazines with advertisements for prints, plywood, glue, figure piece patterns, boxes, blades, and machinery for making jigsaw puzzles.

Both Delta Specialty Co. of Milwaukee and Walker-Turner of Plainfield, New Jersey, introduced high-quality electric scroll saws designed for home workshops in the early 1930s. Prices ranged from $10 to $24, not including the motor. More than a few buyers avoided the extra cost of the motor by hooking the saw up to the motor of an electric washing machine. Some workmen even built their own scroll saws from scratch.

In 1932 small jigsaw puzzle companies were operating all over the United States. The greatest concentration was in the Northeast, where even small towns might have several puzzle businesses in operation. In Maine alone, there were over one hundred puzzle makers.[18] Big cities in the Midwest and West had their share of companies too. Nationwide, more than five hundred small companies operating in this era have been identified, and undoubtedly many more existed whose puzzles and stories have not yet been documented.

The vast majority of these enterprises consisted of one individual, often assisted by a spouse or children, with a scroll saw set up on a kitchen table or in a basement workshop. Most of the cutters were middle-class or working-class people who were trying to supplement their reduced incomes with their puzzle earnings. Some cutters had no other work and had to rely on puzzles as a way to make do.

The quality of craftsmanship of the home workshop puzzles varied tremendously. Some cutters turned out hasty and crude work, with ragged pieces and sawdust tossed into any handy cigar or candy box. Others took more pride in their work; they sanded the edges of each piece, and used specially made boxes and printed labels. Many followed the instructions of Towner Webster, incorporating figure piece designs to make a more sophisticated product. A few went far beyond that, reaching or surpassing the quality of the Parker Brothers Pastime puzzles.

The home-based puzzle businesses were very ephemeral, tiding a family over the worst of the depression. As soon as "real" jobs became available again, virtually all the cutters abandoned their jigsaws and went back to more remunerative employment. Even though most of the depression-era puzzle cutters were active for only a few years, many of their puzzles and their histories have survived, thanks to descendants and customers who have preserved them.

Some of the Best Craftspeople

The vignettes below exemplify the experiences of a few of the best craftspeople.

Carroll A. Towne (1901–1991) of Auburndale, Massachusetts, graduated from the University of Massachusetts in 1928, married, and embarked on a career as a landscape architect. He lost his job after the stock market crash, and hard times ensued. Encouraged by Emily, his fiercely loyal wife who loved to do jigsaw puzzles, he bought a saw for $29.50. Together they began a business selling and renting jigsaw puzzles.[19]

Towne's initials suggested the brand name "Cut by CAT," and each puzzle included his cat-shaped signature piece. He was an imaginative cutter whose puzzles featured many figure pieces and deceptive color-line cutting. Emily did all the sanding, checking, and packaging. She also staved off the tax agents, who came to the door to collect on the proceeds of their puzzle operation. She read them the riot act about harassing a hardworking but poor and struggling young couple, and the flustered G-men retreated.

Later in the 1930s, Towne put his talents to use in his career as a planner for the Tennessee Valley Authority. His interchangeable puzzle maps facilitated the quick preparation of charts to show the geographical distributions of various population characteristics.

Charles Russell (1896–1984) of Auburn, Massachusetts, was fortunate enough not to lose his job as a textile engineer at Crompton and Knowles, but his income dropped dramatically in the early 1930s when his company reduced his employment to only eighteen hours a week. He began cutting puzzles with a scroll saw that he rigged to run off the washing machine motor. He designed hundreds of figure pieces that he cut freehand, with only an occasional glance at his pattern book. His wife Reina glued the pictures, then counted and checked the pieces.

The puzzles sold for ½ cent per piece, either directly to customers or through local retailers such as the Worcester Women's Exchange. Others went into the puzzle club that he started. Members paid weekly dues and got a new puzzle every week. Russell was proud that the efforts paid off:

> We weren't rich, but we were able to buy an automobile and a sewing machine and a few other odds and ends, and we paid for them out of the puzzle money.[20]

Russell continued making puzzles after his retirement in 1960, shipping them to steady customers all over the United States and abroad.

Alden L. Fretts (1897–1980) of Pittsfield and West Springfield, Massachusetts, made his "Yankee Cut-Ups" puzzles with a treadle saw after he lost his job as a draftsman. He also worked as a door-to-door salesman to keep food on the table during the depression. He displayed and sold his puzzles in a shoe repair shop in Springfield, and rented them out at 28 cents for three days. His wife Gladys helped out by sanding the pieces after they were cut, and by assembling each rental puzzle when it was returned to make sure that no pieces had been lost.

Fretts's puzzles are cut from bass plywood and interlock so tightly that an assembled puzzle can be picked up by one corner without any pieces falling out. Most of his puzzles include a number of figure pieces with his signature design, a running dog named Pal, cut in the lower right corner.[21]

Phyllis McLellan (born circa 1907) of Gardiner, Maine, was featured in *What Others Have Done with "Delta" Tools*, a 32-page booklet issued by the Delta Specialty Company. She wrote to the company six months after buying one of Delta's "American Giant" scroll saws and setting it up on her kitchen table.

> The first of January, 1931, I started to make jig-saw puzzles. I am at the present in twenty of the leading gift shops in Maine. My husband is a salesman, and is away most of the week. I make my puzzles in spare time. I found out that I could not keep up with my orders with one machine, so I purchased

Phyllis McLellan was one of hundreds of Mainers who cut jigsaw puzzles in their kitchens and basements to supplement incomes during the Great Depression.
Courtesy of Pentair Tools Group

another. . . . My husband helps with this machine over the week-end. I intend to hire a girl to use this other machine, so I may do twice the business.[22]

The twenty-four-year-old McLellan made high-quality puzzles with figure pieces. She was clearing $35.36 in profits per week, after paying for plywood, prints, boxes, labels, blades, signs, shipping, and other supplies. This was heady stuff at a time when skilled production workers typically earned only $15 to $25 per week, *if* they still had jobs.

Lorraine Riley (born 1907) and **Perry Riley** (1894–1985) began making their "Topsy Turvy" puzzles in Carthage, Missouri, after doing some of their neighbor's Parker Brothers Pastime puzzles. Lorraine had no job and Perry, an electrician, had little work during the depression, so both of them did the cutting. Their puzzles included figure pieces, and they interlocked so tightly that not a single piece would fall out when the puzzle was picked up by the corner.

The Rileys made puzzles for about four years, often cutting three or four sizable puzzles in a day. They sold some for 1 cent per piece, and rented the rest. They built up a stock of almost one thousand puzzles, which they rented from a space in the Ramsey Brothers department store. Demand was highest on weekends, when Carthage citizens would borrow as many as a hundred different puzzles. Many of the puzzles have been preserved at the Powers Museum in Carthage.[23]

Edward Brewer (born 1915) and **William Brewer** (born 1918) were teenagers in high school when they began cutting their "Brewer Brothers" jigsaw puzzles in Cortland, New York. Although their family was in good financial condition, their mother was always involved in making and selling needlework crafts. Ed recalled:

> My mother and father really started us as kids doing it. They were kind of trying to teach us something, I think. We cut puzzles and we did it for four or five years. And helped, maybe, pay our way a little way, not very far, toward college.[24]

Most of the family was involved in the puzzle business. Their mother was the "administrator," their father pasted the pictures onto plywood, and the two boys did the cutting, with occasional help from their sister Barbara. Most puzzles included their "BB" logo and figure pieces.

Although they made some puzzles for sale at 1 cent per piece, most of their puzzles were very large ones that rented for 25 cents for three days. They rented the puzzles through a dozen bookstores across upstate New York, from Albany to Buffalo, rotating their stock periodically from one location to the next.

Bernard J. Roemer (circa 1892–1935) was another puzzle maker whose experiences were documented in the Delta Specialty Company booklet.[25] At the time the thirty-nine-year-old former advertising man was convalescing from an illness in Colorado Springs, Colorado. At the suggestion of an occupational therapist, he made jigsaw puzzles with a coping saw, then moved up to an electric Delta saw in 1930. After six months of experimentation with

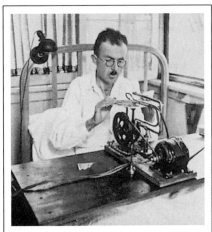

Working from his hospital bed, Bernard Roemer of Colorado Springs built a thriving business of making jigsaw puzzles and writing instruction manuals for aspiring cutters.

Courtesy of Pentair Tools Group

materials and techniques, Roemer started a business from his nursing home bed. His Puzzle Makers company sold "Pike's Peak Picture Puzzles" and other puzzle novelties by mail, sending them to both individual customers and big department stores nationwide.

Because Roemer's health limited him to one or two hours of puzzle cutting per day, he soon branched into the business of supplying other makers with wood, pictures, glue, blades, and other items. He advertised regularly in the home workshop magazines. His greatest efforts went into his mimeographed text, *Production of Fine Picture Puzzles in the Home Workshop: PUZMAK Course in Puzzle Making and Selling.* By 1933 he was selling the 90-page fifth edition for $3. Purchasers could use Roemer's free "Criticism Service" by sending him one of their puzzles for a detailed piece-by-piece critique.

The Jones family of Chagrin Falls and Cleveland, Ohio, began making "Falls Puzzles" after the mechanical engineering business of John Paul Jones (circa 1890–1970) dried up in the early 1930s.[26] His wife, Mary Belle Jones (died 1957), known as "Jimmy" to family and friends, did the cutting and sanding. John bought the pictures, did the gluing, designed hundreds of figure piece patterns, and made rubber stamps to apply the patterns to the wood. The three children helped assemble the puzzles after they were cut, to ensure that no pieces had fallen onto the basement floor.

Their most famous customers were British royalty. John Paul Jones was a childhood friend of Wallis Simpson, the divorcee whose romance with King Edward VIII caused his abdication from the throne. Mrs. Simpson introduced the royal family and other aristocrats to Falls puzzles in 1936. They were such a hit that Harrod's, the London department store, began importing them directly from Ohio. The Joneses also sold some puzzles by mail order across the country, though most of the puzzles were rented through a Cleveland bookstore, Korner & Wood. Every puzzle included their signature piece, a falling girl.

Falls puzzles featured unusually intricate cutting and an extremely high density of figure pieces, at least one out of every four pieces. At one time business was so brisk that Jimmy hired two other women to help with the cutting. The enterprise was so successful that she continued to make and sell Falls puzzles well into the 1940s, long after her husband had returned to engineering.

James T. Browning (1890–1977) of East Orange and West Caldwell, New Jersey, was one of the handful of puzzle makers who continued in business for decades beyond the depression years.[27] A carpenter and contractor by trade, he began making his "U-Nit" puzzles in 1932. Although Browning cut in stacks of three puzzles at a time, he used very fine blades for a high-quality product. The puzzles were backed with a veneer of Spanish cedar and included many figure pieces, some patterned after the Pastime designs.

Browning sold most of his puzzles to retailers such as toy store FAO Schwarz and bookstores Brentano's and Womrath's in New York City. One large order went as far away as a big department store in Rio de Janeiro. He also rented puzzles for a while, both from his home and through various bookstores in northern New Jersey. In the late 1940s his basement workshop was humming with five scroll saws operated by his teenage son, three high school girls, and himself.

When Parker Brothers shut down its Pastime line in the late 1950s, Browning bought many of the prints Parker had on hand. He finally retired in the late 1960s when he was approaching the age of eighty.

Chester W. Nott (1895–1943) made puzzles at home, just for the fun of it and to supply family and friends with the latest entertainment. Nott, a school teacher, took up the hobby after seeing the puzzles rented out by his brother-in-law Henry A. Martin (1898–1958) in Fairport, New York. The two engaged in an informal competition to see who could make the most challenging and attractive interlocking puzzles. They were always on the lookout for interesting pictures. Once Nott and his wife encountered a downed power line while driving to dinner in early January:

> [They] went to the Sheriff's office to report it. Waiting in the empty office, they noticed a December calendar with a great picture. Finally, when no one appeared, they wrote a note about the power line, took the calendar off the wall, and left."[28]

Cardboard Creates a Craze

The puzzle craze took a quantum leap with the introduction of die-cut cardboard puzzles for adults in the second half of 1932. Manufacturers used huge industrial presses to stamp out these puzzles quickly and cheaply. A 300-piece cardboard puzzle sold for 25 cents or less, making the pastime no longer the exclusive province of the middle and upper classes. And millions of advertising puzzles were available for free, even to the poorest and most destitute.[29]

The most intense stage of the puzzle craze began in June 1932 when the Prophylactic Brush Company of Florence, Massachusetts, offered a free 50-piece puzzle to toothbrush buyers. This premium and the simultaneous advertising campaign created a huge increase in sales. The promotion's runaway success caught the attention of hundreds of other makers of consumer products. They followed suit, and a new wave of puzzles deluged the country.

Die-cutting had been used as early as 1890 for small simple puzzles. But as 1932 progressed, advertising puzzles increased in size, to 100 pieces and more. The die-cutting technology improved as well, so the lightweight cardboard puzzles could incorporate the interlocking pieces and figure pieces of the traditional wood puzzles for adults.

Two Boston companies, Viking Manufacturing and University Distributing, realized that cardboard puzzles could compete with the costly wooden ones. People would happily pay for them if the puzzles were attractive (with no advertising on them), challenging, and inexpensive. The two companies' creative genius was the concept of a series of puzzles, with a new picture appearing each week. In an imaginative marketing move, they sold the puzzles through the newsstands that were on city corners everywhere at the time. Customers could pick up the hot new puzzle when they bought the daily paper with its breaking news.

Viking began its "Picture Puzzle Weekly" series in September 1932 with an edition of about twelve thousand.[30] The University Distributing Company released its first "Jig of the Week" puzzle on October 5, 1932, at the bargain price of 25 cents. The box promised: "A new puzzle issued every week, on sale Wednesday."

The weekly puzzle was a sensation in Boston and the rest of New England. Buyers mobbed the newsstands every week to scoop up the latest offerings. By November, distribution had spread across the country as both companies forged alliances with news distributors that had branches nationwide.

The Einson-Freeman Company of Long Island City, New York, already the biggest maker of advertising puzzles, fueled the craze even more in December 1932.[31] Its "Every Week Jig-Saw Puzzle" cost only 15 cents. The box gave instructions for holding a jig-saw race and a jig-saw party. Both events, of course, required the purchase of a separate puzzle for each player.

By the end of 1932, more than two hundred firms were producing die-cut puzzles.[32] The series puzzles multiplied to include such brands as the "Muddle," "B-Witching Weekly," "Duo Jig," "Jigee-Sawee," "Jiggers Weekly," "Juggernaut," "Zigzaw," "Zig-Zag," and "Once-A-Week Dime Jig Saw." During Christmas week, puzzles were completely sold out in at least one city.[33] And that was before the peak of the mania hit a few months later.

In February 1933 the puzzle industry was producing ten million puzzles per week, including about seven million advertising puzzles.[34] Puzzles came in every size and style and were found throughout the country.

Jigsaw puzzles, especially the inexpensive die-cut ones, seemed to take over all aspects of life between June 1932 and March 1933. Not only did they bewitch the solitary puzzler, they also offered a noncompetitive social activity

3 Ways to Play Jig-Saw Puzzles

I. Mental Speed Test

FIRST—Break up the puzzle into separate pieces.
SECOND—Lay puzzle face up on the table, and jumble the pieces thoroughly.
THIRD—Check time when you start and complete the puzzle, and compare with average time schedule, as follows:

AVERAGE TIME SCHEDULE

12 Year Boy or Girl—3½ to 4 Hours
16 Year Boy or Girl—3 to 3½ Hours
Adult (18 years up)—2¾ to 3 Hours

NOTE—Many people, regardless of age, have a special aptitude for solving puzzles quickly. It is, therefore, suggested that you ESTABLISH YOUR OWN FAMILY HANDICAP by actual experience of the various individuals rather than on the basis of comparative age. This is particularly important in playing the exciting JIG-SAW RACE.

2. Jig-Saw Race

FIRST—You must have an individual set for each player.

SECOND—Before starting to play, you should definitely determine the Handicap Time for each player, either according to Average Time Schedule, or based on such other comparative Time Limits as may be mutually agreed upon for each player.

THIRD—100 points are to be credited to every player who completes the puzzle according to his or her Handicap Time. 5 points are deducted for each minute the puzzle is completed ahead of schedule, and 5 points should be added for each minute behind schedule. LOW TOTAL number of points scored decides the winner; just as in any similar contest for speed.

3. Jig-Saw Party

FIRST—Get as many puzzles as there will be players at the party. Assign each player a place large enough to hold the puzzle at the table.

SECOND—Distribute puzzles and place one puzzle, thoroughly jumbled, before each player.

THIRD—Have all players start simultaneously. The first one to finish will receive a prize, or there may be second, third and "booby" prizes.

On the backs of the boxes for its "Every Week" jigsaw puzzles Einson-Freeman promoted jigsaw parties and races that required the purchase of even more puzzles.

for families and friends. Puzzle parties and jigsaw socials abounded in the winter of 1932–33.

As the public rushed to the newsstands to pick up the latest picture puzzle, an element of competition developed. Who would be the first to complete this week's offering? Puzzles that came with "par times" or directions for puzzle races reinforced this competitive tendency. So did several manufacturers' contest sets, packages containing a number of smaller puzzles of equal size and difficulty.

Retail stores organized tournaments and awarded prizes to those who could assemble a puzzle fastest. The Wednesday afternoon contests for women at Hahne's department store in Newark, New Jersey, attracted hundreds of entrants who paid 25 cents each to participate, in the hopes of winning the $5 first prize. The competitions boosted the store's sales so much that Hahne's also added Saturday morning contests for children and considered requests from men for their own event.[35]

At Gimbel Brothers in Philadelphia, men, women, and children competed in one event. A fourteen-year-old schoolgirl, Elizabeth Crawford, defeated all the adults to win a silver cup inscribed "Jig-Saw Puzzle Champion of Philadelphia."[36]

The makers themselves vied to see who could manufacture the largest puzzle. The 10,000-piece puzzle that Parker Brothers had cut in 1928 for Pierrepont Noyes (President of the Oneida Community in New York) was soon eclipsed by an 8 ½ by 13 foot puzzle of 50,000 pieces, made by the Eureka Jig Saw Puzzle Company and displayed at Gimbel Brothers department store in New York. High school students in Longview, Washington, made an even larger one, twelve by thirty feet, with oversized pieces.[37]

The subject matter of puzzles was nostalgic, romantic, exotic and escapist, an antidote for the hard times. Historical images sold well, whether of George Washington, or the Civil War, or King Arthur's time. Landscapes and seascapes, which had not been especially popular in the 1907–10 craze, were favorites during the depression. The penchant for thatched cottages, Venetian canals, Dutch windmills, hunting scenes, and tall ships with billowing sails undoubtedly reflected a yearning for distant and bucolic lands at a time when there was no money for travel.

Human interest stories appealed: the little girl presenting her doll for examination at the doctor's office, or an old-fashioned marriage proposal. Tragedy, however, appeared only in its mildest forms, such as the boy and his puppy in front of the sign proclaiming "No Dogs Allowed." The realities of economics and commerce too were largely absent except in their whimsical aspects. More than one puzzle portrayed a frustrated elderly fisherman furtively buying a string of fish from a barefoot boy.

Movie stars adorned puzzles, adding a touch of glamour and fantasy to puzzlers' otherwise dreary lives. The "Movie Cut-Ups," "Foxagram," and "Star" weekly puzzles featured current films, another popular form of entertainment. Dell Publishing's "Movie Mix-Up!" series sold five hundred thousand copies in the first three weeks alone. Hollywood stars typically received royalties of 1 cent for each puzzle made when they agreed to let their portraits be chopped up.[38]

Contemporary events found their way onto jigsaws. The 1933 opening of the Chicago World's Fair inspired numerous puzzles. So did politics. *Vanity Fair* magazine commissioned caricaturist Miguel Covarrubias to illustrate Franklin D. Roosevelt's inauguration and issued the picture as a 315-piece puzzle in March 1933.

The inclusion of a guide picture with many of the cardboard puzzles enhanced their popularity. Before 1933, puzzles for adults had come in plain boxes with only the title to give a hint about what the completed puzzle would show. The "Jig of the Week" was the first to include a guide picture, on a folded insert in the box. Purists could leave it folded and unexamined, but many novices appreciated the help when tackling a large and challenging puzzle. Guide pictures soon appeared on the boxes as well, creating more interesting packages and helping to market the puzzles.

Puzzles reached into unusual places. Nerve specialist Dr. Henry Reid prescribed jigsaw puzzles to relax his patients in Palm Springs. The Associated Press sent out a bulletin when the puzzle fad spread to the Illinois State Prison. After puzzles became popular in the section holding ex-bankers and brokers, the warden purchased several hundred jigsaw puzzles for the cells filled with burglars and other petty criminals.[39]

Newspapers and magazines were full of cartoons, poems, and stories about jigsaw puzzles. The *Minneapolis Evening Journal* was one of many periodicals that printed pictures designed to be pasted onto cardboard and cut into puzzles at home. *Ballyhoo,* the humor magazine, devoted its entire May 1933 issue to jigsaw puzzles. Newsreels showed stampedes at the puzzle counters in stores, and jigsaws made cameo appearances in *Dancing Lady* and several other 1933 movies. The jigsaw motif extended to popular songs with such titles as "Juggling a Jig-Saw" and "My Jig Saw Puzzle of Love."

Accessories began to appear. Flyers in Viking's "Picture Puzzle Weekly" boxes touted mahogany- or walnut-framed picture puzzle trays in both the regular and deluxe sizes. Patent records for the 1930s reflect the nation's preoccupation with puzzles. Inventors tried to elaborate on the standard puzzle, or to devise better ways to manufacture, assemble, or display it.

Doubly puzzling brands tempted the serious puzzler. The "Cross Jig" had a crossword puzzle on one side and a picture on the other. The "Rebus Puzzle" offered $25 in prizes to those who could solve the rebus on the completed

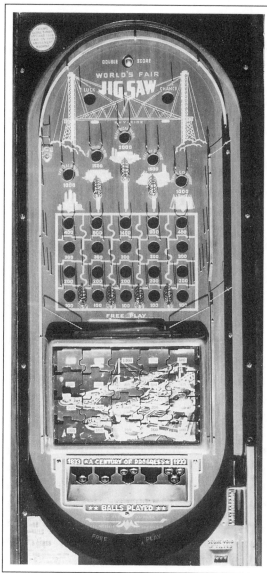

When the balls fall into the right holes, this pinball machine flips over pieces to form an aerial view of the 1933 Chicago World's Fair. Inventor David Rockola was inspired by seeing the popularity of jigsaws in Chicago area speakeasies that year.

Rock-Ola is a registered trademark of Rock-Ola Mfg. Co.

This puzzle came in a slipcase with Walter Eberhardt's novel, *The Jig-Saw Puzzle Murder*. The completed puzzle reveals the identity of the killer, who was not named in the book.

Photo of puzzle from The Jig-Saw Puzzle Murder *© 1933 by Grosset & Dunlap.*

puzzle. Several companies invented games that combined jigsaw puzzles with concepts from bridge.

One of the most intriguing games was the Rock-Ola "World's Fair Jig-Saw" pinball machine, which had a concealed puzzle in its center. The pieces flipped face up when balls landed in the right holes, until the completed puzzle showed an aerial view of the 1933 Chicago World's Fair.

The mystery puzzle, still popular today, first came out in 1933. The most elaborate was Grosset & Dunlap's *The Jig-Saw Puzzle Murder*, a full-length novel by Walter Eberhardt housed in a slipcase with a 200-piece jigsaw puzzle. The story's victim is the host at a party where guests are gambling at a game of jigsaw dominoes. The book did not reveal the killer, but the lurid image on the finished puzzle clearly identified him.

Puzzle fanatics could buy all kinds of products with puzzle elements. Party snapping bonbons ejected puzzle pieces instead of confetti for festive occasions. Fans of the occult pieced their fortunes together with the "Horoscopuzzle," made by the Malcolm Johnston Studio of Cleveland.

Notepaper, postcards, Christmas cards, and greeting cards appeared in jigsaw form. The recipient had to reassemble the pieces to decipher the message. In Delaware, Irénée du Pont had just commissioned artist Frank Schoonover (one of Howard Pyle's most famous students) to do a large painting for the family mansion overlooking the ocean in Cuba. He was so pleased with his newest acquisition, entitled "Pirates Celebrate Ashore," that he had several hundred jigsaw puzzles made from that image. With the letters spelling "Merry Christmas" cut into each puzzle, they served as his Christmas cards in 1933.[40]

Retailers used innovative marketing efforts to sell puzzles. The Union News Company put hawkers on commuter trains in the New York City area to peddle newly issued puzzles.[41] Stores discovered that devoting a table to a puzzle in progress paid off handsomely:

> The sight of somebody fitting a puzzle together attracts [jig-saw puzzle fans] as honey does flies . . . One retailer I have heard of has assigned a clerk to spend his time in the jig-saw department, seated at a table putting the little curly-cues together. He was selected because he can smile and be patient even under a perfect volley of kibitzing. His table is always a center of interest and pulls people from all parts of the store—yea, even in from the sidewalk![42]

Makers of Cardboard Puzzles for Adults

During the 1932–33 phase of the mania, the established game companies such as Milton Bradley and Parker Brothers were quick to add cardboard puzzles for adults to their product lines. But most of the firms supplying the pastimes had never made jigsaw puzzles before. The puzzle craze was a boon that helped them revive their fortunes for a year during the depths of the depression.

The vast majority of the new producers came from the paper box industry, which had been in deep trouble for several years. Because of the general decline in manufacturing output, the demand for packaging had plummeted. Box makers found it easy to capitalize on the puzzle craze, since they already had die-cutting and gluing machines that they could adapt to making puzzles. Dozens of box companies, representing virtually every major city, made cardboard jigsaw puzzles for local or regional distribution in 1932 and 1933.

The Consolidated Paper Box Company of Somerville, Massachusetts, emerged as a major puzzle producer at this time. In addition to making its own "Perfect," "Big 10," and "Big Star" brands, it made boxes for some others, including University Distributing's "Jig of the Week." It continued in the puzzle business for another forty years, one of the few to do so. Most of the other box companies dropped out of puzzle making after 1933.

Printers of all kinds likewise entered the puzzle industry because they already had presses and finishing equipment. Einson-Freeman, for example, had been lithographing point-of-purchase advertising displays before 1932. Labarre Printing Company of West Pittston, Pennsylvania, was a job printer that turned its presses to die-cutting jigsaw puzzles. Calendar manufacturers such as Louis Dow of St. Paul and Thomas J. Murphy of Red Oak, Iowa, saw the logic of converting pictures into picture puzzles.

The lithographers were joined by book publishers such as Saalfield Publishing Co. of Akron, Ohio, Whitman Publishing Co. of Racine, Wisconsin, and Simon & Schuster of New York City. Several greeting card manufacturers—Volland in Joliet, Illinois, Gibson Art Company in Cincinnati, and Hallmark in Kansas City—expanded into jigsaw puzzles. Dennison Manufacturing of Framingham, Massachusetts, added puzzles to its line of labels and party goods. C. S. Hammond of Brooklyn, New York, had supplied maps to puzzle manufacturers in earlier years, but now began to market its own puzzles, both map and pictorial.

One of the more unusual puzzle manufacturers in the 1930s was the Detroit Gasket Company. When there was virtually no demand for its product, the firm adapted its die-cutting equipment to produce "Dee-Gee" puzzles out of the cork that it previously used to make industrial gaskets.

Another entrant into the field was the Upson Company, a wallboard manufacturer in Lockport, New York. It began using its ³⁄₁₆-inch Upson Board to make puzzles as a way to counter the loss of sales caused by the collapse of the housing market in the depression. It unveiled its "Tuco" brand (an acronym for The Upson Co.) just before Christmas 1932, incorporated its Tuco Work Shops division in January, and soon reached production of fifteen thousand puzzles a day.[43] Although Tuco never issued any weekly puzzles and entered the puzzle business a bit later than some other companies, it outlasted most of them by many decades. The last Tuco puzzles were made in the early 1980s. Many puzzlers preferred Tuco's thick fiberboard to the thinner, often flimsy cardboard used by other puzzle manufacturers.

Some of the puzzle makers came from farther afield. The Glenville Unemployed Association of Scotia, New York, consisted of men who had been laid off from the nearby General Electric factory. GE supplied calendar pictures and equipment so they could cut jigsaw puzzles with handheld dies.[44]

Rexall Drug Stores, Liggett's, Kresge's, W. T. Grant, and many department stores contracted with manufacturers to produce puzzles under their own store labels, adding to the number of brands in circulation.

All in all, one trade journal estimated that more than three thousand companies were making jigsaw puzzles in 1932–33.[45] The paperboard industry boomed, of course, while it supplied cardboard for millions of jigsaw puzzles and the boxes to house them.

A New Deal . . . but Not for Puzzles

The depression puzzle craze ended in the spring of 1933. After several years of growing interest and nine months of mania, the passion for jigsaw puzzles was approaching the point of saturation. Political and economic events in February and March combined to make the ending an abrupt one.

The most important event was the inauguration of President Franklin D. Roosevelt on Saturday, March 4, 1933. His first official act that weekend was to close all the banks for a week so that the battered financial system could regroup. Roosevelt's sudden decision caught people without much cash, and puzzle sales fell. The toy industry, however, was sanguine. A report from Denver opined:

> The demand for jigsaw puzzles dropped off slightly during the first part of March, but it is generally believed that this was due to the bank moratorium and that there will be several weeks more of heavy business on the item. The demand has been so strong there that some toy people think not even the coming of warm weather will bring any appreciable drop.[46]

Roosevelt rapidly transformed the country's pessimism into optimism as the New Deal policies took shape in the first hundred days of his administration. Americans were filled with energy, excitement, and high hopes for an economic recovery. Within a month there was a social turnaround, as legislation to legalize beer brought an end to prohibition and opened new possibilities for entertainment. Sitting at home with a jigsaw puzzle held little appeal as spring began to blossom.

The second major event was the imposition of a tax on jigsaw puzzles. Congress had enacted a 10 percent tax on sporting goods and adult games in June 1932. Although jigsaw puzzles were initially designated as a children's item and thus exempt from the tax, the Internal Revenue Service later ruled that puzzles with more than fifty pieces should be taxed.[47]

The extensive reporting requirements, not to mention the tax itself, put an immediate damper on the puzzle industry. The crafters of wooden jigsaws, who had already lost business to the cheaper die-cut puzzles, were devastated. One newspaper reported:

> A tax blight has hit the infant industry of making jig saw puzzles. A number of local people who had taken a flier in the new business as a means of increasing the income have quit. Puzzle for sale signs have come out of the house windows, saws have been stored away and the hum of industry is no more heard in basements of nights.[48]

With the confluence of the tax, the bank holiday, New Deal optimism, warm weather, beer, and simply satiation with puzzles, the mania collapsed.

University Distributing put out its last "Jig of the Week" puzzle in May, and Viking ended its weekly series in early July. Retailers, who had already stocked up on all brands of puzzles, tried to keep the fad alive. Although they were able to market many puzzles as pastimes for summer vacations, sales fell to just a fraction of those in February and March. By the fall, a Boston firm advertised that it was liquidating a million puzzles for the Viking Manufacturing Company.[49]

After the craze ended, puzzles settled back into the comfortable "old standby" position they had occupied in the 1920s. There were some subsequent bursts of puzzle activity later in the depression, in the early months of 1934 and 1937.[50] But these were faint flickers of interest compared with the consuming passion for puzzles of early 1933.

Ironically, the depression years witnessed both the high point for wooden jigsaw puzzles in the United States and the beginning of the end for them. Hand-cut puzzles declined steadily in subsequent years as production costs rose and puzzlers turned more to the readily available cardboard substitutes. By the 1950s, only a handful of companies continued to market wood puzzles for adults in the United States.

5

The Forties and Beyond

JIG SAW PUZZLES ARE AN ESCAPE, TEMPORARILY AT LEAST,
FROM THE SORDID HAPPENINGS WROUGHT BY WAR.

A Christmas 1944 photo shows servicemen overseas working on a jigsaw puzzle.

America's fascination with jigsaw puzzles went through several cycles after the Great Depression of the 1930s. Peaks of popularity came in the 1940s, 1960s, and 1990s. The World War II fad in the forties had some similarities to the depression-era craze. Puzzles were once again an inexpensive home entertainment during an anxious and difficult time.

Patriotic Puzzles

Military might, patriotism, Uncle Sam—these themes have produced some of the most stirring puzzle images. Their heyday came during World War II, when a modest craze for jigsaw puzzles took hold.[1]

World War II had tremendous popular support. Puzzles reflected that spirit with scenes of the U.S. armed forces crushing the enemy. Even puzzles that showed nonmilitary scenes often had a patriotic imprint. The boxes of "Perfect" puzzles carried this injunction: "For Your Country, for Victory, BUY United States Savings Bonds and Stamps."

Several factors pushed up the sales of jigsaw puzzles in the 1940s. The deployment of so many men overseas and strict rationing of gasoline put a big crimp in social life. An evening out for dinner and a show held less appeal when it meant going alone and struggling with transportation. Moreover, women had entered the labor force to replace the absent men. When not working in factories, they were busy tending victory gardens, helping with scrap metal drives, and taking care of all the domestic tasks at home. Inexpensive and widely available, puzzles were an ideal pastime for the home front.

Puzzles once again fit the need for a psychological boost. As one trade magazine noted:

Jig Saw Puzzles are an escape, temporarily at least, from the sordid happenings wrought by war. The intense concentration needed for solving a puzzle takes one's mind off the discomforts resulting from shortages and rationing. Jig Saw Puzzles are a blessed relief from the parlor strategy of arm chair generals and the repetitious accounts of radio news commentators. . . . The desire to be constructive, to thrill in the pride of accomplishment is manifest, as all over the world people are killed and countries laid in ruins.[2]

Puzzles also helped divert the troops. In December 1941, as troop mobilization began in earnest, volunteer groups distributed free jigsaws, books, and magazines to soldiers on trains.[3] Submariners based in New London, Connecticut, took jigsaw puzzles on their missions, courtesy of donations from Isabel Ayer's Picture Puzzle Exchange in Boston "because the submarine boys have the hardest time, the most dangerous job and the least entertainment."[4] The "hurry up and wait" rhythms of war brought long periods of inactivity. One account quoted this letter home from a B-29 bomber crew member in Saipan:

Just received the package of puzzles, and believe me, I had no idea the puzzles would be such a hit. The whole darn hut is busily going daffy with four men working on the jigsaw puzzle and everybody wanting to be next. I wonder when I am going to get a crack at them.[5]

By early 1942 the war effort had claimed most metals, so there were no raw materials to make toy cars, trucks, and the like. Most toy factories stopped manufacturing playthings for the duration and converted their facilities to the production of war materiel.

Companies that made puzzles fared better. Cardboard and wood were in abundant supply during the first few years of the war. By 1944, however, they too grew scarce. Most lumberjacks had left the forests to join the armed forces, and aircraft construction was requiring huge quantities of plywood.

Louis Marx & Company, a major New York maker of metal toys, adapted to wartime by producing both munitions and puzzles. Its "Fighters for Victory" series came out in 1942. Shortly thereafter, Marx turned the puzzle line over to its allied company, Jaymar Specialty Company (owned and operated by Louis Marx's sister Rose and father Jacob). Jaymar later issued the "Modern Fighters for Victory" series showing airplanes, ships, and battle scenes.

Jaymar puzzles had the extra attraction that some of the pieces were cut into war-related shapes. Bombs, jeeps, flags, revolvers, and other figure pieces added interest as puzzlers assembled the scenes. The "Victory" series by J. Pressman of New York City and the "America in Action" puzzles by Leo Hart of Rochester, New York, used the same device. The latter were unusual for the time, using actual news photos of war scenes with informative captions.

Some of the most vivid war scenes appeared on the "Tuco" and "Perfect" puzzles. Artist Kurt Graf's depictions of "Blitzkrieg," "America Fights Back," "Battle of the Don" and other subjects for the "Perfect" line are colorful and full of action. In addition to battle scenes, puzzles featured patriotic images of the Statue of Liberty, Washington landmarks, Uncle Sam, and the American flag.

These and most of the other 1940s puzzles were die-cut from cardboard. Other major brands included "Fighters for Freedom" by Whitman Publishing of Racine, Wisconsin; "All-American" by Dell Publishing of New York City; "Victory" and "Leading American Artists" by J. S. Publishing of New York City; and "Victory" by Saalfield Publishing of Akron, Ohio. Several of these companies also put military and patriotic pictures on smaller puzzles for children.

Map puzzles enjoyed a resurgence in popularity during World War II.

America Fights Back is one of K. Graf's dramatic World War II scenes on "Perfect Picture Puzzles," made by the Consolidated Box Company of Somerville, Massachusetts.

With the news rolling in from distant battlefields, teenagers and adults found a new interest in dissected maps, especially those that featured information about the progress of the armed forces.

After the armistice in 1945, war-related themes maintained their popularity for the next decade. The puzzle subjects were general military ones, however, rather than specific battles. The Korean War of the 1950s generated few puzzles. (The ones from the *M.A.S.H.* television series twenty-five years later show the actors and the camp, but not fighting.) And the Vietnam War was controversial enough that manufacturers must have decided not to risk poor sales by commemorating it on jigsaw puzzles. Patriotic themes on puzzles again came to the fore in this century following the terrorist attacks of September 11, 2001.

Katie Lewin, president of Springbok Editions, reviews proofs for the company's round and octagonal puzzles.

Courtesy of Katherine E. Lewin

Springbok's Surprises in the Sixties

The jigsaws of the 1950s matched the culture of the time. The decade of postwar prosperity, the Eisenhower presidency, and the baby boom was for the most part placid. Puzzles reflected that general contentment. Brands such as "Big Ben" by Milton Bradley, "Guild" by Whitman Publishing, and "Perfect" by Consolidated Box featured comfortable and traditional artwork. The scenic photographs, bucolic farms, and human interest vignettes continued the trend of what had been popular in the 1930s.

The 1960s brought new ideas and upheavals. In American society, the decade witnessed the civil rights movement, assassinations of two Kennedys and Martin Luther King, Lyndon Johnson's "Great Society" program, the first moon landing, war in Vietnam, women's liberation, and hippies. There were big changes in the puzzle world too, though of a very different kind.

Springbok Editions was the company that launched a new puzzle fad in 1964. Owners Katie and Bob Lewin had been intrigued by circular jigsaw puzzles that John Waddington Ltd. produced in Leeds, England. In the early 1960s, with some technical assistance from Waddington, they founded Springbok Editions to produce similar die-cut puzzles for adults in the U.S. (Interestingly, the technology was coming full circle, as Waddington had learned the puzzle business in the 1930s from Einson-Freeman of New York.)

The novelty of Springbok's circular and octagonal puzzles in itself had a strong market impact. But another innovative move by the company, its focus on fine art, was just as important.

Springbok created a sensation with its puzzle of "Convergence," an abstract painting by Jackson Pollock. Full of random squiggles and blobs of paint drippings, it was billed as "the world's most difficult jigsaw puzzle." It captured the public's imagination and sold more than one hundred thousand copies in the first year.[6]

Springbok continued to break the mold with pictures that had never before appeared on jigsaw puzzles. Katie Lewin searched worldwide for striking images that would make challenging and interesting puzzles. "I went through museums with jigsaw eyes," she said.[7] In addition to modern art, she selected unusual subjects such as fifteenth-century Italian religious masterpieces, Kabuki embroidery, a millefiore paperweight, a Roman mosaic, a two-hundred-year-old astronomy chart, and exquisite eighteenth-century Chinese porcelain plates.

Museum curators were delighted to cooperate in this endeavor and supplied educational commentaries to go with the puzzles. Nevertheless, officials at the Albright-Knox Gallery in Buffalo were amazed by the steady stream of museum visitors who came to scrutinize the original of the infamous Pollock painting, after struggling with the puzzle for so many hours. Katie Lewin commented:

You understand a Jackson Pollock better after you have made the puzzle.[8]

The company was the first to commission famous artists to paint special designs for adult puzzles. Maynard Reece's "Wild Flowers," Arthur Singer's

"Water Birds," and Roger Tory Peterson's "Penguins" were among the many titles that reflected the Lewins' long-standing passion for the natural world and ecology. The attractive paintings and the motif of the graceful, lively springbok appealed to a nation sensitized to ecological issues by the recent publication of Rachel Carson's book, *Silent Spring*.[9]

Salvador Dali was Springbok's biggest "catch." Katie Lewin met him (and his pet ocelot) in the lobby of the St. Regis Hotel when he was visiting New York. Her pitch for the custom art, plus the impressive display of Springbok puzzles at the nearby Brentano's bookstore, appealed to Dali's commercial side. He agreed to paint a special Springbok version of one of his double image paintings, an optical illusion with puzzle pieces sprinkled around the edges.

The appeal of Springbok puzzles was not limited to highbrow art connoisseurs. The element of whimsy and surprise in other Springboks appealed to puzzlers who were jaded by the monotony and banality of the jigsaws of the 1950s. One puzzle showed "The Best 18 Golf Holes in America," while headlines from Paris newspapers, Sherlock Holmes, and ladies' hats decorated others.

The company was also the first to cater to the fanatics, the diehards who wanted only the most difficult puzzle without regard to the picture. Springbok gave them a series of 500-piece solid-color puzzles: "Little Red Riding Hood's Hood" (all red), "Close-Up of the Three Bears" (all brown), and "Snow White without the Seven Dwarfs" (all white). The puzzles sold well, although it is unclear how many were actually assembled.

Not only did the Lewins find new and interesting puzzle pictures, but they used state-of-the-art lithography. Bob Lewin had spent his entire career in the printing business. He was the one who made multiple trips to the National Gallery in London and other museums to fine-tune the lithographic proofs until their colors exactly matched the original paintings. Bob's expertise and careful work meant that Springboks outshone the other cardboard puzzles available at the time.

The thickness and appearance of the puzzle pieces themselves attracted puzzlers. Katie Lewin, who drew the designs for Springbok dies, avoided the repetitive gridlike patterns that were common at the time. The circular and octagonal boxes also made Springbok puzzles stand out. Most boxes included several brochures: "14 Tips on Jigsaw Puzzling" (how to assemble puzzles successfully), "The Puzzle Party" (including suggestions for puzzle cookies and jigsaw pizza), and, of course, one showing the other puzzles that Springbok made.

The quality came at a price. Springbok puzzles retailed for $3 to $3.50 at a time when most other brands were selling for less than $1. But a superb publicity campaign overcame buyers' reluctance to spend more. All the weekly news magazines and numerous newspapers across the country featured Springbok and Katie Lewin, famous as the housewife who became president of her own business after her children left home. Her twenty-minute appearance on NBC's *Today Show* just before Christmas in 1964 gave the company free national exposure that was worth a small fortune.

Over time Springbok branched out a bit, putting some images on wood puzzles that were manufactured for the company in England. A special edition for Henri Bendel, the New York women's high-end clothing store, sold for $75.

Hallmark Cards of Kansas City, Missouri, had been keeping an eye on Springbok Editions since its inception. Hallmark had made a few puzzles in the past, including a weekly series in the 1930s and some small jigsaw greeting cards. It had long wanted to market a major line of puzzles for adults in its Hallmark stores, but was reluctant to incur the costs of developing it from scratch. The acquisition of Springbok Editions was the solution.

In 1967 Hallmark made the Lewins an offer they could not refuse. The Lewins stayed on to manage the Springbok division for two years. They retired in 1969, but only temporarily. Within a few weeks Bob Lewin had started up Mill Pond Press in Venice, Florida, to produce limited-edition prints by wildlife artists and others. Mill Pond even published a few wooden "Timber" jigsaw puzzles during the next decade.

The legacy of Springbok Editions has continued. Hallmark made Springbok puzzles for thirty-four years, using the same high-quality manufacturing technology. The new owner soon moved away from museum art, however, relying instead on images produced by its large staff of in-house artists. Hallmark stopped producing puzzles in 2001, thus creating consternation among the hordes of Springbok devotees. The "Bokkers," as they called themselves, mounted an online petition drive to reverse Hallmark's decision.[10] Their persistence helped convince Allied Products of Kansas City to buy the line in 2002 and bring back Springbok puzzles.

Springbok Editions also had a huge impact on its competitors, thus transforming cardboard puzzles for adults. By the late 1960s, major manufacturers such as Milton Bradley, Whitman, Jaymar, Saalfield, Tuco, and Warren were also turning out round and octagonal puzzles for the mass market. E. E. Fairchild of Rochester, New York, marketed "Shape" puzzles with irregular outlines. Although the existing companies did not give up their staple scenic puzzles, all offered a greater variety of artwork.

Further Innovations

Springbok Editions had blown a breath of fresh air into the puzzle industry and demonstrated that creativity was the key to bringing new customers into puzzling. Its success inspired several new companies to develop innovative cardboard puzzles for adults.

The most important was American Publishing Corporation of Waltham, Massachusetts. Herb Kavet and Paul deBoer used all their savings, totaling $380, to found the company in 1962. For several years they eked out a living by making customized games for internal use by United Fruit and other big companies.[11]

In 1965, inspired by that experience, they established their own "Pop Art" jigsaw puzzles. They featured Chiquita Banana, Heinz pickles, and the logos of famous brands such as Campbell's soup, Schlitz beer, and Maxwell House coffee. The packaging, in sealed tin cans, made for novel displays on retailers' shelves. The zany puzzles attracted nontraditional puzzlers and gift-givers of all ages.

Although the use of licensed products had been rising in children's puzzles for decades, it was rare in adult puzzles before American Publishing took up the concept. Kavet and deBoer recognized that the children who had played with television character puzzles in the 1950s had grown up. Now there was a whole generation of adults who would respond to and embrace puzzles of familiar images from the entertainment world, whether television, movies, professional sports, comics, or even commercials.

American Publishing tried to appeal to male puzzlers, who traditionally had been fewer in number than women. Several sports series featured a wide range of action photos of Joe Namath, Wilt Chamberlain, Willie Mays, Bobby Orr, and dozens of other stars and teams.

The "Playmate" series, featuring some of *Playboy*'s famous centerfold nudes, turned out to be best sellers. During the early 1970s, millions of copies went to stores across the United States, and even as far afield as Japan. In an interview with a wire service reporter, Kavet speculated that they were all purchased as gifts for men, and said:

The "Playboy Playmate Puzzles," made by American Publishing Company in the early 1970s, were a hit with buyers of gifts for men.

Reproduced by Special Permission of Playboy Magazine. Copyright © 1967, 1968 by Playboy. All rights reserved.

No one actually does these puzzles. We know that, because we never get any complaints on missing pieces. Statistically you have to have a few complaints. And we never get any. We could just as well fill up these cans with chopped pieces of paper.[12]

Kavet spoke too soon. A few days later, after the story had appeared in hundreds of newspapers, the complaints started rolling in.

American Publishing also went after the young adult market by putting "Woodstock," "Women's Liberation," "Peace," and other contemporary themes on a series of topical puzzles. Later in the 1970s the line expanded to include comic-book superheroes, fantasy (Brian Froud's goblins and Frank Frazetta's science fiction), and some television shows.

American Publishing made puzzles through the 1980s, but other innovators lasted only a few years. Franklin Merchandising in Chicago produced round puzzles showing food (a bowl of popcorn, mixed nuts, a pizza pie), subjects that resurfaced in the mid-1990s in the "Puzzle O's" line by Lombard Marketing of Bloomfield, Connecticut. Gameophiles Unlimited in Berkeley Heights, New Jersey, put fruit crate art and city maps on puzzles for adults. Synergistics Research of New York City marketed a number of novelty puzzles including "Spilt Milk," an all-white puzzle with an irregular edge, and several "Wet Paint" puzzles in solid colors.

International Polygonics and the Puzzle Factory, both of New York City, issued double-sided puzzles. The latter's "Nixon-Agnew Two-Faced" puzzle proved prescient, as both the President and his Vice-President later resigned in disgrace. Although the Puzzle Factory failed in the early 1970s, co-owner Pat Duncan resurrected it a few years later as the Great American Puzzle Factory. It is still going strong in South Norwalk, Connecticut.

The late 1970s brought "Schmuzzle" puzzles, the brainchild of Sam Savage, then an applied mathematics professor at the University of Chicago.[13] Savage was fascinated with the art of M. C. Escher and the tessellations underlying the designs. He concocted a jigsaw puzzle that had 168 identical salamander-shaped pieces. They could fit together in zillions of ways, but only one configuration would complete the puzzle picture.

Solving the technical challenge of manufacturing interchangeable but irregular pieces required both computers and lasers to make the cutting dies. Puzzlers paid little mind to the technological achievements, but simply enjoyed the puzzle that had eliminated the shape of the piece as a clue to the solution and forced them to rely only on the picture. The package encouraged those with less patience to turn the pieces over and use the lizard images as components of fantastic compositions of "schmigure eights" or "schmowflakes." Schmuzzles went out of production in 1983, but in 2003, after a hiatus of two decades, The Canadian Group of Toronto reintroduced them in the North American market.[14]

Mystery Puzzles

A major revival of the mystery puzzle, a detective story combined with a jigsaw, came in the late 1980s. The idea was hardly new. In the 1930s there were more than a dozen brands, none with guide pictures, where the jigsaw puzzle showed a scene from or the solution to the mystery presented in the story. A few stories consisted of just a few paragraphs on the box cover. Most were longer, printed in pamphlets, occasionally even in full-sized hardcover books. Pearl Publishing of New York City issued the "Mystery Puzzle of the Month" in the 1940s, and other brands appeared sporadically through the years.

The designers thought up some ingenious ways to keep the solution concealed until the puzzler was ready to examine it. Einson-Freeman used invisible ink to print the explanations to its "Mystery-Jig" puzzles in 1933; holding the page over a light bulb brought out the printing. Tower Press in England supplied extra pieces for its "Inspector Brown" puzzle—the killer appeared on the scene when the extras were used to replace a section of the original puzzle. In 1967, Hasbro's "Whodunit" puzzles contained 45 rpm records with clues on one side and answers on the other. Printing the solution in mirror writing or sealing it between two pages were other common devices.

Despite all the earlier attempts, the mystery jigsaw only hit the big time in March 1987, when Lombard Marketing introduced the "bePuzzled" series.[15] Founder Mary Ann Lombard used $60,000 in savings and a home equity line of credit to take the plunge into her own business at the age of twenty-eight. The puzzles were bestsellers and reached annual sales of about $8 million a year by the time she sold the company a dozen years later.

The secret of Lombard's success was not at all mysterious: It was careful market research combined with creativity in both design and marketing. The puzzles featured original stories, quality printing and die-cutting, sturdy attractive packaging, and explanations in mirror writing. Lombard enlisted professional mystery authors to write the narratives, including Henry Slesar, who had published his own small line of "Janus" mystery puzzles fifteen years earlier.

Lombard's cold call at the FAO Schwarz flagship store in New York generated a big order in the first month. "Death by Diet," "Feline Frenzy," and "Murder on the Titanic" and other topical subjects were the best sellers. Lombard also used titles such as "To Kill a Lawyer" and "Who Drilled the Dentist?" to appeal to niche markets of professionals who could afford to pay $14.95 per puzzle. The CIA employee store became a repeat customer (for espionage-themed puzzles), as did upscale mail order catalogs, bookstores, and specialty game and toy stores.

The time was clearly right for the mystery puzzle revival in the late 1980s and 1990s. Once "bePuzzled" proved to be a winning line, Lombard extended its reach with frequent new titles. International distribution came with direct sales to Harrod's in London and a licensing agreement with Canada Games. Translations into French, German, Italian, and Spanish helped boost overseas sales to 20 percent of the total. The "bePuzzled Jr." series targeted children of ages ten to fourteen.

Of course, competition reared its head as Milton Bradley, American Publishing, Buffalo Games, Parker Brothers, Pressman Toy Corporation, Western Publishing, and Decipher Inc. all jumped in to issue their own versions of the mystery puzzle. Most of the rivals, however, aimed at the mass market and left Lombard untouched in the high-end market. BePuzzled mysteries continue to thrive since their acquisition by University Games of San Francisco in 1999.

A cousin of the mystery puzzle was one that offered a prize for solving a difficult problem pictured on the completed puzzle, another old idea that came back in force in the 1980s. The leader and the most notable was "Decipher," a double-sided puzzle with no picture on the box whose images formed a sequence of almost four hundred numbers. In 1983 Warren Holland Jr., owner of Decipher Inc. of Norfolk, Virginia, offered a $100,000 prize for unscrambling the coded message by March 1, 1984.[16]

Assembling the puzzle was the easy part. Finding the key to the multiple substitution numeric cryptogram eluded the one hundred fifty thousand people who paid $12 each for the puzzle in the first year. Holland then extended the deadline by a year, periodically issued fresh clues, and watched sales go past two hundred thousand puzzles. Ultimately thirty-six buyers, many using computers, cracked the cipher to reveal a quotation from poet e. e. cummings and to share the prize.

Successors included two "Cryptogifts," sold in the Swiss Colony mail order catalog, with prizes of $25,000 in 1986 and $50,000 in 1987. Two years later, Trivia Games of Seattle upped the ante with a $1 million prize for the solution to "Money Hunt." The 150-piece puzzle came with a 32-page booklet of clues and a map of North America, where the reward had been stashed.

Three-Dimensional Puzzles

"The Jigsaw Puzzle Goes Vertical" said the headline after the "Puzz-3D" line of building puzzles made its debut in the United States.[17]

Three-dimensionality, a decades-old goal of puzzle makers, had hitherto enjoyed only limited success. Gold Seal puzzles of Dundee, Illinois, and J. K. Straus of Brooklyn, New York, had introduced layered puzzles in the 1930s. Thicker wood for foreground pieces made them stand out slightly from the picture's background. In 1953 the M. T. Mathews Publishing Company of New York City was the first to create the illusion of depth by enclosing "stereo glasses" with its specially printed "3D Picture Puzzles."

True depth had been around since the nineteenth century, but only in simple children's puzzles. In Montrose, Pennsylvania, for example, Charles Crandall made his 1884 "Captain Kidd's Castle" from thick wood cut into thirty irregular pieces and supplied with it a miniature cannon. Once a youngster had stacked the pieces to complete the image of the castle facade, a shot from the cannon would knock them over. In 1916 the Harper's Novelty Toy Company of London developed more complex "Toyzenet" puzzles, printed on both sides. The pieces could form a decorated three-dimensional plaything such as a set of dollhouse furniture or a quoits game. The backs of the pieces could be assembled into a jigsaw of a related scene.

The "Skyline" puzzles by Kawin Manufacturing of Astoria, New York, brought real three-dimensional puzzles to adults in the United States in the 1930s. Its "Empire State Building" with over 100 interlocking wood pieces made a fifteen-inch-high, but rather unstable sculptural model of the skyscraper. Other Kawin edifices included the Chrysler and New York Life buildings.

Jaymar made a crude attempt at three dimensions in cardboard in the 1950s with the Disney theme "Band Concert." Minipuzzles of Mickey Mouse, Goofy, and Pluto had tabs that fit into slots in the main puzzle. But the cardboard was not rigid enough to hold the characters upright and keep them from falling on their faces.

Enter Paul Gallant. He solved the twin problems of stability and cost and founded Wrebbit Inc. in Montreal, Canada. Gallant had been trying unsuccessfully to design a three-dimensional puzzle from cardboard when he stumbled across polyethylene foam. He realized that it could be covered with a printed image, cut easily and cleanly into pieces, and then joined to make sturdy assemblies. It was the perfect base for his imaginative puzzles. Gallant patented his technology of mortise and tenon joints, lined up a financial backer, and started manufacturing. By the autumn of 1991, Wrebbit was shipping "Puzz-3D" puzzles to retailers in the United States and Canada.[18]

The early days brought challenges. The first pictures peeled off the foam backing. Gallant had to find a specialist for a crash program to develop a better glue formula. Another hitch arose with the packaging. It took forty minutes per puzzle to separate the puzzle pieces manually. Sometimes Gallant had up to eighty people breaking up and boxing the puzzles, including his mother, his children, and entire ice hockey teams who came in after games. Relief came when a local tinkerer developed a mechanical breaker.

Wrebbit began with jigsaw replicas of famous landmarks—the Capitol in Washington, the Empire State Building, Big Ben, the Eiffel Tower, the Taj Mahal, and mad King Ludwig's Neuschwanstein castle. Each had hundreds of pieces and sold for $25 to $40. Despite the high price, they flew off the shelves.

The construction element of the puzzles appealed to men as well as women. These complex projects were not for young children or the faint of heart. Indeed, once the owners had finally succeeded in assembling them, they usually proudly displayed these architectural trophies in living rooms and dens.

A 1994 marketing partnership with Hasbro's Milton Bradley division gave Wrebbit entry into the retailing giants such as Wal-Mart and Toys R Us, as well as to dozens of countries overseas. Sales soared. The puzzles reached an even broader audience in the late 1990s when Wrebbit had more than one hundred designs, including a juke box, a working Tiffany lamp, *Star Wars'* R2D2 (with a sound chip), and the *Millennium Falcon*. Colorful minipuzzles of fire engines, yellow cabs, and totem poles, together with a special line for kids, meant that puzzlers did not have to set aside a huge block of time to tackle a "Puzz-3D."

Sales peaked in 1998, the year of the "Titanic"—both the film and Wrebbit's 398-piece replica of the doomed luxury liner. 1999 began auspiciously with Wrebbit's dazzling display at the February Toy Fair in New York's Javits Convention Center. Visitors marveled at the immense foam puzzle of the Orient Express dining car, eight feet high and thirty-two feet long. Inside the train, life-size puzzle passengers sat at puzzle tables set with plates and cups made of foam pieces, as scenery filled with "Puzz-3D" buildings rolled past the windows.

But sales plummeted that year, just when major capital investments were also straining the company's balance sheet. Wrebbit survived for a few years through a merger with Irwin Toys of Toronto. Irwin too fell on hard times and shut down in 2002. Gallant bought back the puzzle division, reorganized, and is now rebuilding.[19] He hopes to extend a run that has been amazing by the standards of the toy industry, where the life of most toys is measured in months, not years.

Puzzles Today

At the turn of the millennium, puzzle designers continue their quest for innovations to fascinate their existing customers and bring new ones into the fold. Changing tastes in art and new printing techniques give a distinctive look to twenty-first-century puzzles. Gimmicks (aka "specialty puzzles") have proliferated as companies seek to make their puzzles stand out from the others.

Milton Bradley's "Big Ben" series of landscape photographs remains popular with many puzzlers, even though most of them had not been born when the brand was first introduced in 1941. Wide, panoramic photos sell well, and not just as souvenirs for tourists who want a remembrance of a dramatic city skyline or national park vista. And there are still licensed photos from *Star Wars*, *Lord of the Rings*, and other blockbuster movies.

But for the most part, contemporary artists lead the way in today's puzzle market. Nostalgia, Americana, and whimsy are big. The familiar images of Norman Rockwell and Currier & Ives have been joined by folksy country scenes by Charles Wysocki, Jane Wooster Scott, Mary Engelbreit, and many more. Visual tricks such as cats and other animals in clothing and human poses and Anne Geddes's photos of babies as blooms or butterflies are engaging puzzlers.

Inspiration, mysticism, peace, and fantasy represent another major trend. Thomas Kinkade's creations of soft, luminous cottages vie with angels and motivational sayings for the puzzler who is looking for soothing images. At the other extreme are the dramatic compositions and striking colors on puzzles of wizards, dragons, unicorns, and other magical creatures.

After a lull in the 1970s and 1980s, wildlife and nature paintings have once again come to the fore. Exotic and endangered animals—tigers, pandas, eagles, whales, manatees, and tropical reef dwellers—are favorites, especially the compositions of artists such as Schim Schimmel and Christian Riese Lassen.

Graphics with a twist are popular, because they give puzzlers more than one way to appreciate the picture. Robert Silvers's photomosaics, images made up of thousands of tiny photographs, make difficult puzzles. Glow-in-the-dark inks, glitter, holograms, and shimmering or metallic surfaces all add visual complexity and interest. Built-in activities such as "Find the hidden objects," "Where's Waldo," and crossword puzzles appeal to some puzzlers.

Ceaco of Watertown, Massachusetts, has been particularly influential by pushing the envelope for cardboard puzzles. Carol Glazer, who started her career in the puzzle business as sales director at American Publishing, founded Ceaco in 1987.[20] Since then Ceaco has been a leader in the industry, not only for its choices of artwork but also the interesting ways it has found to make puzzles.

Taking its cues from earlier wooden puzzles, Ceaco brought back figure pieces and devised other unusually shaped pieces to relieve the tedium of the typical gridlike cutting design. Irregular edges, scalloped borders, and puzzles shaped like animals captivated puzzlers too. Ceaco's use of cork-board and thin wood for some of its puzzles increased cost but added a satisfying heft to the pieces.

Clever and bright, colorful packaging added to the appeal of Ceaco puzzles. Cottage-shaped boxes held some Thomas Kinkade puzzles, while small puzzles of Anne Geddes's flower babies came in flowerpots. A "Pot Luck" series with no picture on the box, however, did not go far. Most puzzlers today insist on knowing ahead of time what the image will be.

Buffalo Games of Buffalo, New York, has been another innovator in manufacturing. Founded in 1986 by Paul and Eden Scott Dedrick, this company too sprang from old roots in the puzzle industry. Eden's father, Don Scott, Sr., had produced the last Tuco puzzles in the early 1980s after the Upson Company had sold the line. Tuco's presses, after extensive reconditioning, began to stamp out the Buffalo Games puzzles, many of which have been developed by Scott.[21]

Buffalo Games's "World's Most Difficult Puzzle" series is designed to bamboozle, with images of hundreds of similar objects, such as cats, or dogs, or candies. To further perplex the puzzler, it has the same picture on both sides. Stamping the puzzle twice, from one side for the horizontal cuts and from the other for the vertical cuts, makes it impossible to distinguish a "front" from a "back" side. Puzzlers are apparently undaunted, since the company is still turning out new editions of this fifteen-year-old brand.

Buffalo Games has used the even more confusing technique of interchangeable pieces in its "Talking Puzzle," "Quiz," and several other series. Since all the pieces fit with each other physically, puzzlers must analyze their images and texts to determine whether they really belong together. The company also puts out a successful line of cardboard three-dimensional globe puzzles.

Staying ahead in the puzzle business is a challenge in the twenty-first century. Innovations by one company are quickly copied by rivals. Consumers benefit by having a variety of puzzles available from these companies and others such as the Great American Puzzle Factory of South Norwalk, Connecticut, Ravensburger/Schmid of Salem, New Hampshire, Warren Industries of Lafayette, Indiana, and Sunsout of Costa Mesa, California, just to name a few.

6

Luxury Puzzles

PAR, STAVE, AND MORE

Par incorporated whimsical figure pieces into their personalized puzzles. The top row shows the "PAR" logo and three jesters holding the owner's initials, GCM. The seahorse in the second row is Par's signature piece.

Say "Par" to an old-time New York puzzler, and the enthusiastic response is instantaneous. Par is one of the most cherished names in jigsaw puzzles, having reigned as the premier maker of luxury puzzles for five decades.

Like thousands of other puzzle businesses, Par Company Limited began during the jigsaw puzzle craze of the Great Depression. Unlike the others, Par did not close down when the economy revived. Instead it grew and flourished, building a reputation that is still legendary as the "Rolls-Royce of puzzles."

Par was most renowned for creating beautiful, one-of-a-kind puzzles for the rich and famous—show business celebrities as well as business tycoons and royalty. The company also catered to less famous (but still well-to-do) puzzlers, many of whom bought dozens of Par puzzles over the years.

After Par's founders retired in the 1970s, the baton passed to Stave Puzzles of Norwich, Vermont. Stave now holds the place once occupied by Par in the puzzle world. Stave's success has inspired dozens of makers of fine wood puzzles in the years since. Indeed, the last decade has seen a renaissance of puzzles aimed at the luxury market.

Par's Beginnings

Par puzzles were the creation of Frank Ware and John Henriques. Neither initially envisioned that puzzles would become their life work.[1]

Francis Quarles Ware (1903–1984) was the son of Ada Johnson and Edgar Thomas Ware, an executive with American Tobacco, and grew up in Garrison, New York. He attended The Hill School in Pottstown, Pennsylvania, where he demonstrated his artistic talents with a sketch published in the yearbook. The death of his mother and family financial reverses forced Frank to drop out after his sophomore year. By 1928, however, he was established as the advertising director for Pennsylvania-Dixie Cement in New York City.

He had also met his life partner, John Nunes Henriques (1903–1972). A native New Yorker, Henriques was the son of Grace Green Henriques and Jules N. Henriques, a broker who worked for several years on Wall Street. Little is known about John Henriques's childhood, but by the late 1920s he was selling real estate in New York City and playing an excellent game of tennis in his spare time.

Ware and Henriques lived in New York until the onset of the Great Depression, when both men lost their jobs. With the optimism of youth, they concluded that the hard times would be short-lived. They seized on the dismal situation as a golden opportunity for a six-month tour of Europe.

On their return in 1931, the economy's downward spiral was accelerating. Still jobless, they cast about for a way to keep busy during their forced leisure. Henriques's family had always had a passion for puzzles, and Ware was willing to give it a try. They cut their first jigsaw puzzle, a Matisse print, with a coping saw at the dining room table.

At first the two made puzzles just to amuse themselves and their friends. An early brochure glorified these days:

> The aim was simply a better puzzle . . . not profit. The makers were both puzzle fans of many years standing. They knew the relative merits of the good puzzles on the market. And they knew, too, that certain definite

improvements and refinements in materials, in workmanship were possible. They experimented for months—with pictures printed on different papers—trying many woods and styles of cutting—testing saw blades and glues. They developed rigid specifications. Then they made puzzles which set a new standard.[2]

In 1932, as the unemployment rate approached 25 percent and the contemporary puzzle craze intensified, Ware and Henriques discovered that their friends and their friends' friends would pay to rent and even buy wooden puzzles. So they converted a hobby into a business. With a $35 electric scroll saw, a stock of pictures, and some walnut plywood, they set up a workshop in the basement of the Henriques family home at 419 West 154th Street.

Ware, with his background in marketing, thought their future prospects were good. Despite Henriques's skepticism, Ware proved to be right. They had to work hard, of course. At first they lugged heavy suitcases around New York, as they delivered and picked up the rental puzzles. An early window display of their puzzles near the Harvard Club in midtown Manhattan garnered affluent customers from both industry and the arts. They soon put together the perfect combination of a top-quality product and the clientele that could afford it. By 1936 they had moved their workshop to a posh central location, a two-story penthouse at 18 East 53rd Street, between Madison and Fifth Avenue.

The "Rolls-Royce of Puzzles"

Par's success was all the more remarkable, because while it was raising quality, most of the puzzle industry was rushing in the opposite direction. Weekly cardboard puzzles cost as little as 10 cents, and advertising puzzles were free.

How could Ware and Henriques compete when they sold a 500-piece Par puzzle for $7.50 or rented it for 75 cents per week? Quality and customization were the answers. Par built its reputation on unique personalized creations, using unusual prints, tricky cutting, impossible target times for completion, and top-of-the-line materials.

The Prints

Ware and Henriques shared similar tastes in art and were bored with what they called "the idiot variety of the old tavern scenes."[3] They tried to wean their customers away from the scenic pictures and sentimental vignettes that then dominated traditional puzzles. Instead they introduced puzzles featuring modern art by Picasso, Dali, Dufy, and Leger, among others. They were partial to the very colorful impressionists, especially Matisse and Van Gogh.

The pair also favored the striking posters that advertised railroads, airlines, circuses, and theater. Judging by the many travel posters that appear on Par puzzles, Ware and Henriques must have regularly checked the foreign tourism offices and travel agencies in New York for new stock. Pan American Airways posters, showing destinations all around the world, were staples of their print collection.

Par customers could visit the premises and make their own choices from the vast selection of prints. Or, as did many, they could describe their general tastes to Ware and Henriques, who would then surprise them with an appropriate picture. The partners also kept "ready cut" puzzles on hand to accommodate urgent needs of puzzlers who were willing to take "pot luck."

Par encouraged orders that used the buyers' submissions: photographs, original art, Christmas cards, and the like. An original painting by Gene Davis, cut into pieces by Par, appeared on the cover of *Art in America*.[4] Another time, a friend of Picasso asked the partners to dissect a print of the artist's "Still Life with Black Bust." When Picasso received the gift puzzle, he reportedly loved it. Other customers requested special puzzles for their children, made, for example, from the covers of *Mad* magazine.[5]

Although the partners drew the line at hard-core pornography, they sawed up more than a few *Playboy* centerfolds. Par cut its share of thatched cottages, Currier & Ives reproductions, and other traditional pictures too. Ware complained:

We had very little success trying to steer people away from junk, and now we make mostly hunting scenes.[6]

He particularly disliked seascape puzzles, with their vast and boring expanses of blue sky and blue water.

The Cutting

Ware and Henriques brought exceptional artistry to their puzzles. They adopted the best of the old cutting techniques and perfected new ones to keep their puzzles interesting and challenging. Each contributed complementary talents to their craft. While Ware was the better artist, Henriques did the faster and more intricate cutting.

Ware designed the hundreds of unique Par figure pieces: dancers and athletes in all sorts of poses and, of course, their signature seahorse piece. Interestingly, Par's first signature piece was a backward swastika, an old Hindu character. When Hitler and the Nazis appropriated that symbol, they searched for a replacement trademark with happier associations.

Drama critic and customer Alexander Woollcott suggested the seahorse, which has appeared in every Par puzzle since then. Occasionally, buyers who wanted more challenging puzzles asked Par to omit the figure pieces, but they always found a seahorse or two nestled among the pieces. A stylized sketch of two seahorses served to sign each item of Par's voluminous correspondence. The same sketch in gold ink decorates many later puzzles.

Custom-made puzzles featured the owners' monograms and significant dates. Par tailored the figure pieces to the owner's interests: an elephant for a staunch Republican, baby carriages for an expectant

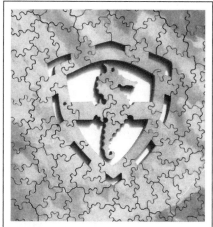

Par used drop-outs to highlight the signature seahorse in some puzzles.

mother, or a Christmas tree for a holiday gift. Some Par buyers placed standing orders to receive a puzzle each month, so Ware was continually creating imaginative new ways to cut their initials.

The Duke of Windsor was perhaps Par's most famous buyer of personalized puzzles. Each of his puzzles had to include the initials "H.R.H." (for "His Royal Highness"), the Windsor crest, and silhouettes of his four cairn terriers. Puzzles for the Duchess always contained a "W.W." monogram, patterned after her signature.

Par used a variety of cutting techniques to tease and perplex its customers, especially in the custom-made puzzles. Common tricks included splitting the corners, cutting fake corners in the middle of the puzzle, or cutting along the color lines.

The most creative cutting involved the "drop-out" and the irregular edge. Par appears to have invented the sneaky "drop-out," a gap within a puzzle, often to accentuate the initials of a monogram or to show off the details of a figure piece. Puzzlers go crazy when first encountering this device; only after a lengthy and futile search for the odd-shaped piece comes the realization that the void is deliberate.

The irregular edge was an old trick, but one that Par elevated to a new art form. Most puzzlers were used to traditional rectangular puzzles and tackled them by first sorting out the corners and edges to frame the image. When faced with Par's irregular edges, they hardly knew where to begin. Ware and Henriques did keep the rectangular outlines for prints of art masterpieces, not wanting to violate the artist's conception of the picture. But they had no such scruples with other material.

An accident at the very beginning led them to irregular borders and thus freedom from the tyranny of the straight and narrow. Their wirehaired terrier chewed the edges of a puzzle they had just finished cutting. Loath to discard their work, they made a virtue out of necessity and snipped off the damaged parts.

Irregular edges were particularly useful when they dissected posters. If "Come to Spain" was emblazoned across the top, the partners simply cut away the unwanted words, and often the entire background. They embellished some edges with names, dates, flying birds, or other creatures. They could cut the same poster in different ways, depending on the order. The 750-piece version would be trimmed more and have a totally different edge from the larger 1,200-piece one.

Par Time

Each puzzle label gave a "par time," a norm like par for a hole in golf. It challenged puzzlers to prove they were "up to par" by completing the puzzle within that time limit. Initially Henriques, a *very* fast puzzler, assembled each puzzle after it was cut. "Par" represented his time. In later years, they just estimated par, being much too busy to assemble each and every puzzle.

Par time was a constant source of frustration to the customers. Few could match it, and occasionally a client would challenge it. Henriques's standard bet was $25 that he could indeed make par on his own puzzles. He always won. Some puzzlers, feeling too pressured by the time on the box, asked that it be eliminated. "Par" on their labels consisted of cryptic phrases and their initials: "ask J M W" or "E B knows."

Double entendres enlivened some labels. "Sheer Bliss," a pastel collage of wedding mementos, was one of Par's most popular puzzles. Ware and Henriques sold dozens of copies as anniversary gifts, each giving the par time as "forever and ever." On their largest puzzle, a 10,000-piece monster, they set par at "days and nights"; they truly had no idea how long it would take to do.

Par times were specially infuriating to those who usually assembled puzzles by referring to the picture on the box. Par puzzles came in plain black boxes with no guide pictures. The partners delighted in teasing puzzlers with corny titles that gave only a hint of the true subject. "Mad Meadows" turned out to show the 1939 New York World's Fair in Flushing Meadows. "Bobby's Beat" represented a London street scene. "High IQ" was the title for a map of Cambridge. A fall foliage scene became "Turn Coat." And a picture of Jenny Lind and P.T. Barnum was known as "The Nightingale's Knight."

Materials

Ware and Henriques were always secretive about how they actually made their puzzles. They welcomed customers and reporters into the office, but absolutely refused to let anyone view the gluing, designing, cutting, or finishing. The wooden cut-out letters on the workshop door said it all: "SCAT."[7] Nevertheless, they were quite happy to boast about their success in finding high-quality materials.

For precision cutting they used extremely fine German blades, only seven thousandths of an inch thick. Ware recalled that chemists worked for five years to develop a glue that met the partners' precise requirements. It took longer to solve the plywood problem. At first, Ware and Henriques used three-ply walnut backed wood, but they found that walnut splintered too much. They soon switched to three-ply Honduras mahogany, which they used at least through the 1940s. During the 1950s they began working with five-ply mahogany that was less likely to break.

At one point when their normal supplier was unable to obtain any mahogany, Par even imported whole logs directly from a Belize plantation. A customer in the diplomatic corps helped with the importing arrangements, perhaps to minimize delays in receiving his next puzzle. Customer connections also led them to a manufacturer who made plywood sheets to Par's exacting specifications.

Par's Customers

While outstanding quality was the key to Par's reputation, Ware and Henriques were also unsurpassed at finding buyers who cherished and could afford that quality. Ads in *The New Yorker* and the *New York Times* helped in the early years, but weren't necessary for long. The partners' flair for publicity and word-of-mouth recommendations from satisfied buyers served them much better. They soon built up a customer list that read like a *Who's Who* of high society, both in New York and around the world.

They had some luck at the beginning when Norman Bel Geddes, a leading stage and industrial designer, rented one of their puzzles. Not only did he and his children (including actress Barbara Bel Geddes) become excellent customers, but they spread the word to all their friends and associates in the performing arts. Over the years, Par cut puzzles for Jimmy Durante, Humphrey Bogart, Bing Crosby, Yul Brynner, Marlene Dietrich,

James Garner, Marilyn Monroe, and Gary Cooper, just to name a few.

Ware and Henriques moved in literary, publishing, and broadcasting circles too. Among their customers they numbered CBS executives, *Encyclopedia Britannica* editor Franklin Hooper, the chief editor for *Harper's Magazine*, and mystery writer Mary Roberts Rinehart. Some of these notables insisted that Par send them puzzles in unmarked boxes, to conceal their addiction to jigsaws from their highbrow colleagues.

Time magazine founder Henry Luce and his wife Clare Boothe Luce, playwright and ambassador, were among Par's best customers and supporters. Mrs. Luce never set foot in the Par office because the partners repeatedly refused to divulge any of their trade secrets for cutting puzzles. Yet she remained friendly, sending them neckties decorated with seahorses. The connection paid off handsomely in terms of publicity, as Par received major spreads in Luce publications such as *Life* and *Sports Illustrated*.[8] Luce also commissioned the partners to cut a small puzzle for use in a *Time* advertisement.

Par's mailing list included business tycoons and politicians as well. Edsel Ford kept puzzles aboard his yacht. Charles M. Schwab, founder of Bethlehem Steel, ordered them for his private railroad car. Par puzzles graced the mansions of Rockefellers, Vanderbilts, du Ponts, Astors, Goulds, and Crowninshields. Wendell Wilkie and Dwight D. Eisenhower owned Par puzzles.

For each famous customer who was willing to be named in Par publicity, there were dozens more who preferred anonymity. Par guarded their privacy closely and opened up the company files only once, during World War II. The FBI and the British Intelligence Service were hunting for Axis spies who were sending secret messages to Trinidad in hollowed-out wooden puzzle pieces. They exonerated Par's clientele, however. Most likely, the spies could not afford Par's premium prices and had to resort to lower-quality puzzles for their communications.

Par's Rental Puzzles

The customized puzzles were the most fun and commanded the top prices, as high as $1,500 in the 1940s.[9] But the rental puzzles provided a solid base for

Par's operations for more than thirty years. Within Manhattan they used messengers to deliver and collect the puzzles. An early Par brochure promised, "A phone call or note received before 6 p.m. brings a puzzle to your door the same day."[10] More distant customers, located throughout the country, depended on the U.S. mail.

One woman rented ninety puzzles a year for over a decade without ever losing a piece. As with earlier puzzle libraries, Par kept careful records to make sure that she never got the same puzzle twice. Other regular customers included lighthouse keepers and many New Englanders who had a long puzzling tradition. The Broadmoor Hotel in Colorado Springs kept Par puzzles out on tables for their guests. Rentals soared during World War II as gas rationing kept people at home. Escaping into a puzzle brought a respite from worries about the news from the front.

Rental rates were quite reasonable, though still more than the price of a cardboard puzzle. By 1964 Par was charging $3.75 a week for a standard-size 750-piece puzzle that would fit on a card table.

Having discovered early on how difficult it was to make replacements when pieces got lost, Ware and Henriques set policies to minimize the problem of damage. They encouraged their Manhattan customers to leave each puzzle assembled until Par's messenger arrived to pack it. Puzzles that went farther afield were checked upon their return, sometimes with the help of relatives who loved to assemble puzzles. Renters who damaged puzzles had to purchase them. And the partners had no compunction about cutting off the supply to those who repeatedly lost pieces or allowed dogs to chew them to bits.

Par periodically culled its rental collection, selling off the worn puzzles at discount prices. In 1964 the partners offered used 750-piece puzzles for $18, $25.50, and $33—much less than the $125 price tag for a new puzzle. Buyers could specify only the price they would pay; the actual title they received was a matter of chance. A few years later, weary of the hassle, the partners shut down the rental operation entirely.

The rental puzzles are easy to identify because each has a serial number on the label. They tend to be more traditional puzzles, both in subject matter and cutting. While some had irregular edges, many were rectangular. Of course, none of the rentals had the monograms, dates, and other personalized touches that made Par famous.

The Par Partners

Ware and Henriques, though financially successful, were not the typical New York businessmen of the time. Many who knew them described them as eccentric and zany. It was not just that they worked in blue jeans instead of suits. They also had strong, independent, and fun-loving personalities. They enjoyed challenging and fooling their customers. Basically, they had a great career entertaining people and answering only to themselves.

They made one puzzle that gamblers loved. "48 into 49" was a borderless map of the United States cut out of plain bakelite (an early plastic) along state lines. The pieces had no writing on them, and nothing about the cutting revealed which side was up. More than one owner used it for bar bets, challenging the unsuspecting to put the map together in less than fifteen minutes. Even those who could sort out all the rectangular states in the middle had trouble with Michigan's Upper Peninsula, the forty-ninth piece.

The partners liked to tease and joke with people, about everything from puzzles to life in general. They could be witty, irreverent, outrageous, and sometimes quite rude. They spoke their minds and didn't tolerate fools gladly, even the ones who were spending thousands of dollars on puzzles. They went so far as to refuse puzzle orders on occasion. Henriques said:

We aren't unreasonable, but if we don't like people, we won't do one.[11]

Once he even threw a particularly obnoxious customer's money down the stairs after him.

On the whole, people liked the pair and found them amusing and interesting. Ware and Henriques were very outgoing and became personal friends with many puzzlers. Their bookshelves were full of first editions inscribed by authors who were Par customers. *New Yorker* cartoonist Charles Addams presented them with a special drawing in appreciation of the many

Par puzzles he had enjoyed. When Norman Bel Geddes designed the General Motors Futurama exhibit at the 1939 World's Fair, he enlisted Ware to help him build the displays.

Ware and Henriques worked hard, often six days a week. They were proud of their ingenuity, self-reliance, and independence, being self-taught in art, cutting puzzles, and repairing machinery. They felt it was inappropriate to ask their underlings to tackle the most difficult tasks. The partners did the heavy lifting, not just figuratively but literally too, as when they carried a heavy workbench up the stairs. (The elevator stopped on the fifteenth floor, one flight shy of their workshop.)

Yet they took plenty of time to enjoy their leisure. Great fans of the arts, Ware and Henriques were regulars at New York theaters, concert halls, and movie houses. While hobnobbing with the glitterati, not only did they produce some dazzling personalized puzzles, but they also made some brilliant investments. As backers of Broadway musicals, they astutely picked smash hits such as *Cabaret*, *The Music Man*, *Mame*, and *Fiddler on the Roof*.[12] They spent many weekends at their country home in southern Vermont.

Though Ware and Henriques did not conceal their homosexuality, neither did they flaunt it. Their public behavior was discreet, as was considered proper for that era. They took care that visitors to their workshop were comfortable, regardless of their sexual orientation. The male elevator operator in the 53rd Street building once began flirting with a teenage boy who worked at Par after school, sweeping the floors and cleaning. When the partners learned about the incident, they made sure that the elevator operator was replaced.

Latter-Day Pars

Once Ware and Henriques had established their niche, they stayed there. One industrialist was so taken with Par puzzles that he drew up an elaborate plan for expansion into mass production. The partners would have nothing to do with such schemes, preferring to continue on a small scale in their rather cramped quarters on 53rd Street. The two did all their own cutting during the 1930s, although they employed up to five assistants at a time to help with delivery, packing, shipping, and cleaning.

One of the young helpers, Arthur Gallagher (1922–1989), started as a Par messenger in the late 1930s.[13] He served in the military during World War II, then returned to the company for a career. During a nine-month apprenticeship, he progressed from the basics of puzzle making to its finer points. Over the years Gallagher took on more of the production cutting, while Henriques concentrated on the custom cutting. The partners regularly rewarded him with complimentary tickets to Broadway hits.

When Henriques died in 1972, Ware felt some of the zest go out of his work and decided it was time to retire. But a feature story that summer in the *Wall Street Journal* brought in so many orders that he kept going a year longer than he had intended.[14] In 1974, he gave Gallagher the entire business—saws, wood, pictures, and the invaluable mailing list. Ware spent his retirement years pursuing his interests in theater and books, but interestingly kept not a single Par puzzle in his Sutton Place South apartment. He died in 1984.

Gallagher relocated the business to North Massapequa, close to his home on Long Island, and operated it on a smaller scale. Working by himself, he could cut about one hundred twenty-five puzzles per year, roughly one-third of what Par had been producing a few years earlier. One of his sons helped for a while, but had no desire for a career in the puzzle business. Gallagher eventually found his own apprentice, John Madden, who became the third generation trained in the art and secrets of cutting Par puzzles.

By the early 1980s, poor health forced Gallagher to retire as well. He had developed emphysema, most likely due to decades of cutting puzzles before dust masks became standard safety precautions. Gallagher turned over the business to Madden, who still operates it part-time from his nearby home in Wantagh.

Stave Puzzles

Meanwhile, Ware's retirement had created consternation among aficionados of luxury puzzles. The lucky ones could still get puzzles from Gallagher's modest operation. But he could not satisfy all the Par customers on the mailing list. Many found themselves cut off completely.

One devotee, a wealthy insurance executive who was suffering from Par withdrawal symptoms, approached Strategy House, a small manufacturer of inexpensive cardboard puzzles in Norwich, Vermont. He showed a Par puzzle to the owners, then asked if they could cut its equal. When he offered $300 for a Par-quality puzzle (one hundred times the $3 that each cardboard puzzle brought in), they lost no time getting into the wood puzzle business.

That twist of fate launched Stave Puzzles, now entering its fourth decade. Stave quickly assumed the mantle of the leader in luxury puzzles. Not only did Stave match Par's quality, but it went beyond, bringing still new innovations and new concepts to fascinate puzzlers worldwide.[15]

Steve Richardson, Stave's owner, was no stranger to quality wood jigsaw puzzles. As a child he loved to do them with his grandparents, who always had Pastime puzzles spread out on a table in their house in Rhode Island. He was thrilled at the age of ten when his grandfather gave him an electric scroll saw. But young Richardson kept cutting his fingers along with the wood, and his mother became exasperated by the trips to the doctor for stitches. Oblivious to her son's potential as a world-class puzzle maker, she threw the saw into the trash. Richardson grew up to receive an M.B.A. from the University of Michigan and spent several years in the corporate world.

Then came the "Rolaids episode." During one particularly long and grueling commute on the Garden State Parkway, Richardson had a flash of insight: Life could be better away from the corporate treadmill. He moved to Vermont for a slower-paced lifestyle and a computer analyst job at a small company. An unexpected layoff six months later left him with a surfeit of time on his hands and a scramble to find something that would support his family. By 1971 he and Dave Tibbetts, a graphic artist and another victim of the pink slip, had teamed up to form Strategy House, a small game company.

They had modest successes with "NFL TV Football" (distributed by International House of Pancakes) and "Xaviera's Game" (named after Xaviera Hollander, who wrote *The Happy Hooker*). They also produced die-cut cardboard jigsaw puzzles, including a series of *New York Times* crosswords made in jigsaw form and several customized puzzles for Vermont businesses.

They turned to wooden puzzles in 1974. It took months of experimentation with saws, woods, and other materials before the two felt confident enough about their skills to buy a one-inch advertisement in *The New Yorker*. They also changed the company name to "Stave," a combination of their first names that coincidentally means "to break up." That first ad generated a $6,000 order from a customer who subsequently bought over $1 million worth of Stave puzzles. The rest, as they say, is history.

Tibbetts moved on to other creative endeavors (including children's puzzles) in 1976, leaving Richardson operating the company with just one or two employees. He is so much the company's persona that more than a few customers think his first name is Stave, not Steve.

Richardson's first goal for Stave Puzzles, just to match the quality of Par puzzles, was quickly achieved. Each Stave puzzle used an attractive print mounted on specially made mahogany-backed plywood. Personalization was a key ingredient, with puzzles featuring customers' names, monograms, special dates, and favorite figure pieces. Irregular edges accentuated the distinctive elements of puzzle images and played havoc with the typical puzzler's strategy of starting with the corners and edge pieces. Stave's signature piece, a clown, appeared in every puzzle. Of course, there was no guide picture on the box.

The second challenge was to sell puzzles at the stratospheric prices required for such a labor-intensive product. While the initial Stave price of 50 cents per piece ($250 for a 500-piece puzzle) seems low by the company's current standards, back in the late 1970s it was not easy to find puzzlers who were willing to shell out hundreds of dollars for a single puzzle.

Richardson proved to have a real flair for marketing and publicity. His first major coup came in 1975 when the Horchow Collection, an early high-end mail order catalog, devoted a full page to an exclusive Stave puzzle. By 1980 a front page feature in the *Wall Street Journal* noted that Stave counted members of the du Pont and Mellon families among its customers.[16]

The list of celebrities has since expanded. Queen Elizabeth, Barbara Bush, Stephen King, Julie Andrews, Tom Peters, and Bill Gates all own Stave puzzles. And the marketing drive never ceases. Regular reading in the Stave workshop is the annual *Forbes* listing of the world's billionaires. Richardson says, "We pick up another one or two each year."

Richardson's creativity as a puzzle inventor surpassed even his talents in marketing. Soon he went beyond what Par had achieved. He commissioned artists to create original art and to hand-color their prints for limited-edition puzzles. Jim Schubert's "Winter Fantasy" design, a hit in 1978, was followed by the "Dollhouse Village" set of five puzzles. The "collect 'em all" crowd had to shell out $15,000 for this charming grouping. The company has since collaborated with about two dozen artists, creating puzzles in which the cutting meshes perfectly with the picture.

Dimensionality was another Stave innovation. Richardson began with two-layer puzzles, such as the stunning "Midsummer Night's Dream," hand-painted by Henri Loustau. The next step was "pop-ups," ballerinas, trains, and other pieces that stood up when fitted into slots in a puzzle. But the progression to a full-blown three-dimensional creation in 1991 was a bit shakier. Customers loved the bright, whimsical picture of the $1,595 "Flying Horses Carousel" in the catalog, but became disillusioned when it arrived. Most found they did not have the perfectly steady touch needed to make the eleven-inch-high merry-go-round stand upright without teetering. Stave subsequently stopped making the carousel and retreated to 3-D constructions that topped out at just a few inches.

Even at the beginning Richardson recognized that while some puzzlers were looking for relaxation, others were not satisfied unless they had to knock themselves out to solve a puzzle. For the latter group he offered cutting tricks such as dropouts, fake corners, the "nightmare cut" (very squiggly), and rebuses built into the puzzle. Company catalogs repeatedly describe Richardson as the "Chief Tormentor" and the puzzles as "diabolical."

Since diehard puzzlers quickly caught on to these standard tricks, Richardson had to design harder and harder puzzles to keep them happy. Too many customers were taking advantage of Stave's money back guarantee. They asked for refunds on the grounds that a $500 puzzle had not delivered $500 worth of entertainment. Making the puzzles bigger ratcheted up the difficulty level, of course, but raised costs at the same time. Richardson faced a real dilemma: How could he satisfy the seemingly insatiable appetite for frustration, while not driving potential buyers away with even higher prices?

His big breakthrough came in 1983 when he designed his first "two-way trick" puzzles. By stack-cutting two layers of a puzzle at a time and artfully using dropouts, Richardson could make a puzzle with interchangeable pieces. "Go Fish," the first such puzzle, had 150 pieces painted by Stephanie Loeffler. It had more than a million possible configurations, but only one was correct. Essential components of Stave trick puzzles include both specially designed artwork that leads the puzzler to put pieces together the *wrong* way, and precision cutting at critical points in the picture.

Since then the ongoing battle between puzzle inventor and puzzle solver has escalated steadily. A metamorphic puzzle, for example, makes two pictures. One designed by Andrea Farnham features a Christmas wreath as the fairly straightforward first solution. But to convert it into a Christmas tree, some pieces must go in upside down!

Stave enlists a few of the most talented puzzlers among its clientele as "testers" for the trick puzzles, especially the most difficult ones. These are marked with four or five lightning bolts in the glossy company catalog and come with a bottle of aspirin thoughtfully tucked into the puzzle box. The staff counsels customers about whether they are up to these monsters, and tries to dissuade casual puzzlers from even attempting the two- or three-bolt puzzles.

Yet some puzzlers inevitably get in over their heads and phone Vermont in despair, begging for help. Richardson and his "gang" of helpers relish these pleas for mercy. They dole out hints one at a time, sometimes over several months, to keep the callers moving toward a solution. Naturally, they deliver some ritual teasing and taunting along with the clues. They seem to be happiest when the customers turn the tables and play some tricks of their own (a thank-you note sliced into bits, or worse), and when satisfied puzzlers send them chocolate treats. (Godiva brings cheers from the predominantly female staff.)

Richardson admits he went too far in 1989. He designed an April Fools' Day puzzle called "5 Easy Pieces." It was easy enough to assemble any four of the pieces, but the fifth piece was always too big to fit in. Indeed, the

Steve Richardson's April Fools' joke in 1989 was *5 Easy Pieces*, a puzzle that was impossible to assemble. The clown signature piece appears in every Stave puzzle.

© *2004 Stave Puzzles, Inc.*

puzzle was impossible to solve, and there was an outcry of "foul play." Richardson had to refund the full purchase price of $89 to each of the thirty buyers. He immediately discontinued production, so "5 Easy Pieces" may well be the rarest of all Stave puzzles.

Richardson now makes sure that every puzzle has a solution. But his goal is to create a puzzle that is solvable, yet is so difficult that no one else *can* actually find the solution. Although he hasn't quite succeeded yet, the Stave puzzle contests of recent years show that he is getting close.

At Stave's twentieth anniversary party in 1995, he challenged puzzlers to assemble his most fiendish trick puzzle, "Olivia," within ten thousand seconds (just under three hours). None of the contestants was able to win the $10,000 prize, although the six finalists did exact a little revenge by mashing whipped-cream pies in Richardson's face. Those who tackled the 1997 challenge puzzle, "Fred and Ginger," likewise came up empty-handed. A few determined puzzlers eventually solved both puzzles, but required days, not minutes, to do so.

The personal touch and service are key factors in Stave's success. Regular customers are treated like extended family and are invited to periodic celebrations. Even new customers get special attention. A Philadelphia man phoned late one afternoon, insisting he must have a customized gift puzzle for his mother by the following day. Richardson explained that all the staff had gone home. There was simply no way to cut and ship the puzzle so it would arrive in time. The desperate customer pleaded, and offered to come to Vermont to pick up the puzzle. Richardson, lacking the heart to turn him away, said, "You start driving, and I'll start cutting." He had just dissected the last piece when the man arrived late that night. The overtime effort created a loyal customer who has bought a Stave puzzle every year since.

Richardson used to wonder if something Freudian was going on: Was he still trying to prove something to his mother so many years after she took away his first saw? Today, he is confident of his position as the best known and most successful maker of luxury jigsaw puzzles. Indeed, he was the first recipient of the prestigious Spilsbury Award for innovation in jigsaw puzzles, presented by the Association of Game and Puzzle Collectors in 2001.

Richardson is secure in the knowledge that it's not just technical ability that produces a fine puzzle. It requires his rare combination of creativity, artistry, business savvy, humor, and the willingness to take risks, together with a personality that thrives on the challenge, stimulation, and pressure that customers provide. Richardson is also adept at encouraging the same talents in his employees, giving ample credit in the Stave catalog to their many creative contributions.

Modern Competitors

Just as Par inspired Stave, so has Stave's success spawned a host of puzzle makers who have sprung up to compete with him in recent decades. His influence is so pervasive that even the manufacturers of inexpensive cardboard puzzles have imitated his designs. But his real mark has been in the sphere of high-end wood puzzles, where aspiring makers have studied his ideas on how to build a thriving business. Stave's current prices, around $6 per piece, provide room for others to find a market for their puzzles at $1 to $3 per piece. A handful of full-time puzzle cutters and several dozen part-timers now offer customized wood puzzles for the connoisseur. More than a few have ties to Stave, either as former employees or as former customers.

Two of the most successful appeared in the late 1980s. Betsy Stuart's fondness for the wood jigsaws crafted by her Uncle Tuck during the Great Depression led her to found Elms Puzzles in Baltimore in 1987.[17] Her initials are E. L. M. S., and every puzzle includes a signature piece of an elm tree. In 1990 she moved to Harrison, Maine, where she and her staff make quality wood jigsaw puzzles in the tradition of Par and Stave.

One of the company's most popular features is the Elms Puzzle Club, which has several hundred members. They can rent Elms puzzles, thus getting a steady stream of new puzzles at a fraction of the cost. Some join the club just so they can participate in the periodic sales of used puzzles when the rental stock is renewed.

Jim Ayer took a different tack when he founded J. C. Ayer & Company in Marblehead, Massachusetts, also in 1987.[18] He too had enjoyed wooden puzzles as a child, but recognized that cutting them by hand would be very costly. Building on his experience from a career in mechanical engineering, he worked almost a year to devise a computer-controlled water jet cutting system. Amazingly, if you put water under enough pressure (fifty thousand pounds worth), it will cut through plywood. The automated system is ideal for making many puzzles with the same pattern. Once Ayer has created the cutting design on the computer, the only labor needed is to push the start button on the machinery for each puzzle.

Ayer's puzzles are complex, including many figure pieces and sometimes irregular borders. He can customize them to a client's taste by going back to the computer and creating a new cutting pattern. Because of the narrow nozzle, the pieces fit tightly and stay together when a puzzle is picked up by a corner.

In the 1990s more companies joined the ranks of producers of luxury wood jigsaw puzzles. The most visible full-timer is MGC Puzzles of East Haddam, Connecticut. Owner Mark G. Cappitella, unlike the others, had no previous experience with wood puzzles, but had long pursued a wood-working hobby.[19] After being laid off from his job in 1995, he experimented with jigsaw puzzles, making simple ones as holiday gifts for family and friends. When he later came across an article about Elms, he was astounded to learn that its top-quality puzzles brought hundreds, even thousands of dollars. He started selling his own puzzles in 1996, did some cutting for Elms for a few months, then gave that up when his own business began to take off.

Cappitella too specializes in customized puzzles with irregular edges, monograms, figure pieces, and all the other tricks developed over the years. One of his biggest innovations was to develop the potential of the Internet for niche marketing. Whereas other companies relied on printing expensive catalogs, Cappitella built an elaborate, high-profile website. It draws in affluent customers who can afford both computers and hand-cut puzzles. A self-taught web designer, Capitella is now so proficient that MGC Puzzles shows up at the top of virtually any Internet search for wooden jigsaw puzzles.

The vast majority of the new puzzle makers are part-timers. Their websites are popping up in large numbers, a dozen new ones in each of the last few years. They are a heterogeneous lot, including both retirees and younger people with day jobs. Some cut a few dozen puzzles each year, while others toil over the jigsaw on a daily basis. Most are longtime aficionados of fine wood puzzles, but a few are newcomers to the field.

The new cutters have had varying degrees of success. More than a few have fallen by the wayside, having underestimated the work and commitment needed to develop their products, find customers, and build a business. Others seem to be on their way to posing some formidable competition to the older companies. Some of the more active operations in the United States today include Fool's Gold Puzzles in Harrisville, New Hampshire, Jardin Puzzles in Stow, Massachusetts, Sunbonnet Puzzles in Lebanon, Missouri, and Custom Puzzle Craft in San Diego, California.

A handful have begun to make jigsaw puzzles as an adjunct to other artistic pursuits. Amy Finley Scott is an established artist, with several one-woman shows to her credit at New York City galleries.[20] In 1977, she was planning a Christmas dinner for fourteen, but realized that she would have to wash dishes after the main course in order to serve dessert. How to keep the guests entertained in a cramped New York City apartment during the break? She worked till 3 A.M. that Christmas Eve, painting on wood, then cutting up the result. The jigsaw puzzle was a hit and launched Scott into a new artistic dimension. She makes jigsaws on a very limited basis, mostly on commission. She most enjoys creating images that weave together the special interests of the buyers.

Is Stave worried about losing business to all the newer makers of modern luxury puzzles? Not at all. Steve Richardson declares that a vibrant industry creates a buzz and attracts new customers who have never seen such puzzles before:

> We work aggressively to get some pretty decent PR for ourselves. The downside is that it opens the door and it creates energy out there for the competitors. But they in fact create some form of energy for us.[21]

Everyone wins.

7

Pieces of Marketing

THE ADVERTISING PICTURE GAINS A GREATER
EFFICACY BY BEING A SCRAMBLED PICTURE.

Courtesy of PMC Group—Pro Corp.

The Prophylactic Brush puzzle that pushed the Great Depression puzzle craze into high gear featured Frances Tipton Hunter's delightful painting of a child brushing a terrier's teeth.

McLoughlin Brothers copyrighted the large *Fire Engine Picture Puzzle* in 1887. The dramatic scene shows McLoughlin's building in New York City at right. Naturally, the fire is at a rival firm down the street.

The two layers tell the story of Cinderella's transformation, in this puzzle made by Waco-Tex around 1960.

Parker Brothers published this puzzle in 1899. Along with the toys, Santa brings *The Battle of Manila* and other bestselling Parker games.

Each piece in this 1994 fish puzzle is a distinct ocean creature. The manufacturer, Pieceful Solutions, put educational text on the back of each piece. © *Pieceful Solutions*

Winter Recreation is the title of this colorful 96-piece puzzle made by Madmar Quality Company around 1920.

Frances A. Cooke of Weston, Massachusetts, used a 1912 magazine cover by F. X. Leyendecker for this 187-piece puzzle.

Charles P. B. Jefferys made this 187-piece puzzle from a cartoon about the war in Cuba in 1898.

ABOVE: *Kentucky Belle* is one of Margaret Richardson's "Perplexity" puzzles. The 908 pieces and the cutting along color lines make it extremely difficult.

RIGHT: C. M. Coolidge's series of dog pictures were a big hit with puzzlers. Parker Brothers sold this one in 1919.

Valdemar T. Hammer, an amateur working in Branford, Connecticut, in the 1910s, chose artwork by Howard Chandler Christy and a courtship theme for this romantic puzzle.

This puzzle probably began life as a wall calendar around 1908. The maker is unknown.

Black to Move—Black to Win was made by the Leisure Hour Puzzle Co. of Melrose, Massachusetts. The artist, Harry Roseland, is known for his unusually sympathetic portrayal of African-Americans in the early 1900s.

Beauty and the Beast is a "Get-A-Fit" picture puzzle, sold by the Mrs. Vanity Fair store in New York City. Artwork by Jessie Willcox Smith was very popular for puzzles during the first puzzle craze.

LEFT: *Roller Coaster* was one of many puzzles cut by a member of the Fifield family in Swampscott, Massachusetts, during the second and third decades of the twentieth century.

BELOW: *David Copperfield Leaving Margate* is one of many "Pastime" Parker's puzzles that showed Dickens coaching scenes, painted by Albert Ludovici Jr.

Maxfield Parrish's painting of *Cleopatra's Barge* originally decorated Crane's Chocolate boxes in 1917. Parker Brothers used it and other beloved Parrish prints on some "Pastime" puzzles.

Mooning is the title of this whimsical portrayal of honeymooners. George W. Fiss Jr. of Philadelphia, Pennsylvania, cut the 649-piece puzzle in 1910. It circulated widely among family and friends.

RIGHT: The woman
who cut this "Pastime"
puzzle for Parker
Brothers cleverly cut
two L's on Lindbergh's
flying jacket to stand
for "Lucky Lindy."

*Courtesy of Goes Litho-
graphing Co., Chicago
60621: Charles B. Goes IV,
president. Prints sold as
True Color Prints.*

ABOVE: *Start Something*, a 229-piece wooden
jigsaw by the Tryawhile Puzzle Company circa
1930, continued the earlier style of cutting on
color lines.

RIGHT: Harriet M. Eagleson of Watertown,
Massachusetts, made *The Y.M.C.A. Girl "Over
There"* and hundreds of other puzzles for family
and friends in the 1910s and 1920s. She cut
several figure pieces, including her "HME" signature piece in the lower right corner.

ABOVE: Carroll A. Towne's puzzles often included pieces that spelled out a message, in this case "Venice City of Romance!"

Courtesy of Goes Lithographing Co., Chicago 60621: Charles B. Goes IV, president. Prints sold as True Color Prints.

LEFT: Parker Brothers made this puzzle of *Old Glory* during World War I, long before the Nazis turned the swastika from a benign symbol into a reviled one.

Street in the Orient, a "sculptured" puzzle manufactured by Joseph K. Straus in the 1930s, has two layers so the people and buildings stand out from the background.

Courtesy of Goes Lithographing Co., Chicago 60621: Charles B. Goes IV, president. Prints sold as True Color Prints.

The University Distributing Company issued Louis Remy Mignot's painting of Washington and Lafayette at Mount Vernon as the twentieth puzzle in its "Jig of the Week" series in February 1933.

Irénée du Pont was so pleased with his new painting by Frank E. Schoonover that he had several hundred copies printed and made into cork-backed jigsaw puzzles. They served as his Christmas cards in 1933.

Courtesy of the Schoonover family

During the 1907–10 puzzle craze, postcard manufacturers supplied perforated cards with envelopes. The sender could write a message, separate the pieces, and mail it to a puzzled recipient.

Jimmy Durante leads a host of stars in *Hollywood on Parade*, a small puzzle die-cut by the Consolidated Lithographing Corporation of Brooklyn, New York, in the 1930s.

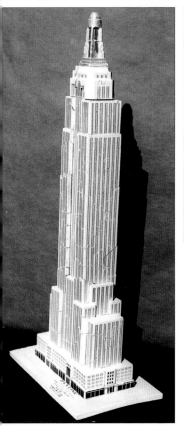

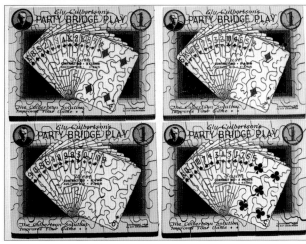

ABOVE: The 1933 *Ely Culbertson Party Bridge Set* came with "Instructions to Hostess" for combining jigsaw and bridge play.

LEFT: This wooden 119-piece three-dimensional puzzle of the Empire State Building is one in the "Skyline" series, made in the 1930s by the Kawin Manufacturing Company of Astoria, New York.

Jaymar Specialty Company imitated the makers of wooden puzzles by including figure pieces in its die-cut "Modern Fighters for Victory" series. *Subtracting a Zero* has pieces shaped like bombs, guns, and other military items.

Marx Toys and Entertainment Corp.

Springbok Editions turned the puzzle world upside down in 1964 when it published *Convergence* by Jackson Pollock and marketed it as "the world's most difficult jigsaw puzzle."

LEFT: *Forward America*, made by Tuco Work Shops in 1942, shows President Franklin D. Roosevelt surrounded by flags, with a scene of American military might at the bottom.

RIGHT: The Puzzle Factory in New York City designed many double-sided jigsaws, including the *Nixon-Agnew Two-Faced Jigsaw Puzzle.* © 1970 The Puzzle Factory

Elms Puzzles in Harrison, Maine, often paints decorative edge pieces by hand, as on this romantic image, titled *Hearts and Flowers*. *Artwork © Carolyn Bucha, puzzle and border © Elms Puzzles, Inc.*

ABOVE LEFT: Frank Ware was always coming up with new ways to cut a customer's initials or nickname into a Par puzzle.

ABOVE: The soaring bird cut into the edge of *Pilgrims' Progress* broke up the monotony of the blue sky and made the puzzle more challenging for those who tried to start with straight edge pieces.

LEFT: Ware and Henriques frequently cut messages around the borders of Par's personalized puzzles, such as this 850-piece scene called *Camelot*.

RIGHT: Par's 775-piece *Double Exposure* features a completely irregular edge. The reflection of the owner's monogram follows the motif of the artwork.

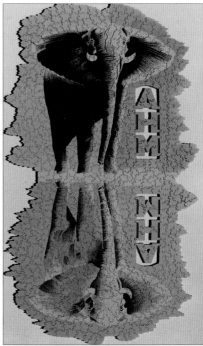

BELOW: In this detail from Par's *Stepping Out*, the band member pieces, accentuated by drop-outs, mirror the image of the travel poster.

Par sold dozens of copies of *Sheer Bliss*, each puzzle personalized with the appropriate wedding anniversary date and the couples' initials. Par time is "forever and ever."
Courtesy of Gus and Marty Trowbridge

In Stave's
St. Nick's Knacks,
the trick is to fit all
the gifts back into
Santa's bag.
© *2004 Stave Puzzles,*
Inc.

The *Tristram Coffin Mansion* is one of five puzzles in Stave's limited edition *Dollhouse Village* designed by Jim Schubert. The package includes a story booklet about the goings-on in the village. © *2004 Stave Puzzles, Inc.*

RIGHT: Jim Ayer cut *Coughing Bear* out of wood, using a sophisticated computer-controlled water jet mechanism.

BELOW: The C. I. Hood Company used Louis Wain's *Wedding in Catland* on this circa-1900 puzzle. An essay about the curative powers of Hood's Sarsaparilla appears on the reverse side.

ABOVE: The *Boston Globe* inserted this cardboard picture, printed with instructions for cutting it up, into its Sunday newspaper around 1908.

LEFT: The Yells Funeral Home in Geneva, New York, gave out free jigsaws during the puzzle craze of the 1930s.

The Russell Manufacturing Company of Middletown, Connecticut, commissioned artist Tony Sarg to do this premium puzzle for Rusco brake linings.

Courtesy of Dana Corporation/Raytech Corporation

ABOVE: Buyers of Singer sewing machines received puzzle giveaways from salesmen during the first decade of the twentieth century.

LEFT: Hills Brothers Coffee distributed this dynamic 200-piece advertising puzzle in 1933.

Courtesy of Sara Lee Corporation

ABOVE LEFT: At Stave's twenty-fifth anniversary party in 2000, guests tested their mettle on this oversized trick *Crab Shack* puzzle, designed by Dee Rogers. © 2004 Stave Puzzles, Inc.

ABOVE: Amy Finley Scott, a New York City artist, painted and cut *Night Gifts* in 1993.

© Amy Finley Scott, New York, New York

LEFT: Scott Stafford of Medford, New Jersey, created this customized wedding proposal puzzle. Happily, Jennifer chose the "yes" piece to fill the heart-shaped gap.

Photo copyright by Julie A. Gray, Hatfield, Pennsylvania; puzzle copyrighted by Scott Stafford; courtesy of Jeff Garber and Jennifer Swope

Jigsaw puzzles and advertising—the connection goes back to the 1880s. The masters of media on Madison Avenue are always seeking novel, creative, and memorable pitches for products. Inspired by dreams of puzzlers who spend hours fitting together the pieces of a company's name and its products, they periodically seize on jigsaws to carry their messages. Virtually every consumer good and service, from baby foods to funeral homes, has appeared on advertising jigsaw puzzles. Promotional puzzles thus record the history of daily lives and values in the past.[1]

Publicists in advertising's multifaceted world classify the jigsaw puzzle as a "premium," a gift from the seller to attract customers. Familiar examples include the toy in the cereal box, the dessert mold offered with a package of pudding mix, and the tote bag given with a new magazine subscription.

Jigsaw puzzles offer some advantages over other premiums, even over other kinds of puzzles. Their images can easily depict the products, logo, and message of the promoters. They appeal to both adults and children. Because puzzles are often passed along from one person to another, they tend to reach a large audience. And unlike mechanical puzzles, usually a solitary pursuit, jigsaws can engage and entertain several people at once. One early trade magazine enthused:

Perhaps the outstanding asset of jig-saw puzzles, from the advertiser's point of view, is that they lose none of their essential appeal by being made the base of an advertising picture. In fact, the advertising picture gains a greater efficacy by being a scrambled picture, since it is not only permitted to enter but is welcomed into the inner sanctum of the prospect's leisure and since it commands the prospect's attention for a longer period of time than it otherwise could.[2]

The premium has a cost, however, and that cost adds to the price of the merchandise. So why would buyers prefer a higher priced product *with* a puzzle to a lower priced item without? One executive explained how advertising puzzles boosted sales during the Great Depression, after earlier price cuts had failed to do so:

Few people could afford to go out nights as they used to in flusher times. The majority had to stay home—and if an advertiser could furnish the means to turn tedium and boredom into a happy forgetting of cares, he would win both the public's gratitude and business. . . . Regardless of its actual monetary value, a trifle that the public really wants constitutes a greater inducement to purchase than a considerably larger concession in cash. Possibly it proves that we are all far more childish than any of us would care to admit—but it is nevertheless almost as axiomatic as the well-known truism about two and two.[3]

The psychology of the giveaway, the search for distraction from worries, and the appeal of inexpensive home amusement are just as relevant today as they were in the 1930s.

Mail in Three Box Tops

Companies have devised all sorts of ways to distribute their advertising puzzles, many of which bring back revenue or other benefits for the issuer. Buyers obviously prefer the free premium obtained at the time of purchase—simply buy the product and get the premium instantly. For example, in the 1930s Rexall Drug Stores gave away a 200-piece puzzle with any purchase of Rexall Milk of Magnesia toothpaste, Klenzo Shaving Cream, or Rexall Orderlies ("the original chocolate flavored laxative").

Sometimes the premium is already in the package, such as Cracker Jack's prize. Or it may be part of the packaging, such as puzzle pieces printed on a cereal box for kids to cut out and reassemble. Sunday newspapers in 1908–1909 and in the 1930s often included lithographed pictures marked with lines showing how to cut them into puzzles.

Quite a few manufacturers, however, require more than one purchase. To get a Hood's puzzle in 1891, the buyer had to mail in three trademarks cut from Hood's Sarsaparilla wrappers. In 1932 General Mills promised a Jack Dempsey puzzle in exchange for a coupon and two Wheaties box tops. The coupon, published in several magazines and coded to identify the date and source, was a clever device that enabled General Mills to determine which ads generated the most response. The returned coupons could also generate a list of targets for future direct mail advertising.

Several companies that sell gum, cigarettes, and other items in small packets have used "collect 'em all" promotions to encourage repeat buying. In the 1980s, for example, each of Leaf's packets of Donruss baseball cards contained 3 pieces of a 63-piece puzzle of a baseball star. Those intent on completing the puzzle had to make twenty-one purchases—usually more because there was no way to tell which pieces were inside until the wrapper was removed.

Advertisers also create "self-liquidating" premiums, in which they sell the premium at or above its cost, but the item is available only from the issuing company. The "25 cents for handling" demanded for many children's premiums in the 1950s actually covered the cost of making the items and mailing them third class.[4] Self-liquidating premiums have expanded over time from mail-in offers to products sold in company gift shops and catalogs. Disney and Warner Brothers later took this concept to a new level, selling souvenirs not only in theme parks, but also in retail stores and then on the Internet. Prices on their puzzles more than cover the cost of production, thus generating healthy profits.

A special class of premiums aims at businesses, rather than consumers. Manufacturers regularly hand out promotional jigsaw puzzles to retailers at trade shows. Ingersoll-Rand created the epitome of the advertising puzzle, cut with the company's water-jet cutting process. Not only did it advertise, but the tiny pieces also demonstrated the capabilities of the company's technology to prospects in industry. And companies occasionally present puzzles to employees as mementos, or for team-building exercises. Business-oriented premiums usually have much smaller production runs than advertising puzzles for consumers.

The growth of licensed properties in the last few decades has generated a huge category of puzzles that look like advertising puzzles, but in fact are really regular merchandise. Established puzzle companies negotiate and acquire licenses, make the puzzles, and sell them through many different retail outlets. American Publishing Company of Waltham, Massachusetts, was one of the first to do this, with puzzles showing Heinz pickles, Chiquita bananas, and other familiar products in 1965. Hallmark, Jaymar, and others joined in a few years later. April House in Lenexa, Kansas, published a clever "Puzzle Cheer" series, puzzles of familiar whiskey and cordial bottles that were packaged in liquor boxes. The purist would not include these commercial products in the advertising puzzle group.

Another gray area includes advertising images that appear on homemade and unlicensed puzzles. For over a century, children have used scissors to cut up magazine covers or calendars to create picture puzzles. Makers of wooden jigsaw puzzles similarly have taken prints from those sources and others, including posters, cigar-box lids, and fruit crates. When the advertising message is not trimmed from the picture, it is tempting, but not accurate, to call these advertising puzzles.

Although some collectors may spurn them, future historians will surely be interested in both the homemade and the commercial puzzles. They serve to reflect society's patterns of consumption just as much as the true advertising puzzles do.

Early Advertising Puzzles

The first American advertising puzzles appeared more than a century ago. "Silent Teacher" puzzles were the most abundant before 1900. A series of upstate New York companies (The Union Sectional Map, G. N. Tackabury, E. J. Clemens, and C. E. Hartman) sold wooden dissected maps under this brand name for three decades, beginning in 1877. By the early 1880s, they had begun making reversible puzzles, backed with advertising for either Sherwin Williams paints or White bicycles and sewing machines.

Sherwin Williams and White most likely paid the manufacturers to fill the blank space on the puzzle backs with the attractive color prints that promoted their products. (No records remain to document the business relationship between the puzzle makers and the advertisers, so it is possible that the makers bought the advertising prints because they needed paper to back their puzzles. However, the lithographs came from Cleveland, Ohio, and there were surely cheaper sources of backing paper closer to the puzzle factories in New York.)

A few other advertising puzzles appeared in the 1880s, notably those issued by the John Shillito Company of Cincinnati in its Third Floor Christmas Department. Shillito contracted with Peter G. Thomson, who made games and puzzles from 1883 to 1887, to make two sliced cardboard puzzles showing both the exterior and the interior of their "Mammoth Dry Goods Warehouse." Few of these puzzles survive today, because distribution took place for only a few years in the Cincinnati area.

Several firms published advertising puzzles during the 1890s, the most prolific being C. I. Hood & Co. of Lowell, Massachusetts. The "Rainy Day and Balloon Puzzle" first went out to buyers of Hood's Sarsaparilla in 1891. Brochures inside the puzzle box claimed that the tonic cured everything from boils and dyspepsia to scrofula and malaria. The drink was extremely popular over the years, not the least because its 16.5 percent alcohol content made users feel better.[5] The company issued several editions of the puzzle, each with slight variations in the lithography or die-cutting. By the time C. I. Hood closed its doors in the early 1920s, it had published five other puzzle titles, including the "Wedding in Catland," illustrated by Louis Wain, and the "Auto Race."

Hood made a technical contribution too. In the 1890s the firm was the first in the United States to die-cut cardboard puzzles into curved and interlocking pieces. Hood's puzzles were thus more interesting to assemble than the earlier sliced cardboard puzzles, yet still very inexpensive to produce.

Another innovation came from the Dr. Miles Medical Company a few years later. Its cardboard map puzzle of the United States included pieces shaped like letters, spelling out the name of the company and its "Nervine" tonic.

A spate of advertising puzzles appeared around 1908–10, an outgrowth of the full-scale craze for puzzles that fascinated adults in those years. Some companies, including Pratt Food and Singer Sewing Machine, packaged their puzzles in envelopes, which cost much less to manufacture than the boxes used in earlier years.

Mailing costs fell too. In 1909 Richard T. Peckham invented a new production method that made it possible to ship intact puzzles flat in an envelope. It was up to the recipient to trim the uncut puzzle edges with scissors and separate the pieces.[6] The American Lithographic Co. of New York City used Peckham's patent to make puzzles for many companies, including Metropolitan Life Insurance, Berry Brothers varnishes, Knotair Hose, and Famous Biscuits.

The pieces of this Berry Brothers floor varnish advertising premium stayed together until the recipient trimmed the uncut puzzle edges with scissors to release them.

The next two decades were relatively quiet for advertising puzzles, with a few striking exceptions. The Victor Talking Machine Company made a big splash in 1922 with two puzzles showing musicians and artists who performed on the Victrola label. The company, perhaps unaware of earlier advertising puzzles, falsely claimed:

> We are the first national advertiser to make the consumer 'set up' his own advertisement in this way.[7]

One round puzzle resembled a 78 rpm record, even down to the small spindle hole in the center. The firm's magazine encouraged retailers to give away jigsaws at expositions, county fairs, circus grounds, dinners, and other entertainments. Victor Talking Machine sold the puzzles to phonograph dealers for $15 per thousand, less than their cost to the company.

The American candy industry found some interesting ways to integrate the puzzle into the package itself. Gibson's Candy "Kross Kut Puzzle

Distributors for Victor Talking Machine Company gave away copies of *Try for a Speed Record* to woo customers in 1922.

Package" had the assembled puzzle nestled into the lid and sealed with a transparent wrapper. Once the candy was removed, the box served to house the puzzle. In the mid-1920s the Face Corporation of Philadelphia made a changeable face puzzle whose "blocks" were actually hollow cardboard boxes that held candy.

Revival of Premium Jigsaws in the 1930s

The heyday of the advertising puzzle came in 1932 and 1933, the depths of the Great Depression. By the middle of 1932, both businesses and consumers were in dire straits. Most Americans were not in a position to buy very much, despite attempts to lure them into stores with price cuts. In a desperate move to revive its sales, Lambert Pharmacal, the parent of the Prophylactic Brush Company, sought help. It turned to the Einson-Freeman Company, a specialist in display advertising in Long Island City, New York.

Einson-Freeman designed and made prototypes of four different premiums, including a jigsaw puzzle.[8] Experiments revealed that the jigsaw puzzle had the biggest impact. Sales increased by an astounding 400 percent in the test markets, even when the company raised prices of its Pro-phy-lac-tic toothbrushes substantially. Lambert Pharmacal enthusiastically ordered a million puzzles and accompanying countertop and window displays and began to distribute them to retailers in July 1932.

Einson-Freeman was quick to capitalize on this success. It pitched advertising puzzles to its regular customers, and promoted them in trade publications. It created customized designs and cutting dies for jigsaws showing such products as Cocomalt, Toddy, Sunshine Biscuits, Sapolin Paints, and Westinghouse Lamps.

For smaller companies, especially regional and local ones with lower budgets and limited markets, Einson-Freeman produced a line of inexpensive stock puzzles. The scenic and human interest pictures were unrelated to the product and carried no text; only the envelope displayed the advertising message and the name of the company. They cost five cents each for a nine-by-twelve-inch puzzle and four cents each for a six-and-a-half-by-eight-and-a-half-inch puzzle, for up to a thousand puzzles. Quantity discounts orders brought costs down, to as little as 2 cents each on orders of one hundred thousand or more puzzles. Interestingly, some larger companies also used the stock puzzles; they felt that their customers preferred puzzle images that were untainted by advertising.

Dozens of other lithographers and box-making companies soon adapted their presses and die-cutting equipment to puzzle production. Established puzzle companies such as E. E. Fairchild and Regent Specialties in Rochester, New York, and Western Printing and Lithography in Racine, Wisconsin, joined in as well.

In February 1933, journalists reported that seven million free advertising puzzles were going to American homes each week, in addition to the three million puzzles being sold commercially. Einson-Freeman alone accounted for 30 percent of the production.[9]

Puzzles clearly had struck a special chord. One magazine observed:

> The jig-saw puzzle was a good thing for the mental condition of the people at the end of the third year of the depression. It took them out of themselves. Solving a jig-saw puzzle provided a comforting measure of personal satisfaction for persons whose major problems seemed at the time impervious to all solutions.[10]

The hundreds of promotional puzzles of the depression years touted every imaginable product and service: beverages, foods, tobacco, vitamins, autos, clothing, jewelry, hardware, furniture, carpets, houses, cleansers, coal, furnaces, farm supplies, banks, insurance, restaurants, hotels, hospitals, dairies, tourist bureaus, individual stores, and theaters. Some of the more unusual ones advertised funeral homes, and even a prison. Almost all were die-cut from cardboard, though there was a sprinkling of hand-cut wood puzzles too.

For the first time there were links between broadcast media and advertising puzzles. Pepsodent's puzzles featured two radio comedies that it spon-

The Personal Finance Company's puzzle explained how the firm could solve clients'
financial problems during the Great Depression.

Photo by Harry L. Rinker

sored, *The Goldbergs* and *Amos 'n' Andy*. WLS in Chicago created two advertising puzzles around its *Prairie Farmer* show to immortalize the Barn Dance
crew and Uncle Ezra. Other tie-ins with radio personalities included Gene
and Glen (Sohio), Gambling's Gang (Thom McAn), the Flying Family (Cocomalt), Jack Armstrong (Wheaties), Dick Daring (Quaker Oats), and
Chandu the Magician (Beech-Nut Gum).[11]

Quite a few puzzles pertained to current events, such as the souvenir of
President Franklin D. Roosevelt's inauguration in March 1933. Nash, the
auto manufacturer, and several other exhibitors at the 1933 Chicago
World's Fair handed out jigsaw puzzles showing their products and displays.

With so many puzzles being produced, it was a challenge for individual
advertisers to make their own premiums stand out. Great graphics helped.
Esso (now Exxon) hired Theodore S. Geisel to design a puzzle promoting its

Dr. Seuss's artwork for Esso made a colorful *Foiled by Essolube* premium puzzle in 1932–33. The envelope identified the Karbo-nockus and Oilio-gobelus, along with three other monsters that threatened motorists.
Courtesy of Exxon Mobil Corporation

products. In one of his earliest "Dr. Seuss" creations, the artist depicted a motorist who uses Essolube to foil the Moto-munchus, Karbo-nockus, Oiliogobelus, and other fantastic Seussian monsters. The Hills Brothers Coffee puzzle had an irregular edge—its coffeepot shape accentuated the advertising message. RKO produced another knockout with its colorful shaped puzzle promoting its 1933 hit, *King Kong*. RCA Victor's puzzle of Nipper came in a box designed to look like a radio console and contained figure pieces of gramophones, dogs, and the letters "VICTOR."

Other packages commanded attention. The envelope for the Sunbeam Mixmaster puzzle made an appeal to everyone with these words:

Lots of fun for the idle and for busy people in their spare moments. Great for those who can't sleep. Fine for youngsters, middle-aged—even those who are going about in their second childhood. Good for the knock-kneed, the bow-legged, the straight-legged, the flat-chested, the stoop-shouldered, the straight-as-an-arrow. In fact, to all mankind, in every walk and station of life, it brings new and interesting moments that take the mind away from the hum-drum and cheerless aspects of life, that are disappearing every day now.

Richfield Oil imprinted the envelopes for its six "Goofy Golf" puzzles with advice from pro Alex Morrison on "The Grip," "Starting the Backswing," and other tips. Several companies, such as Toddy drinks and Goodrich tires, created advertising pieces in which the completed puzzle served as a game board.

Money was the attraction of some puzzles. DeVoe & Raynolds promised $1,000 in cash for the entry with the best final lines to the limerick printed on its Superkleen brush puzzle. McKesson & Robbins's competition required contestants to complete both a jigsaw puzzle and a crossword puzzle, compile a list of the company's products, and write a short advertising slogan. The $250 prize undoubtedly inspired thousands to submit entries at a time when the prevailing wage was 25 cents per hour.[12]

The Buffalo Baseball Club put photographs of twenty different team members on puzzles and gave away ten thousand of each. Winning serial numbers on the puzzles entitled the recipients to game tickets, box seats, and season passes.

Many puzzles stimulated competitions among puzzlers, even without prizes. Einson-Freeman began the practice of printing average completion times on the envelopes, for adults and for children of different ages. Other puzzle manufacturers emulated that presentation. White Rose Tea's 49-piece puzzle prescribed targets from forty minutes for a six-year-old to sixteen minutes for an adult. The envelope also included a section on "How to have a puzzle race," by setting handicaps for family members of different ages. Other advertisers recommended that each player use a separate puzzle.

When the Great Depression puzzle craze ended abruptly in the spring of 1933, advertising puzzles declined more gradually. One reason was that newsstands, which bought commercial puzzles from the distributors on a returnable basis, sent back their unsold puzzles in March and April of 1933.

The manufacturers managed to recycle quite a few of these into advertising puzzles by pasting new wrappers onto the boxes. Both Salada Tea and Pippins Cigar bought up surplus stocks of "Jig of the Week" and "Movie Cut-Ups" puzzles for free distribution to their customers.

Advertising Puzzles Since 1940

During wartime shortages of the 1940s, the few advertising puzzles that appeared took on the themes of the times. The Ward Baking Company gave away jigsaw puzzles to customers who pledged to eat Ward's Tip-Top Bread for a week. Its "Patriotic" series included puzzles of the Statue of Liberty, the Capitol in Washington, and the military academies. The packages gave a few facts about each location and urged:

During the 1940s patriotic themes appeared on advertising puzzles, such as this one for Ward Baking Company's Tip-Top Bread.

> We hope you will continue to eat Enriched Tip-Top and help make yourself strong and healthy the way Uncle Sam wants every girl and boy to be. Yours for Victory, Ward Baking Co.

The travel and entertainment industries have made much more use of advertising puzzles in the last few decades than they did in earlier years. Today's puzzles now promote theme parks, cruise ships, convention centers, casinos, sports events of all types, television shows, movies, music, and individual performers. Many of these are actually commercial merchandise, often made under licensing agreements, and sold in gift shops or concession stands at individual venues. Puzzle postcards are common souvenirs that show tourist attractions and entertainment personalities.

Other subjects of modern advertising puzzles include prescription drugs (usually passed out by the pharmaceutical companies to doctors), and nonprofit organizations. Symphonies, colleges, and local Chambers of Commerce have all designed fund-raising puzzles to give to supporters in exchange for contributions. They and others have also produced puzzles that serve as invitations to events.

Fast-food restaurants began to take off in the 1960s in the United States. They now issue dozens of premium puzzles each year. From McDonald's, Wendy's, and other national franchises to regional ones such as Jojo's, virtually every one offers a child's meal with a premium, often a puzzle. Electronic products—computers, chips, software, and consulting firms—are other newcomers to the advertising puzzle world in recent years.

Absolut Vodka, known for its imaginative campaigns showing bottle images, used a puzzle to create a buzz in the world of advertising. Each one of the five hundred thousand copies of *New York* magazine on February 25, 1991, included a page holding a 54-piece "Absolut Solution" jigsaw puzzle.[13]

Contests continue too. Some retailers send out a single puzzle piece to customers and tell them to bring it into the store. The person whose piece fills the gap in the store's puzzle wins the prize.

Puzzle Themes in Advertising

Pictures of puzzles turn up in advertising as frequently as the puzzles themselves. The image lends itself to marketing to both consumers ("Puzzled about which long distance deal is best? Sign up now with us.") and to businesses ("We can supply the missing piece to your productivity puzzle.").

Nonprofit advertising adopts the same theme. Fund-raisers tug at

donors' heart strings by using puzzle images to conjure up the tragic conse-
quences of the incomplete campaign: "A vital piece will be missing from our
project without *your* support." A World War II poster warned, "Bits of careless talk are pieced together by the enemy" and showed a hairy Nazi hand
fitting the last piece of intelligence into place.

Although relatively few advertising puzzles deal with economic issues,
finance and money predominate in ads that use puzzle images. Perhaps
this is because so many of them appear in trade magazines aimed at businesses. But consumers get puzzling financial information too. MasterCard
has run several television and print campaigns that show pieces coming together to make its credit card.

Many covers for magazines, books, catalogs, movies, and music feature
puzzle designs. While the cover image is not advertising per se, it is a crucial marketing tool. Puzzle pieces are a natural for decorating the dust
jackets of mystery novels; they suggest the sleuth's task of finding all the
bits to identify the killer. Some products employ jigsaw images as logos
and on their packages. In the 1990s Microsoft used interlocking puzzle
pieces to emphasize how all the components of its *Office* suite fit together
perfectly.

Puzzles of the Future

What changes will the future bring for the advertising puzzle?

Technological advances will continue to expand their use. Although puzzle manufacturers have traditionally required an order of at least one thousand puzzles, advertising puzzles are feasible for much smaller-scale
promotions today. Several firms now make blank assembled puzzles that
can be purchased by the dozen or in larger quantities. The user can then
feed the blank puzzle through a standard laser printer or inkjet printer and
imprint it with any images designed on or scanned into a computer.

The Internet has already affected the premium industry, and will do so
in the future. Online retailers began to give away advertising puzzles in
the late 1990s. Some examples, such as the one from Amazon.com, have

the extra attraction of a magnetic backing. As small playthings for the refrigerator door, they are ideal for keeping the company's name in front of the consumer's eye.

Globalization will accelerate the spread of innovations from other countries. While American and European advertising puzzles generally follow the same trends, the beer mat puzzle is one type that is popular in Europe and Canada but has not yet reached the United States. Breweries supply these large coasters, either square or shaped like puzzle pieces, to bars. A patron who collects a complete set of four to eight mats can assemble them into a decorative advertising message, usually for alcohol or tobacco products. Another fashion that is popular abroad is the collectible phone card. Puzzle sets, including anywhere from two to twelve cards that together form a picture, are beginning to appear in the United States. And of course, we can expect more and more puzzles produced in large quantities under agreements between puzzle companies and owners of trademarks and licensed characters.

The pieces of the jigsaw are clearly integral to the puzzle of modern marketing.

8

Collecting and Collections

THE JOURNEY IS AS MUCH, IF NOT MORE, FUN
THAN THE ARRIVAL AT THE DESTINATION.

Courtesy of Verl Cook

When Verl Cook of Midland, Michigan, arrives at antique shows, dealers know immediately what he wants to buy.

Puzzle collectors come in all shapes and sizes, from the casual to the fanatical, from the generalist to the specialist, and from young to old. Retired bartender Charley Lang covered all the walls and ceilings of his California home with more than one thousand assembled jigsaw puzzles totaling more than one million pieces.[1] On the other side of the country, the Bush family keeps their modern custom-made wood puzzles at Camp David, the presidential retreat, and at their summer home in Kennebunkport, Maine.

Dedicated and acknowledged collectors regularly seek out new prizes. Many focus on one type of puzzle, perhaps wooden jigsaw puzzles of the 1930s, children's puzzles, or advertising puzzles. Some buy only the products of a single company—Pastime, Par, and Tuco all have their devotees. A few have even narrower interests: one Arizona man's mission is to own all thirty-two of Tuck's Zag-Zaw puzzles made from Albert Ludovici's illustrations of coaching scenes for Charles Dickens's novels.

Casual collectors enjoy doing puzzles and have accumulated them over time, yet they do not see themselves as collectors. Why do they accumulate so many puzzles? Some just cannot bear the thought of getting rid of a puzzle after struggling to complete it for weeks, even months, and finally triumphing. Some save a handful of favorites, and periodically spread out the pieces to enjoy the puzzle again. Others keep the closet full of puzzles for children and then grandchildren to enjoy. Still others think their old puzzles are now worth a small fortune, and deserve a better fate than a 10-cent price tag in their next yard sale. More than a handful are unabashed pack rats.

Quite a few people collect jigsaw puzzles just for the graphics and do not really enjoy assembling them. Usually the puzzle is an adjunct (or even peripheral) item to another interest. A superhero collection, for example, often includes a Superman puzzle. In other cases the individual finds the artwork on the puzzle irresistible: Charles Wysocki, Maxfield Parrish, illustrators of children's books, and modern fantasy artists are favorites.

Studies of the history of collecting and the psychology of collectors have scrutinized the behavior of all these types. Scholars have posed questions such as: Why do humans seek material possessions beyond those needed for survival and comfort? Why do some covet a collection of related objects— indeed, of *old* related objects? Does a collection confer more status than other displays of affluence? Does it soothe fundamental insecurities and pains that were never resolved in childhood? Does the thrill of the hunt hearken back to earlier hunting and gathering instincts, or to the spoils of war and conquest?[2]

The answers to these questions are still unresolved.

Little Gloats

The hunt itself has many elements that appeal to human nature. One cannot simply walk into a retail store and find shelves full of antique puzzles at standard advertised prices. It is a more complex process with both satisfactions and disappointments.

A few times at flea markets I have hit the mother lode and needed help to lug several cartons of puzzles to my car. Offsetting those days are the ones when the search is fruitless, and I have to resist the temptation to buy meaningless puzzles just to avoid going home empty-handed.

Occasionally a puzzle purchased as a consolation prize turns out to be a real gem. In 1979 I made a special trip to New York City for a big auction.

I had arrived loaded for bear, namely fourteen Par puzzles, but was outbid on all of them. In frustration, I bid on the only other puzzle lot in the auction. It was only after I reached home, many hours later, that I realized I had some real prizes. I had snagged a very scarce English "Maids of Kent" puzzle *and* a marvelous nineteenth-century, hand-colored German puzzle that assembled into a freestanding castle. These hard-won treasures mean more to me than others that required little effort to find.

The satisfaction of getting a bargain is just as often counterbalanced by the chagrin of paying too much. More than once I have paid a premium for a puzzle I had never seen before, only to observe several other copies selling at much lower prices in subsequent weeks. Usually that is not a coincidence— the high price paid for the first one to sell encourages other owners to offer their copies for sale.

Apart from the results of the hunt, there is the competitive element and the race for bragging rights, or "little gloats," in the parlance of English collectors. One of my most satisfying finds was a huge cache of scarce depression-era puzzles for less than $1 apiece, in a glass dealer's booth. It was all the sweeter for being a few miles from the home of a hostile rival, and just a day after he had beat me out for some choice puzzles at a major auction.

Fortunately, most puzzle collectors are a congenial group, willing to share the wealth of their knowledge and information. All but a few of my fellow collectors are friends first, and rivals second. (Of course, it *is* best if their interests and mine do not overlap completely.) I cannot easily count the number of fellow collectors who generously have loaned me puzzles to study, allowed me to photograph their extensive collections, and continue to send me notes and photos of their interesting finds.

Finding Old Puzzles

Collectors can buy antique and collectible jigsaw puzzles at a variety of prices. Die-cut puzzles from the 1950s and 1960s are readily available, often for a few dollars. Top-of-the-line Par puzzles, some eighteenth-century children's puzzles, a few scarce advertising puzzles, and a handful of others sell for prices in the thousands of dollars. Rarity, high visual appeal, collectible subject matter, superb craftsmanship, and top condition all command the highest prices in the puzzle world.

The source also affects the price. There is a clear feeding chain in the antiques and collectibles business. A puzzle might go through half a dozen middlemen before reaching its ultimate destination in the hands of a collector. Yard sales, thrift shops, and the swap table at the town dump are the starting points in the chain and feature the lowest prices. At the end of the chain are the specialty antique dealers who see customers only by appointment. In between are local and regional flea markets, country auctions, specialty auctions, antique shows, and antique shops. Collectors can find puzzles in all these hunting grounds if they so choose.

The big tradeoff is hours versus dollars. It takes a tremendous amount of time and effort to pick through all the dross at yard sales in search of the few gems that go for rock-bottom prices. Buying from a specialized antique dealer minimizes the time spent, but maximizes the price paid. After all, the dealer and the intermediaries have put in hours of work to transfer the puzzle from its starting place as an individual's castoff through the links of the chain. To make it worth their while, they all must be able to sell the puzzle for more than what they originally paid.

Prices are not set in stone, however. Bargaining is a fact of life and part of the fun in most places where puzzles are sold, from yard sale to antique show. A courteous "Can you do any better on the price?" will often generate a discount of 10 to 20 percent. Some marked prices, however, are so "ambitious" that the gains from normal bargaining are questionable. Since a lowball offer offends some dealers, it is best preceded by some soothing words about the true value of the item. Still, at the end of a long, tiring day, sellers may come down even more, just to avoid the hassle of packing and lugging their inventory home.

Serious collectors cultivate the dealers who regularly supply them with puzzles. Sometimes it even makes sense to buy an unwanted puzzle to encourage a dealer to keep searching on one's behalf. Knowledgeable, friendly, and dependable sellers are great allies in unearthing rare treasures. Over time, the best of them become cherished friends, rather than just agents. They love the sociability of weekend flea markets and shows. Many have their own collections and love to share their valuable perspectives on market trends.

For years, my favorite hunting grounds were the big outdoor antique shows that take place periodically during the warm months of the year. One famous northeastern example is Brimfield, Massachusetts, a small village on U.S. Route 20 between Worcester and Springfield. Three times a year—for a week in May, July, and September—it boasts about five thousand booths. The dealers range from the local part-timer who finds stock at nearby yard sales to the full-time specialist who crisscrosses the nation several times a year to sell at high-end antique shows. Big or small, they all set up at more than twenty individual markets, located in the yards, parking lots, and fields that line both sides of Route 20.

Buyers come from as far away as Europe and Asia to forage along this narrow mile-long strip. As they dart back and forth across the road in search of treasure, normal traffic slows to a crawl, often to a standstill. Even drivers with no interest in antiques pause to gawk at the flamboyant displays of merchandise, as well as the colorful characters. Determined buyers sport outfits that proclaim their interests. Clothing imprinted with "I buy jigsaw puzzles" or similar messages helps eager customers connect with the right dealers.

The availability of jigsaws at big outdoor markets has declined in recent years, however. Weather, of course, has always been a threat to both buyers and sellers. Many a puzzle at Brimfield has been drenched by rain, faded by the sun, or scattered by wind gusts. But the advent of online markets has hurt the outdoor show more than the forces of nature. Brimfield has now lost so many dealers in paper goods that some puzzle buyers now refer to it as "Grimfield."

This dramatic transformation in the antiques and collectibles market began in the late 1990s when eBay pioneered the online auction business. Dealers have moved online to display their wares to a much wider audience than they could reach before. Even though some dealers still enjoy selling person to person and have no intention of sitting in front of a computer, the wired dealers regularly visit these holdouts and scoop up items they can resell for a profit online.

Collectors too have embraced eBay. Its ability to display millions of items, coupled with a very efficient search engine, means that anyone sitting at a computer can view puzzles on sale around the world at any given moment. No more waiting months for the big antique show—the contents of the world's attics are available 24/7. Collecting need no longer be a question of wearing out shoe leather and refilling the gas tank. Today the major risk to some shopaholics is repetitive stress injuries from the keyboard and mouse. One can now build a world-class collection in a few years, rather than decades, given sufficient funds and determination.[3]

Collectors used to search locally or regionally. Today they can buy puzzles from all over the nation, and from abroad as well. Californians, who always had trouble finding old and antique puzzles in the west, compete vigorously online with easterners. Shipping costs are so inexpensive for jigsaw puzzles that they hardly constitute a deterrent.

Online auctions have thus brought some standardization to what was formerly a thin and disorganized market. There is less room for a series of middlemen, since so many of the sellers offer their finds directly to the final buyers on the Internet. Regional differences in prices, previously quite large, have narrowed considerably within the United States because there is so much awareness of the online market. Bargains in puzzles are now hard to find, though some still turn up in remote locations or with unlikely sellers who specialize in something else.

Online auctions are not without their hazards—it is much more difficult to evaluate a photo of a puzzle on a computer screen than an actual puzzle sitting on a dealer's table at a show. The standard warning of "caveat emptor" to auctiongoers applies with even more force to eBay. Buyers need to take online auction descriptions with a very large grain of salt. Sellers on eBay grossly overuse some terms, thus transforming their meanings. For example, "unique" has a dictionary definition of being "the only one." The word simply cannot be applied to mass produced goods. But on eBay, "unique" is jargon for "I haven't seen another one in the past month."

However, reproductions and fakes, a real danger in some fields, are not a big issue for jigsaw puzzle collectors at this time. The prices of most vintage puzzles are still considerably less than what it would cost to reproduce them today. B. Shackman, a novelty manufacturer in New York City, is the biggest seller of reproductions; most are die-cut from cardboard and clearly marked on the package. They can, of course, pose problems when sold without the original packaging.

The Bane of the Missing Piece

Sooner or later, usually sooner, every puzzler must confront the disappointment, even the tragedy, of the missing piece. Despite our best efforts, the puzzle cannot be solved and must remain imperfect. The illusion that we *can* bring perfect order out of chaos is shattered, and we are brought back to the real world.

Some losses, thankfully, are only temporary. A common experience after lengthy searching midway through a puzzle is to conclude that a distinctive piece is lost. Yet somehow it turns up later right in front of our eyes, or perhaps lurking under the rug, or tucked into the pocket of a mischievous fellow puzzler who is staking out the right to put in the last piece. Fanatical puzzlers have been known to pluck pieces from the innards of dismantled vacuum cleaners after a sleepless night spent eliminating all other possible hiding places.

If a new jigsaw turns out to be defective, manufacturers will usually supply a replacement puzzle. This is a fairly common occurrence—in one major factory, not to be named here, loose pieces that did not make it into the boxes are always scattered on the floor below the presses.

But for the collector, the missing piece is a fact of life. There is rarely a guarantee that a box full of old puzzle pieces actually contains them all. Puzzlers experience a special rush when, at the very end, an antique puzzle turns out to be complete.

The best way to be sure that old puzzles are complete is to buy ones that are already assembled. But that sacrifices the fun of putting the puzzles together. And the dealers who sell preassembled puzzles charge premium prices to compensate them for their efforts, as well as for all the incomplete puzzles that they have purchased but cannot resell easily.

If an old puzzle is loose in the box and the seller does not guarantee its completeness, the odds are better than even that at least one piece is missing. Favorable signs include: a recently dated notation on the lid that the puzzle is complete and a sturdy undamaged box that is carefully tied up in string. If the label says the puzzle has 243 pieces and there are exactly 243 pieces in the box, so much the better. The extremely cautious shopper may even insist on assembling small puzzles before buying them, though dealers at crowded shows tend to discourage this practice for obvious reasons.

Buying an entire lot of puzzles, instead of selecting just one, can be wise, because pieces often get mixed up between boxes. I once bought a shopping bag full of old wooden puzzles for $80. When the first three puzzles that I assembled each lacked several pieces, I began to rue the purchase. But the fourth brought some encouragement. Although it too was defective, that box held pieces that filled the gaps in the first puzzle. By the time I finished, I realized that none of the twenty boxes had contained a complete puzzle. Yet I managed to reunite enough pieces to get five complete puzzles out of the lot.

Most collectors keep a box of extra pieces found with old puzzles, in the hopes that these orphans can eventually be returned to their original homes. Success is almost as unlikely as winning the Powerball jackpot, but it can happen. One midwestern collector bought two wooden puzzles that had originally been part of the same rental library, run by an Ottumwa, Iowa, drugstore that had burned down in the 1940s. One puzzle turned up at a flea market in St. Louis, and the other came by mail from Ottumwa. She could hardly believe her eyes when the five pieces needed to complete the Iowa puzzle turned up in the box from St. Louis![4]

Collectors occasionally can construct one complete puzzle by merging two incomplete puzzles of the same subject and brand. But that is never a sure thing, even with mass-produced cardboard puzzles. The manufacturer could have used different dies to cut each puzzle, or rotated the die one hundred eighty degrees, or the die could have struck the picture in different places. In the last two cases, the piece will fit, but the picture will not match.

Even if two puzzles are truly identical, there is still the risk that both lack exactly the same piece.

Puzzles with missing pieces are worth less than complete ones. One missing piece will reduce the value by 20 to 50 percent, depending on the size of the puzzle and whether the missing piece is central to the image.

A few dedicated and very patient souls take on the job of puzzle restoration, cutting replacement pieces and painting them. These social workers of the puzzle world treat afflictions, cure defects, and rehabilitate puzzles that might otherwise be discarded. Then they take care to place these "clients" with those who will truly cherish them. Although repairs are anathema in some collecting fields, they are perfectly acceptable and even desirable in jigsaw puzzles, as long as they are clearly marked on the back. Reversibility, a key precept of modern conservation, is not a problem with replacement pieces. If the original piece turns up later, the replacement can be discarded.

The tools for making replacement pieces are basic: an X-Acto knife for cutting cardboard pieces and a scroll saw for wooden pieces. (Appendix A describes the process of making puzzles in some detail.) Restorers trace the outline of the missing piece onto plywood, cut it out, and then use watercolor pencils or acrylic paints to recreate the image. Artistry and imagination are essential, especially if there is no guide picture to work from.

Ridding an old puzzle of musty odors and mildew is more difficult than recreating a lost piece. Spreading the pieces on a tray and airing them outside on a warm, dry day can help, but it is essential to cover them with a fine screen or netting so they do not blow away.

Damaged boxes usually need either cleaning or reconstruction. Collectors can do their own simple cleaning of the glossy labels that adorn children's puzzles. A gentle application of a lukewarm solution of soap and water with a cotton pad can do much to remove years of accumulated grime. (It is important to test an inconspicuous spot first, because some color printing will run.) Do *not* use soap and water on cardboard boxes, however; that will weaken them. Instead, remove the dirt with a soft, dry brush. Rebuilding boxes with structural damage is best left to an expert. Even small repairs with tape can ultimately damage a box if not properly done.

How to Display a Collection

Some puzzles are so attractive and their completion represents so much of a triumph that it is simply impossible to put them back in the box. But the question of how best to display them without damaging them is a puzzle in itself.

The puzzle glue that comes with many cardboard puzzles is an easy but inherently destructive approach. Once the pieces are glued together, no one else can ever enjoy playing with the puzzle. Furthermore, sunlight will soon fade the puzzle if it is hung on the wall. So glue is barely tolerable, but *only* for puzzles that are currently on the market and can easily be replaced. It should never be used for scarcer items. Plastic box frames offer a convenient alternative that allows for easy rotation of puzzles. Professional framing with acid-free mats and protective UV glass is an even better, albeit expensive, solution.

Collectors with large numbers of puzzles often invest in the metal flat files that artists and architects use to store drawings. Each large, shallow drawer is ideal for displaying several layers of puzzles assembled on mat board. Even so, most serious puzzle collectors wind up with shelves stacked with many boxes full of pieces.

Although puzzles and their containers are made from materials that will deteriorate over time (wood and cardboard are definitely *not* acid-free), they are amazingly resilient if treated with some simple precautions. Do not stack the boxes more than five deep, to avoid crushing. Keep them in a dry area where the temperature is stable. Avoid damp basements and hot attics, both of which are hazardous to the boxes and their contents. For very valuable puzzles, follow museum practices and use archival materials such as acid-free paper or Mylar to protect the puzzle picture and box labels. (Collectors who cannot afford to follow museum practices are still performing a valuable service by preserving puzzles that might otherwise be thrown away.)

Taking photos of the assembled puzzles before returning them to their boxes allows a collector to savor, show off, and study favorite puzzles without going to all the effort of reconstructing them. (Hint: Personal experience proves that taking the puzzle apart *before* inspecting the finished photo almost guarantees that the photo will be ruined!)

Since puzzlers tend to be an organized lot, some continue beyond the photo to catalog each of their puzzles. A page in a loose-leaf notebook serves well to hold a photo and description of each puzzle. Computer users can use a spreadsheet program to enter descriptive characteristics and sort easily. The pros use sophisticated databases that allow for the integration of digital images as well.

Catalogs are also useful for insurance purposes in case of loss due to fire, flood, or theft, and should include purchase prices. Determining the current value of a puzzle is not easy. Price guides are often inaccurate, even in the year they are published, and quickly become outdated. Instead, ask puzzle dealers or auctioneers to recommend an appraiser. Or check eBay, which is a good source of information on recent sales of comparable puzzles.

Sharing

Much of the fun of collecting is sharing with other collectors. The principal organization for North American puzzle collectors is the Association of Game and Puzzle Collectors. The AGPC holds both an annual convention and regional events where members attend seminars, buy, sell, swap, and play with puzzles and games. The organization publishes a quarterly newsletter, sponsors a computer listserve, and maintains an archive of information about puzzles, games, and the companies that made them. The Ephemera Society, the Antique Advertising Association of America, and the Antique Toy Collectors of America are other groups that include significant numbers of puzzle collectors.

There are several ways to learn about the history of the puzzles you have collected. The bibliography and the list of websites at the end of this book give some good starting points. Fellow collectors and dealers are an excellent source of information too. For delving further into the history of a particular company that made jigsaw puzzles, local libraries and historical societies are the best resource. Many of the techniques of genealogical

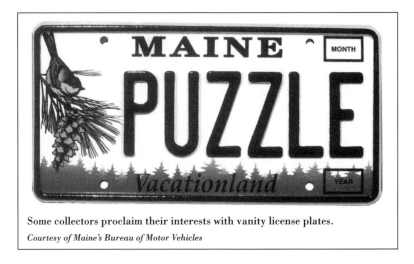

Some collectors proclaim their interests with vanity license plates.
Courtesy of Maine's Bureau of Motor Vehicles

research apply just as well to research on small companies. Searches of old city directories or local newspapers can turn up more detailed information about an individual company.

You may well unearth some new stories to go with your puzzle collection, and with luck you will be able to find some puzzle makers or their descendants to interview. That is the time to get out the tape recorder or video camera and save the history before it disappears, in the same way that people interested in genealogy preserve family stories.[5] Write up a summary, and keep it, along with any relevant photos or mementos, with the puzzle itself.

Some Perspectives on Collecting

This chapter began with some unanswered questions about the nature of collecting, and specifically about collecting puzzles. While I still do not have all the answers, a quarter-century of active collecting has taught me a lot about puzzles, history, markets, people, and myself.

Collecting itself is similar to doing a jigsaw puzzle. Whether one is collecting the puzzles or the history that goes with them, it is a process of finding pieces, and putting them in order to understand and enjoy the overall picture. In both cases the journey is as much fun as the arrival at the destination, if not more.

While it can be satisfying to complete a collection, I find it more interesting and exciting to have an open-ended collection. I now am certain that I will never attain my goal of having a representative puzzle from every American manufacturer. Even finding the names of all those who have made puzzles over the centuries is a metapuzzle that will surely remain incomplete. My collection of both puzzles and stories can never become a lifeless museum exhibit. It will continue to grow and change.

Collectors are not only historical preservationists, they are also the ultimate recyclers. In a society that has gone overboard on packaging and on throwing out serviceable but outdated items, collectors help keep landfills from overflowing. In the case of puzzle collectors, this social service furthers our own interests too. We are getting the best of both worlds, because the quality of old puzzles often exceeds that of comparably priced new ones.

Collecting *can* escalate. Indeed, collectors often use the same vocabulary as any addict: the next fix, a big hit, dealing to support a habit, and so on. For most, it is a harmless preoccupation, with no need for a twelve-step program. But clear signs of trouble include spending beyond your resources and paying others to put your puzzles together because you do not have time to assemble them all. An occasional puzzler truly gets hooked, sacrificing personal relationships to the habit. One fanatic reported:

> [He] gave me a choice—him or jigsaw puzzles. I just couldn't see him asking me to give up something I enjoy that much. . . . He'd ask me what I had done all day and I'd answer "500 pieces." I guess that was hard for a businessman to understand.[6]

The man in question became her ex-husband. Much-needed counseling followed, a few years later.

9

The Sum of All the Pieces

A CHALLENGING STIMULUS AND COMFORT FOOD FOR THE MIND

Britain's 2003 stamp celebrating the Genome Project uses the jigsaw image to suggest that complex scientific mysteries are solved piece by piece.

J ohn Spilsbury and his fellow map dissectors could not have envisioned how puzzles would evolve over the years.

In 1760 a few aristocratic youngsters pieced puzzle maps together. We now have a democratization of the jigsaw. Its extension into entertainment for masses of children and adults reflects a general affluence and availability of leisure that was unheard of two hundred fifty years ago. The range of artwork on today's puzzles would astonish the early manufacturers, as would modern technologies and production methods. And of course, they would be fascinated by the jigsaw's visual record of cultural, social, political, and economic changes through the centuries.

Jigsaws Are Ubiquitous

Puzzles have spread throughout the globe. Annual jigsaw puzzle sales exceed $300 million in the United States alone,[1] and are much higher overseas. Puzzlers everywhere are snapping up jigsaws and their accessories. Puzzle totes and roll-ups hold the *rompecabezas* in Latin America, *pintu* in China, *golovolomka* in Russia, and *yapboz* in Turkey. Puzzles packaged with glue and frames sell especially well in Japan, where the *jigusoh pazuru* has become a popular decorating object.

It is now possible to buy all sorts of household objects shaped like puzzle pieces: picture frames, soap, place mats, clocks, ottomans, throw rugs, and coffee tables. Jigsaw designs adorn quilts, bedding, tablecloths, and key chains. True fanatics can wear puzzle piece pins, cuff links, bracelets and earrings, to go with their puzzle-themed sweaters, ties, shirts, and dresses. Their model is perhaps Mattel's "Puzzle Craze Barbie" doll, who wears chartreuse slacks decorated with puzzle pieces, and carries a miniature puzzle—of herself, of course—in a tote bag. A dress made entirely of cardboard jigsaw puzzle pieces was featured at a 2003 Rhode Island School of Design fashion show.[2]

A Rhode Island School of Design fashion show in 2003 featured this dress made entirely out of jigsaw puzzle pieces.
Providence Journal photo by Kathy Borchers

In anticipation of the final puzzle, a Dutch artist has built a jigsaw coffin, consisting of interlocking hollow pieces. He has prepared an elaborate ritual for his future mourners, asking that they place his ashes into the pieces, take them home, then periodically remember him by gathering to reassemble the pieces and "make him complete" again.[3]

Jigsaw puzzles have found their way into the media too. They turn up regularly in television shows and movies, as both background objects and featured subjects.[4] *The Puzzle Place,* a children's television series, has a set designed around jigsaw pieces. *Survivor* and *Everybody Loves Raymond* are examples of prime-time hits that have built puzzles into their plots. Jigsaws have bit parts in many films.

Occasionally, as in *The Jigsaw Murders* (1988), they play a central role. (A risqué puzzle at a detective's bachelor party provides the first clue to the identity of a dismembered and headless corpse. Once the nude model's face is revealed on the assembled puzzle, the scene switches to the puzzle factory, where investigators track down her name.)

The print media use the puzzle image frequently, both in words and in pictures. "Last Piece of Jigsaw in Place" is the headline above a report on the building of a complex new telescope.[5] But it could just as well refer to the hiring of a key player for a sports team, the rise of a political candidate, or a medical breakthrough. Writers, cartoonists, and speakers use symbolic puzzle pieces when dealing with difficult and confusing topics. In her closing argument at the O. J. Simpson trial, Marcia Clark placed pieces of the prosecution's case into an oversized jigsaw puzzle on display for the jury.[6]

Puzzles show up in creative writing. Georges Perec's novel *Life: A User's Manual* is centered on an artist who has his paintings cut into jigsaw puzzles. Shel Silverstein's *The Missing Piece* brings the search for life's meaning and completeness to the child's level, as does David F. Birchman's *Jigsaw Jackson.*[7] A nineteenth-century poem reads, in part:

> *Though now, like a dissected map,*
> *Our life confused appears,*
> *It seems to gather into shape*
> *When viewed in after years.*[8]

And songwriters, from Kate and Anna McGarrigle ("Jigsaw Puzzle of Life") to the Rolling Stones ("Jig Saw Puzzle" in *Beggar's Banquet*), have adopted puzzle motifs.

Artists portray jigsaw puzzles and puzzle themes. Naturally, there is a monumental puzzle piece sculpture outside the building that houses Hallmark's creative department in Kansas City. It reflects not just the company's history in the puzzle industry, but also how pieces come together in the development of a new idea. More recently, John Stokes III and Bob Archer created a fourteen-foot-high puzzle tree as part of San Diego's 2003 celebration of urban landscapes.[9] Other artists work with smaller bits. Mel Andringa

This tree sculpture was part of San Diego's celebration of urban landscapes in 2003–2004. Artists John Stokes and Bob Archer designed the foliage as oversized puzzle pieces that can all fit together.

Photo © 2004 by John S. Stokes III

of the Legion Arts Company in Cedar Rapids, Iowa, does performance pieces, including "The Sistine Floor" and "Puzzle Pictures." In the latter he takes puzzles stamped from identical dies and interchanges the pieces to patch together novel designs. Jess Collins, Al Souza, and Ian Skoyles glean secondhand puzzles from thrift shops and transform the pieces into collages that create coherent images out of disordered fragments.[10]

The Best Puzzles

Of all the billions of jigsaw puzzles made in the past two and a half centuries, which is the *best*?

It is tempting to try to identify the pinnacle of puzzledom, to enshrine the single superlative jigsaw in the world. But the task is impossible. Tastes, abilities, and styles of puzzling vary so widely that there is no one answer to the question of which is best. An adult's choice does not match a seven-year-old's. The best could be the biggest, the most difficult, the most beautiful, or simply a childhood favorite.

My personal answer is to look for challenging puzzles without a guide picture on the box. But I am not a diehard who will work happily on a jigsaw puzzle for months, staring at it for days at a stretch without being able to fit any pieces in. Although I have assembled a few very difficult solid color puzzles, I did not enjoy them. I need the promise of an interesting and attractive picture at the end.

I also look for challenges and rewards as I progress into the puzzle. What intrigues me the most are unusual pieces and the surprising ways that they fit together. I savor the notion that the puzzle designer has created an irregular border or imaginative figure pieces to tease and perplex me. As I wend my way through a puzzle, I feel that I am gaining some insight into the designer's mind and engaging in a game. The other player, though absent, is an active participant.

It is not just the puzzle alone that must be judged. A jigsaw may be deemed "best" due to the circumstances—the puzzlers had a special and memorable experience while assembling it. I have discovered great pleasure in some relatively ordinary puzzles, just because I enjoyed the company of my fellow puzzlers.

Even incomplete puzzles can be fun. Once, at a Salvation Army thrift store, I found a large bucket full of pieces. They obviously came from many different children's puzzles. Some were wood and some cardboard, with varying thicknesses and colors on the backs. It seemed that some parent in a cleaning frenzy had swept out the kids' room and put all the pieces into this pail. I paid out 50 cents and reaped several hours of delightful entertainment. By the time I finished sorting them all, I had three complete puzzles (and of course many more incomplete ones).

The Significance of Jigsaw Puzzles

A review of the history of jigsaw puzzles tells us much about ourselves and our culture. History, art, education, technology, the economy, work, leisure, and entertainment all are reflected in the last two hundred fifty years of jigsaws.

Puzzles provide a fascinating window on the past. The subject matter, originally limited to "dissected maps," has grown to encompass virtually every possible topic. Indeed, the images on puzzles mirror our lives, both realistic and idealized, as they depict current events, the fine arts, literature, icons of popular culture, and everyday life. Puzzles deal with political topics such as monarchies, revolutions, elections, war, and slavery. They proudly depict the achievements of new technologies from steam engines to space exploration.

The images reflect tastes in both fine and commercial art—from Rembrandt and Picasso to calendar pictures and Disney cartoons. Jigsaw puzzles also play a role as persuaders, when businesses distribute promotional puzzles that picture their products. Old advertising puzzles remind us of long-forgotten goods, such as Hood's Sarsaparilla and Essolube.

Puzzles illuminate trends in education and learning. American children today learn geography by piecing the states together, just as their counterparts in the 1700s tried to assemble the counties of England or the countries of Europe. Though the maps have changed over the centuries, the process is the same. Yet modern children's puzzles are much more than a textbook lesson in picture form. Preschool puzzle designs consciously promote a variety of skills that will help youngsters excel in their future schooling—hand-eye coordination, dexterity, pattern recognition, concentration, persistence, and logical problem solving.

The puzzles themselves embody the achievements of the Industrial Revolution and later technological developments. Puzzle makers first used handheld fretsaws, then progressed to treadle machines, electric saws, die-cutting presses, and now computer-controlled lasers or water jets. Printing has evolved from hand-colored engravings to simple lithography and finally to modern four-color printing.

The puzzle industry too has changed over the last two and a half centuries, along with the rest of the economy. For the most part, the small companies and the artisans of the past have been supplanted by large companies that mass-produce puzzles and increasingly rely on offshore production in low-wage countries. The big chain stores account for the bulk of sales, leaving much less room for local and specialty retailers.

Still, individual craftspeople working alone or in small workshops have always played a major part in the production of puzzles, especially the wooden ones that are cut one piece at a time. The craft is a bit like quilting, where the object is to take preexisting images and transform them into a different medium that is both imaginative and attractive. The puzzle makers' artistry and creativity in finding new ways to perplex and please puzzle solvers remain important today.

The industry has been open to both men and women for more than a century. Women of all classes played the major role in creating wood puzzles during the first great puzzle craze of 1908–10, both as individual crafters and as factory workers. Male puzzle makers were more prevalent during the 1930s craze, as they sought to replace income lost due to the Great Depression.

Puzzles shed light not just on working lives, but also on our use of leisure time. In fact, puzzling has been most popular during economic downturns, when people have more leisure time than they really want. During the 1930s jigsaw puzzles became popular as never before. As unemployment skyrocketed, people turned to them for inexpensive entertainment and solace. The joy of bringing order out of the chaos of scattered pieces seems to be enhanced when the problems of the world appear most intractable.

Inspirational speakers, from business consultants to coaches to preachers, use the metaphor of the jigsaw to explain how to move from chaos to order with an overall vision, a system for sorting through the pieces, trial and error, persistence, and insight. Puzzles appear in team-building exercises designed to teach workers how pieces of the whole fit together. They also celebrate achievements, as during the 2003 commencement ceremonies at the University of New England. Speaker Yoko Ono presented a piece of a "Blue Sky" puzzle to each graduating student, together with an invitation to a reunion ten years hence to assemble the puzzle.[11]

Puzzling Payoffs

Jigsaw puzzles offer amusement, satisfaction, and beauty to the solver. But do they have any practical importance? Does skill at doing jigsaw puzzles carry over into the realities of everyday living? Without a doubt. Puzzlers develop their concentration, visual perception, memory, logic, and organization—all traits that help with problem solving, regardless of one's occupation. Dexterity too is a must for many tasks.

Several professions involve jobs remarkably similar to doing a jigsaw. Architects fit components into fixed footprints of buildings. Archeologists and restorers of antiquities piece together the fragments of ancient scrolls, papyri, and ceramics. Detectives and accident investigators face real-life "jigsaw puzzles" that inevitably are complicated by lost pieces. After the disastrous explosion of TWA Flight 800 in 1996, experts reassembled all the parts that could be recovered. It took them months to complete this giant three-dimensional puzzle and pinpoint the cause of the catastrophe.

Perhaps the most challenging job to utilize puzzle-related skills is the on-going attempt to reconstruct the documents the East German secret police shredded and stuffed into sixteen thousand paper sacks during the final days of the Communist regime. Fifty civil servants, working full-time for eight years, succeeded in assembling the papers in only three hundred sacks. Since the project would last another four hundred fifty years at that rate, the solvers have brought in the modern big guns—computers.[12]

Computer programs to solve jigsaw puzzles have been around since the mid-1960s. The federal government supported early developments in this field with grants, because precise shape recognition was vital to computerized defense systems. Until recently, all the programs used the brute force method. Start with one piece, then pick up a second and try it all possible ways. If the shapes do not fit together, discard the second one and try to match a third piece to the first, and so on. The computer's robotic method used no insight about the meaning of the images. It was just as likely to try to match an eye with a cloud as with a face. Without some logic to narrow down which matches are tried, the number of possible combinations explodes exponentially as the number of pieces increases. Solving a 500-piece puzzle becomes a protracted process despite the fastest microprocessors.

Computer programs today are beginning to get a handle on how to use colors and patterns, as well as shapes, to complete a puzzle.[13] In 2001, scientists unveiled software that had successfully pieced together priceless Giotto frescoes that had been shattered by a 1997 earthquake in Assisi, Italy. This program compared the pieces with photographs taken before the earthquake.[14] Algorithms to manage such a complex assembly without a guide picture are still under development.

What about computer programs that create puzzles? The first basic ones appeared in the 1980s. Today there are dozens of video games and websites that put a dissected picture onto a screen for the puzzler to reassemble. The player can choose the image, the number of pieces, and the shapes of the pieces.

Many programs offer double-sided puzzles, animation, and music as well. In 2003 Veo began selling an inexpensive digital camera that could take photos, then convert them into computer puzzles for emailing to family and friends.

Computer puzzles have developed a loyal following, including many who scour the Internet on a daily basis for free puzzles. After all, the computer saves time by turning all the pieces face up, and it *never* loses a piece.

The Future

What lies ahead? How will the jigsaw puzzle change between now and its five hundredth anniversary in 2260? Will it actually survive the twenty-first century and the growing computerization of our lives? Can a jigsaw still provide pleasure when the solution is electronically available in an instant? Will craftspeople continue to cut creative designs into one-of-a-kind puzzles?

Of course it will endure! Jigsaw puzzling is not about the solution. Puzzling, as we have seen, is really about the process, about the satisfaction of bringing order out of chaos. It is also a sensory experience, as well as a mental one. For most people a jigsaw is simply not right if they cannot pick up the pieces with their fingers, feel the edges, and turn them around and upside down. The virtual jigsaw that requires manipulation with a mouse is lacking in comparison. Nor is it compatible with casual puzzling—a

The author posed with this huge jigsaw sculpture in Kansas City, Missouri.

few pieces a day—or with social puzzling and conversation. And for assembling pieces of an unknown image, particularly ones that are not cut into the typical four-sided puzzle pieces, the human brain is likely to outperform the computer on puzzles of any size for some years to come.

The traditional jigsaw will still have a place, indeed many places, in contemporary life. It is an instrument of playful learning for young children, as they develop skills ranging from concentration to pattern recognition. One company spokesperson declares:

> Kids have to have a tactile experience. They will always sort pots and pans and play with puzzle pieces.[15]

For adults and older children, the jigsaw puzzle will continue to offer a variety of rewards. In some circumstances, the puzzle provides a challenging stimulus for the synapses in the brain. At other times it soothes, and becomes comfort food for the mind. Future puzzlers will not be limited to the fanatics who practice night and day for the next championships. Or to the types like Bill and Melinda Gates, who buy two copies of the same puzzle so they can race each other.[16] Or even to the very affluent who spend thousands of dollars on personalized jigsaw creations. The puzzlers of tomorrow will include casual players as well as hard-core devotees. They will span society, from young to old, and from rich to poor.

The craft of puzzle making will continue to coexist with mass production and new technologies. Designing individual bits and cutting them one piece at a time brings a unique kind of satisfaction for the creator and the solver of the puzzle.

What *is* certain to change is the puzzle artwork.

Just as Spilsbury would not recognize today's jigsaw images of animated film characters, spacecraft, skyscrapers, and modern fashions, we too would be astounded if we could preview the jigsaw puzzles of two hundred fifty years in the future. We will have to wait to see them, of course, one piece at a time.

Making Jigsaw Puzzles for Fun or for Sale

The two boys at left are using jigsaws in the well-equipped woodworking shop at Camp Dudley in Westport, New York, circa 1930.

Courtesy of Camp Dudley, YMCA Inc.

So you have a great idea for a jigsaw puzzle—how can you take it from concept to reality? Maybe you want to make a special puzzle or two for family and friends. Perhaps you envision a small jigsaw puzzle business. You might even have thought up such a blockbuster that you are ready to take on the giants of the industry. Whatever the case, this appendix will help. It introduces the basics of modern puzzle making, provides an overview of the puzzle industry, and lists some additional resources that those who are considering a business venture should consult.

I have always been fascinated by manufacturing processes. Perhaps it has something to do with my career in education, where the "output" is so intangible. Exams and term papers are at best imprecise reflections of learning. I watch youngsters with satisfaction and joy as they graduate, but I cannot physically inspect their minds. I never really know exactly how successful my teaching has been and what effects it has had.

With puzzle manufacturing, on the other hand, there is a product that can be picked up, turned over, weighed, measured, and boxed. Mistakes are glaringly apparent. And a well-crafted puzzle gives great satisfaction, both to the maker and to those who play with it.

The scale of production has a big impact on the details of manufacturing process. A large factory uses heavy machinery, and requires different modes of handling, compared with a small operation. In one major plant, for example, operators who feed cardboard puzzles into giant presses wear safety gloves that are tethered to a post behind them. When they are wearing the gloves, it is impossible to put their hands too far forward where the press might sever fingers. In contrast, a home workshop set up in the corner of a basement can use small tools that pose less risk of injury.

The principles of jigsaw puzzle manufacturing are the same, regardless of the scale. The requirements are simple: a picture, a rigid backing, adhesive, and a cutting tool. Even a young child can make a rudimentary jigsaw with scissors and paper. But for a thicker and more satisfactory puzzle for adults, clumsy scissors cannot suffice. Today's makers cut puzzles with saws, dies, lasers, water jets, and routers. The next sections give the basics of those technologies in brief.

The methods for making children's puzzles are essentially the same as those for adult puzzles, with the addition of extremely important safety standards. Since young children put everything in their mouths, children's puzzles *must* conform to the Consumer Product Safety Commission's standards for toys. The sections on small parts and nontoxic materials are particularly relevant for jigsaw puzzles. Furthermore, toddlers and preschoolers are just developing fine motor control, so puzzles for them are usually noninterlocking with thicker backing, a wide kerf (space between the pieces), and rounded corners. Tray puzzles that contain the pieces within a frame are most suitable for the under-three set. Many crafters use published patterns for children's jigsaw puzzles.[1]

Wood Hand-Cut Puzzles

Anyone who has the patience to put a jigsaw puzzle together probably also has the patience needed to cut one up. The traditional way, using a saw, is also the simplest: Paste a picture to a thin wood board, then cut it into pieces. Although power scroll saws (sometimes called jigsaws) have replaced the handheld fretsaws of the 1760s, this process is still very time-consuming. It is ideal when the maker wants every puzzle to be unique. This technology is known as "hand-cutting," despite the use of a saw, because the operator cuts each piece one at a time.

Several dozen companies today cut customized wood puzzles. Typical prices for a 100-piece puzzle are rather daunting, anywhere from $75 to $400. Readers with more time than money and those who are thinking about making puzzles for sale can use the instructions below to make a wood puzzle at home. They are simplified from the procedures that commercial makers use for puzzles for adults. Of course, all woodworkers must consult and follow the instructions and safety precautions described by the manufacturers of specific brands of machinery, glues, finishes, and other materials.[2]

The puzzle recipe calls for the following ingredients, all of which can be found in hardware, woodworking, or discount stores:

- A picture on good-quality paper. Photos make excellent puzzles, as do many calendar prints. If you are using a published (or unpublished but copyrighted) picture for a puzzle that you intend to sell, you must first obtain permission from the copyright holder.

- Scroll saw. Many brands and sizes are available, at prices ranging from $75 to $1,200. A saw with a sixteen-inch "throat" (the distance from the blade to the back post that supports the upper arm) can cut puzzles up to twenty inches square. The most versatile saws are those that use standard five-inch-long blades with plain ends (*not* pin ends). Do not use a handheld jigsaw with the blade anchored at only one end.

- Blades. The best blades are fine ones, from .008 inch to .012 inch thick, and with twenty-five to thirty teeth per inch. The thinner the blade, the narrower the kerf, and the more tightly the puzzle pieces will fit together.

- Safety equipment. Woodworkers must always wear safety glasses (or goggles or a face shield) and a dust mask while cutting wood, to protect eyes and lungs while cutting. Commercial manufacturers and active amateurs install dust collection systems as well.

- Plywood. High quality ¼-inch (5 mm) plywood, with no surface flaws or interior voids, is best. Puzzle makers traditionally have favored bass plywood, because it has a clear grain and is easy to cut. Baltic birch, mahogany, and cherry are good alternatives, but are harder woods and cause more blade breakage. Plywood is superior to solid wood, which tends to warp and can break easily along the grain of the wood at interlocks.

- Adhesive. Yellow woodworking glue or white glue works well. Do not use rubber cement, because it will discolor the picture over time. Very active puzzle makers will find it worthwhile to invest in a dry mounting press, such as those used by commercial makers.

- Finishes. A finish on the picture surface (such as acrylic floor wax or an art fixative) protects the puzzle when it is in use. A finish on the back (such as brushing lacquer or polyurethane) enhances the puzzle's appearance.

- Wide painter's tape or self-stick removable two-by-four-inch address labels to use for patterns. (Nonremovable labels and tape will *not* work.)

- A sturdy and attractive box to house the finished puzzle.

• Miscellaneous implements and supplies. Paintbrushes or sponge applicators (one to two inches wide) for the glue and finish, a hard rubber or plastic squeegee, a sponge, and sandpaper.

To prepare the puzzle, cut a piece of plywood one inch wider and one inch longer than the picture. For example, an eight-by-ten-inch picture needs a nine-by-eleven-inch plywood board. If the plywood is rough, sand it on both sides. Apply a finish to the more attractive side—this will be the back of the puzzle—and let it dry.

The next step is gluing. Dampen the back of the picture with a moist sponge to minimize rippling when the paper comes in contact with the glue. Apply a thin, even coating of glue to the unfinished side of the plywood. Then place the picture on the glued surface. Use a squeegee to smooth out any air bubbles and wrinkles, starting in the center and working gently toward the edges. Be careful not to tear the damp print. Sponge off any excess glue, and let the mounted print dry overnight. Then apply two coats of a protective finish to the print.

Before cutting the puzzle, decide on the overall design. It can be interlocking throughout, push-fit (noninterlocking), cut on color lines, with figure pieces, or any combination thereof.

Figure pieces and other distinctive shapes make a puzzle more interesting, but also easier to assemble. Several books of copyright-free silhouette designs are good sources of ideas for figure pieces.[3] To create figure pieces, names, or dates, first draw the outlines of the patterns on painter's tape or removable self-stick labels. Press each pattern lightly onto the picture in the desired place.

Begin cutting by trimming the excess wood from the edges of the picture. Cut picture side up, so the burr created by the blade is underneath. Then make some main cuts to divide the puzzle into manageable sections. If the puzzle is to interlock, the main cuts must consist of loops. For very large puzzles, it may be necessary first to cut from the edge to the center, then remove the blade and start over with a second cut from the opposite edge to the center.

Strip cutting in a gridlike pattern is typical of commercial puzzles. The solid lines show the first vertical cuts. The horizontal cuts (dotted lines) are made next. The pieces interlock on all sides, and there are no figure pieces.

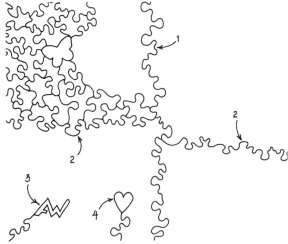

Puzzle cutters can show their creativity with random cutting. Cuts 1 and 2 are main cuts that divide the puzzle into manageable sections. Cuts 3 and 4 are for signature and other figure pieces. The rest of the cuts are varied. Note the split corner and disguised edge piece in the upper left corner.

Cut any figure pieces next. After completing each piece, gently peel the pattern off the picture. Be careful not to pull off the picture along with the pattern. Then cut the rest of the puzzle freehand. After a little practice, it is easy to develop a style for freehand sawing. The satisfaction of getting "into the zone" with cutting matches that of assembling a puzzle. But blades quickly get dull, slowing down the cutting and producing ragged edges. Change the blade as soon as you feel resistance.

To ensure that pieces do not get lost, assemble the puzzle on a board or nearby table as the pieces are cut. When the puzzle is complete, turn it over and sand the back to remove the burr. While taking the puzzle apart to box it, count the pieces. On the lid of the box, paste a label giving the title, number of pieces, the date, and the cutter's name.

Some commercial makers speed up production and reduce cost by cutting several wood puzzles together in a stack up to two inches high. Since they must use thick blades to make the cuts, stack-cut puzzles have very wide kerfs. This technique works well for children's puzzles, whose wide kerfs make it easier for small hands to maneuver the pieces. Most puzzlers consider stack-cutting to be a disadvantage for adult puzzles, where tightly fitting pieces are desirable.

Die-Cutting Puzzles

Die-cutting is a process, much faster than hand-cutting, that stamps out an entire puzzle at once. The sharp steel rule die looks like a giant cookie cutter, and it fits into a heavy flatbed or roller press (like a printing press). This technique works for puzzles made out of cardboard, rubber, foam, and extremely thin wood.

Puzzle companies began using steel rule dies to cut cardboard puzzles in the 1890s. Once the die has been manufactured (a time-consuming process done by specialty die-makers), it can stamp out tens of thousands of identical puzzles before the steel rule gets too dull or breaks. The big commercial puzzle makers make large financial investments in their equipment. They need not just the presses and their dies, but also printing presses for the

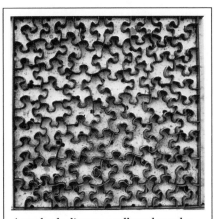

A steel rule die cuts cardboard puzzles by stamping out all the pieces at once. It resembles a giant cookie cutter.

pictures, gluing machines, and machines that break up the puzzle pieces and box them.

An individual consumer who seeks one or two puzzles has several alternatives. Personalized, one-of-a-kind cardboard puzzles have been around since the 1930s. Currently they are available from several mail order catalogs (Miles Kimball and the like), most photo processors and some copy stores, as well as from many websites (new ones seem to pop up each month). The customer supplies the photo or other artwork, either as a camera-ready original or as a digital image.

Recent advances make it possible now to create a puzzle from photos or other graphics with a home computer. Several companies produce inexpensive precut blank puzzles or heat transfers that can be fed through a color printer or copier. Office supply stores carry International Paper's "Invent It" kits and similar brands. Web sites such as those of Joslin Photo Puzzle and Compoz-A-Puzzle are sources for others. (See Appendix B.)

Another option is the "Community Puzzle," made by Biggwood of Hamburg, New York. This puzzle can be customized the old-fashioned way—with pens, pencils, paint, or rubber stamps. Community Puzzle packages contain dozens of fully interchangeable interlocking four-by-four-inch blank pieces, plus edge pieces. They are excellent for school, fund-raising, or training projects, where each participant can decorate one piece.

For a large order, for example fifty to two thousand identical puzzles, it is most economical to contact advertising specialty companies that can deal directly with factories that manufacture puzzles. The Yellow Pages of the phone book lists local representatives under "Promotional Products."

For even larger-scale production, there are two options. Subcontracting puzzles to a company that specializes in die-cutting is one possibility. In fact, some of the major jigsaw puzzle companies do not own any manufacturing equipment. They rely instead on suppliers who can produce thousands of copies of an identical puzzle at very low cost. The customer provides the artwork and sometimes the printing as well. Some well-known subcontractors include: Calbox of Hartford, Connecticut, Edaron in Holyoke, Massachusetts, Warren Industries in Lafayette, Indiana, and Joslin Photo Puzzles in Northampton, Pennsylvania.

The second option, of course, is to set up one's own puzzle factory. It is now possible to do this on a relatively small scale with equipment from Graffiti Graphics in Victoria, British Columbia. In the 1990s owner George Ciesek, after beginning as a die maker, decided to branch out into the jigsaw puzzle business.[4] He developed a roller press that works on household electric current. Business was so brisk that the company was swamped with work.

Disinclined to go into large-scale puzzle production, Ciesek took another tack, and started manufacturing more presses to sell to others. While he still makes some puzzles, his sales now are mainly to entrepreneurs who use his die-cutting machinery and dies in small workshops. One example is a car dealership that photographs customer and salesperson standing in front of each newly purchased car. It then creates a puzzle from the photo and presents it to the customer as a thank-you gift. The Graffiti Graphics equipment and supplies packages range in price from $6,000 to $17,000.

Computerized Technologies

Computer-controlled cutting—with lasers, water jets, or routers—represents the most advanced and complex technology being used for jigsaw puzzles today. A few companies have used these methods to automate the production of wood puzzles. The large investment required for the equipment makes sense only for firms with high sales volumes.

For all three methods, computer software must first translate the entire cutting pattern into a program, a sequence of commands for the motors that drive the equipment. The program can then produce identical puzzles over and over again, like a die, but without any limits imposed by dullness or breakage of the steel rule.

Laser cutting is very fast. The Wentworth Wooden Jigsaw Company, located in an industrial park nestled in a corner of an old English country estate, is the largest manufacturer using this technology for jigsaw puzzles, producing one hundred thousand puzzles per year.[5] The laser machine can cut a 500-piece puzzle with a wide kerf in under ten minutes. (For a narrower kerf, it must cut more slowly.)

The laser's disadvantage is that it leaves slight burn marks on the bottom of the puzzle. Wentworth camouflages the burns with a dark stain on the back of its puzzles. In an incongruous mix of the traditional and the modern, the wife of the estate's gamekeeper stains the plywood boards by hand before they go to the high-tech laser machines for cutting. And inmates at the local jail stitch cloth bags to contain the pieces inside the boxes.

Water-jet cutting uses a .007-inch-diameter nozzle that emits a very fine jet of water under fifty thousand pounds of pressure. Because of the spray, it is necessary to protect most puzzle pictures with a clear laminate. Water jets cut more slowly than lasers, but still much faster than saws, thus reducing the cost of a wood puzzle well below $1 per piece. J. C. Ayer of Marblehead, Massachusetts, pioneered water-jet cutting of jigsaw puzzles in the United States and specializes in high-end puzzles, often one-of-a-kind. (See Chapter 6.) Others, such as Peter Parker in Pinehurst, North Carolina, mass-produce smaller "Stamples" puzzles made from postage stamps.

Puzzle companies use computer-controlled routers mainly to cut tray puzzles for preschoolers. Routers produce very loose-fitting pieces, which are especially desirable for young children.

Overview of the Industry

Learning the basics of manufacturing is just the first step in starting a puzzle business. Finding customers and convincing them to buy the product is just as important. New companies *can* break into the industry and succeed, but it takes a combination of good products, hard work, and sometimes a bit of luck.

Would-be puzzle producers have it easier than some start-ups. The toy and gift industries are relatively open to new companies. Each February about fifteen hundred companies, including two hundred fifty puzzle manufacturers, exhibit their wares for retailers at the International Toy Fair in New York City.[6] They range from small, one-person operations to giants such as Hasbro and Mattel.

New puzzle companies must know the market, especially the segments that are relevant to their particular products. The puzzle industry has grown over the last decade, albeit slowly during the recession that began in 2001. Retail sales of jigsaw puzzles in the United States are estimated at $333 million for that year.[7] The September 11 terrorist attacks had the immediate effect of dampening consumer spending just before the all-important holiday season began. (Puzzle industry revenues peak during the fourth quarter of each year—half to three-quarters of the year's sales occur during the prime gift-buying months of October, November, and December.)

A resurgence in puzzle sales occurred after 2001 as the slow economy and anxieties about terrorism and war led buyers to seek out low-cost items for home entertainment. The major companies have seen steady, though not spectacular, growth in the last few years. But several medium-sized firms, including Nordevco of North Adams, Massachusetts, and Fink & Co. of Hope, Arkansas, could not survive the financial roller coaster and went out of business.

It comes as no surprise that the puzzle industry is experiencing the same trends that affect other businesses today. Economies of scale in marketing, advertising, and distribution continue to drive consolidation into ever larger firms. Hasbro, for example, now owns many puzzle companies that stood alone in the past. Milton Bradley, Parker Brothers, McLoughlin Brothers, Selchow & Righter, and Playskool are just a few of the brands that have wound up in Hasbro's hands through a series of mergers and acquisitions over the last century. The largest pieces of the market in terms of value go to

Hasbro (48 percent), Mattel (15 percent), and Ceaco (12 percent). Other significant players in the industry are Warren Industries (a subsidiary of Rose Art), Patch Products, and Lights, Camera, Interaction![8]

Because short-lived fads dominate much of the toy industry, there is still room for small, new companies with innovative ideas. Every year brings thousands of new products, as each company strives to introduce a modern classic that will have the staying power of Barbie dolls and Monopoly. But the truth is that most toys have life spans measured in months, not decades. The smash hits of just a few years ago—Tickle Me Elmo, Pokemon, Furby, and 3D puzzles—have already faded. Even during their peak popularity, best-sellers suffer because competing companies bring out similar products and sometimes virtually identical knockoffs.

The narrow time window for sale of most toys means that the biggest profits accrue to the firm that starts a new toy craze. The industry thus has developed a tradition of extraordinary secrecy to protect new ideas. Patents and copyrights, while offering some barriers to intellectual property theft over the long term, are less relevant for toys, since consumer tastes change so quickly. Indeed, the Patent and Trademark Office files are full of inventions that received patents, yet were commercial failures; some never even made it into production.

Jigsaw puzzles are a classic category with steadier sales than most toys. Manufacturers must come up with new artwork regularly, but they do not have to invent totally new playthings. Market research shows that the puzzle image is the dominant factor in the purchasing decision, with the degree of difficulty being the next most important.[9]

The wide variety of consumer taste along both dimensions offers good opportunities to fill certain niches. Springbok Editions found a large market in the 1960s with its fine art and natural history images. Twenty years later Lombard Marketing revived mystery puzzles, appealing to puzzlers who wanted both a detective story and the surprise element of not having a guide picture on the box. And in the late 1990s W. B. Adams Company of Lansdale, Pennsylvania, specialized in puzzles showing African-American artwork and history.

Difficulty depends not only on the number of pieces but also on the abilities and interests of the puzzler, so demographics are crucial. About 64 percent of the puzzles sold are for children age twelve and under, with the rest being for teens (4 percent) and adults (32 percent). The majority (60 percent or more) of adult puzzlers are women, and most are over age thirty.[10] Ronda Tidrick, Art Director for Warren Industries' "Rose Art" puzzles, divides the adults into two types:

> Either they want a thorough challenge or they want to escape and relax.[11]

The former are the ones who seek out the 10,000-piece puzzles and sometimes even do puzzles upside down.

Like other leisure-time products, today's jigsaw puzzles rely heavily on licensed properties for their subject matter. Most children's jigsaw puzzles feature television or movie characters through agreements with Disney and other entertainment conglomerates.

Licensing has become more important for adult puzzles as well, as tastes shifted from the scenic photos of the fifties to today's emphasis on reproductions of paintings and prints. Norman Rockwell and Charles Wysocki, always popular on puzzles, have been joined by newer artists such as Bill Bell, Alexander Chen, Jane Wooster Scott, and Josephine Wall. Thomas Kinkade's art empire now extends to jigsaw puzzles. Since the 1994 revision of United States copyright law, jigsaw puzzle companies typically have paid royalties for the images they use, unless they employ in-house artists to design their own artwork.

Recent decades have demonstrated that there is plenty of innovation in the puzzle industry too. Die-cut puzzles broke away from traditional rectangular outlines with all the interlocking pieces in a gridlike configuration. They adopted some of the elements from hand-cut wood puzzles. The irregular edges, figure pieces, and odd-shaped pieces revived interest and sales. Three-dimensional foam puzzles, introduced by Wrebbit of Montreal, had huge success. Their architectural character brought in many male buyers who had not been fans of traditional flat jigsaws.

Wrebbit's success at selling puzzles for $20 to $40 and more had a spillover effect, according to one industry insider:

> Wrebbit's Puzz-3D changed the industry in regards to acceptable price points. The consumer is now willing to pay more, and this opens up lots of new possibilities.[12]

Other manufacturers have since moved into special printing effects and other touches that cost more, but for which there is now a ready market.

Today it seems that virtually every mass-market toy sold in the United States comes from China. But offshore manufacturing is somewhat less important for jigsaw puzzles than for other segments of the toy industry. While most inexpensive children's puzzles come from low-wage countries in East Asia, production of high-end wood puzzles (for both adults and children) and many die-cut puzzles still takes place within the United States. Domestic manufacturers can deliver products more quickly, with lower freight costs, and with less vulnerability to international disruptions.

Selling a product is usually harder than making it. This adage holds true for jigsaw puzzles. While Hasbro and Mattel can sell through the likes of Wal-Mart, Target, or Toys R Us, small manufacturers rarely can get shelf space in the giant retail stores. Furthermore, the majors are putting pressure on other retailers. Two important specialty toy chains, FAO Schwarz (including its Zany Brainy subsidiary) and KB Toys, went into Chapter 11 bankruptcy within a few weeks of each other during the winter of 2003–04.

There are still some good alternatives for marketing, although the number of outlets is shrinking. Independent toy, gift, book, craft, and museum stores are always looking for quality puzzles from new companies, especially puzzles that are *not* being mass-marketed. Mail order catalogs offer another outlet. Catalogs such as those from Bits and Pieces and the Spilsbury Puzzle Company even specialize in puzzles.

Niche marketing through websites has proved to be a boon for some puzzle firms, notably those with specialized products (such as personalized puzzles) or very expensive hand-cut wood puzzles. Most find it helpful to offer some puzzles through eBay or other online auction services as a way to publicize their work. Some makers of wood puzzles, especially those for children, do well on the craft show circuit.

Resources for Puzzle Entrepreneurs

Budding entrepreneurs can find more detailed information on the puzzle industry both in print and on the Internet. Reference librarians at public and university libraries can provide invaluable help in locating sources, either in their own libraries, through interlibrary loan, or on the Web.[13]

Several trade magazines focus on the toy and gift industries. *Playthings* and *The Toy Book* are monthly magazines of the toy trade. Each publishes an annual feature on puzzles and games. *Playthings* also issues an annual directory of toy manufacturers and suppliers to the toy industry. Several other trade magazines cover puzzles, including *Specialty Toys & Gifts, Giftware News, edplay, Educational Dealer, License!,* and *The Licensing Book.*

Trade shows offer a great venue to scope out the market. The Toy Industry Association (TIA) organizes the International Toy Fair each February so manufacturers can display their products to the buyers for retail outlets. The show includes participation by the American Specialty Toy Retailing Association (ASTRA) and is so large that it completely fills New York's cavernous Javits Convention Center. The Game Manufacturers Association (GAMA) show takes place in March, usually in Las Vegas. Both shows include seminars and presentations for exhibitors and attendees. The show directories are invaluable references that list exhibitors and other suppliers to the industry.

Many puzzle makers also exhibit each May at New York's National Stationery Show, held in conjunction with the Surtex licensing show. In June the International Licensing Industry Merchandisers' Association (LIMA) sponsors another show that offers opportunities to view and license work by artists and studios. There are also gift shows for the trade: a major show in August in New York, plus regional ones in Boston, Atlanta, Chicago, Dallas, Los Angeles, and other major cities throughout the country.

It is beyond the scope of this book to cover general information on starting and running a business. Libraries are full of publications that cover every aspect of that topic. Still, it is worth mentioning that governments are a fount of information and services. At the federal level, our tax dollars support the resources provided by the Small Business Administration, the Departments of Commerce and Labor, the Patent and Trademark Office, the Copyright Office of the Library of Congress, and the Consumer Product Safety Commission, among others.

At the state and local level, entrepreneurs can get help, including both advice and financial assistance, from government agencies and organizations that support business development. Other important resources include the business school of a state university, the state's extension service, the local Chamber of Commerce, and the local chapter of Service Corps of Retired Executives (SCORE).

Selected Websites for Puzzlers

All these sites were operational and current when this book went to press. But the Internet evolves and changes rapidly. Use a search engine to find new sites that have emerged since this book was printed, or to find old sites that have moved to new locations.

JIGSAW PUZZLE HISTORY—GENERAL
In addition to general histories, several sites offer detailed histories of specific companies.

Anne Williams' Puzzles: http://abacus.bates.edu/~awilliam/publications.htm
Bob Armstrong's Old Jigsaw Puzzles: www.oldpuzzles.com
Joe Seymour's Puzzles: www.icollectpuzzles.com
Canadian Jigsaw Puzzles: http://canadajigsawpuzzle.tripod.com
Japanese Jigsaw Puzzle Manufacturers: http://imaginatorium.org/shop/mfrs.htm
Mystery Jigsaw Puzzles: www.public.iastate.edu/~pellack/Mysteryjigslist.htm
Puzzlehistory.com: www.puzzlehistory.com
American Jigsaw Puzzles: www.jigsaw-puzzle.org

JIGSAW PUZZLE HISTORY—SPECIFIC BRANDS AND COMPANIES
See also the general sites listed above.

Heye Puzzles: www.heyepuzzles.com
Parker Brothers Die-cut Puzzles: www.it.ilstu.edu/~brown/favpuzzs/puzzpb.html

Springbok Editions (pre-Hallmark): http://home.att.net/~mike_helland

Tek Method and Cadaco "Cluster" and "Jumble-Fits" Puzzles: www.azplerp.com

Tuck Puzzles: www.home.zonnet.nl/g.h.bekkering

Tuco Puzzles: www.lockport-ny.com/History/Upson.htm

Tuco Puzzles: http://geocities.com/timessquare/ring/1432

PUZZLE COLLECTIONS IN NORTH AMERICAN MUSEUMS AND LIBRARIES

Only a few of these institutions display jigsaw puzzles on their websites, but all welcome visitors. To be sure of viewing specific puzzles, call ahead for an appointment.

Abby Aldrich Rockefeller Folk Art Museum:
   www.history.org/history/museums/abby_art.cfm

American Antiquarian Society: www.americanantiquarian.org

Connecticut Valley Historical Museum: http://quadrangle.org/CVHM.htm

Fresno Metropolitan Museum: www.fresnomet.org

Indiana University, Lilly Library (a few jigsaw puzzles): www.indiana.edu/~liblilly

Peabody Essex Museum: www.pem.org/homepage

Princeton University, Cotsen Children's Library: www.princeton.edu/~cotsen/

Margaret Woodbury Strong Museum: www.strongmuseum.org

New-York Historical Society: www.nyhistory.org/

Old Sturbridge Village: www.osv.org

Osborne Collection, Toronto Public Library:
   www.tpl.toronto.on.ca/uni_spe_osb_index.jsp

Smithsonian National Museum of American History: www.americanhistory.si.edu

Toy and Miniature Museum of Kansas City: www.umkc.edu/tmm/

University of Waterloo Museum and Archive of Games:
   http://healthy.uwaterloo.ca/~museum

U.S. Library of Congress (map puzzles): www.loc.gov/rr/geogmap

Yale Center for British Art: www.yale.edu/ycba

COLLECTOR/ENTHUSIAST ORGANIZATIONS AND RESOURCES

Association of Game and Puzzle Collectors: www.agpc.org

Benevolent Confraternity of Dissectologists:
   www.btinternet.com/~philip.tyler/Jigsaw/

Northeast Document Conservation Center: www.nedcc.org

Tips on how to do jigsaw puzzles: www.jigsawjungle.com/code/puzztips.htm

Chat group (mainly for online puzzles):
  http://groups.yahoo.com/group/jigsaw_puzzle

Antique Advertising Association of America: www.pastimes.org

Ephemera Society: www.ephemerasociety.org

SOURCES FOR ANTIQUE AND COLLECTIBLE PUZZLES

eBay (online auctions): www.ebay.com

Maloney's Antiques and Collectibles Resource Directory: www.maloneysonline.com

PUZZLE LENDING LIBRARIES AND RENTALS

British Jigsaw Puzzle Library: www.britishjigsawpuzzlelibrary.co.uk

Elms Puzzles Inc.: www.elmspuzzles.com/club.html

RESOURCES FOR HISTORICAL RESEARCH ABOUT JIGSAW PUZZLES

Library Index: www.libdex.com

Links to libraries: http://dir.yahoo.com/reference/libraries

Links to Repositories of Primary Sources:
  www.uidaho.edu/special_collections/other.html#othus

American Association for State and Local History: www.aaslh.org

Cyndi's List of Genealogy Sites: www.cyndislist.com

Social Security Death Index, free search: www.familytreelegends.com/ssdi

MANUFACTURERS OF WOODEN JIGSAW PUZZLES

Companies in the first group of listings below specialize in wooden jigsaw puzzles for adults. Many can also make children's puzzles. They do mainly custom work and special orders, and are not available in retail stores. The list includes full-timers, as well as part-timers who make at least fifty puzzles per year.

AuPuzzle: www.aupuzzle.com

J. C. Ayer & Company: www.ayerpuzzles.com

BellArt: www.bell-art.com

Black Bear Puzzles: www.blackbearpuzzles.com

Custom Puzzle Craft: www.custompuzzlecraft.com

DougsPuzzles.com: www.dougspuzzles.com

Elms Puzzles Inc.: www.elmspuzzles.com

Firebird Puzzles: www.firebird-puzzles.com

Fool's Gold Puzzles: www.foolsgoldpuzzles.com

Jack-in-the-Box Puzzles: www.jitbpuzzles.com

Jardin Puzzles: www.jardinpuzzles.com

Jemidanny Handcut Wooden Jigsaw Puzzles: www.jemidanny.com

MGC's Custom Made Wooden Jigsaw Puzzles: www.mgcpuzzles.com

PG Puzzles: www.pgjigsawpuzzles.co.uk

Par Puzzles: www.parpuzzles.com

PrimePuzzle.com: www.primepuzzle.com

Purple Martin Puzzles: www.purplemartinpuzzles.com

Rainy Lake Puzzles: www.rainylakepuzzles.com

Robert Longstaff Workshops: www.longstaff.co.uk

Southern Puzzle Company: www.southernpuzzles.com

Stave Puzzles Inc.: www.stave.com

Thingamajigsaw Puzzles: www.thingamajigsaw.com

WC Puzzles: www.wcpuzzles.com

Wentworth: www.wooden-jigsaws.com

Michèle Wilson: www.pmwpuzzles.com

Children's puzzles are so widely available that only a few web sources are listed here, for brands that are not generally carried in retail stores.

Damhorst Toys Ltd.: www.damhorsttoys.com

Every Buddies Puzzles!: www.kidpuzzles.com

Mamasoes: www.mamasoes.com

The Puzzle Man: www.thepuzzleman.com

TAG Toys: www.tagtoys.com

Zoodonyms (name puzzles): www.zoodonyms.on.ca

JIGSAW PUZZLE RETAILERS

Most of the retailers listed specialize in die-cut cardboard puzzles, although a few also carry wood puzzles.

Are You Game? www.areyougame.com

Nancy Ballhagen's Puzzles: www.missouripuzzle.com

Bits and Pieces: www.bitsandpieces.com

Jigsaw Jungle: www.jigsawjungle.com

Old Game Store: www.theoldgamestore.com

Puzzle House: www.puzzlehouse.com

Spilsbury Puzzle Company: www.spilsbury.com

CUSTOM AND PHOTOGRAPHIC DIE-CUT JIGSAW PUZZLES

These are some of the established sites. New ones pop up all the time. See the list of wooden puzzle makers also.

The Community Puzzle: www.communitypuzzle.com

Compoz-A-Puzzle: www.compozapuzzle.com

Joslin Photo Puzzle: www.jigsawpuzzle.com

Morphoto: www.angelfire.com/biz2/morphoto

National Puzzle Co.: www.nationalpuzzle.com

Snapshot Puzzles: www.snapshotpuzzles.com

Up in Pieces: www.upinpieces.com

ONLINE VIRTUAL JIGSAW PUZZLES

This is just a sampling of the many sites that are available.

JigZone: www.jigzone.com/

Shockwave: www.shockwave.com/sw/content/jigsawpuzzles

RESOURCES FOR PUZZLE BUSINESSES

Consumer Product Safety Commission: www.cpsc.gov

Drescher Paper Box (die-cutting subcontractor): www.drescherpuzzle.com

Graffiti Graphics (die-cutting equipment): www.puzzlemachine.com

Service Corps of Retired Executives: www.score.org

U.S. Department of Commerce: www.commerce.gov

U.S. Copyright Office: www.copyright.gov

U.S. Patent and Trademark Office: www.uspto.gov

U.S. Small Business Administration: www.sba.gov

TOY TRADE ASSOCIATIONS AND SHOWS

American Specialty Toy Retailers Association: www.astratoy.org

Entertainment Software Association: www.theesa.com

Game Manufacturers Association (GAMA): www.gama.org

Intellectual Property Owners Association: www.ipo.org

International Licensing Industry Merchandisers' Association (LIMA):
    www.licensing.org

National Stationery Show: www.nationalstationeryshow.com

New York International Gift Fair: www.nyigf.com

Surtex (licensing art and design): www.surtex.com

Toy Industry Association: www.toy-tia.org

TOY TRADE MAGAZINES AND MARKET RESEARCH

Adventure Publishing (publishes *Toy Book, Toy Report, Licensing Book, Licensing Report, Specialty Toys & Gifts*): www.adventurepub.com

Bloom Report: www.thebloomreport.com

Fahy-Williams Publishing (publishes *edplay* and *Educational Dealer*): www.fwpi.com

Playthings Magazine: www.playthings.com

NPD Group (market research): www.npd.com

Toy Directory: www.toydirectory.com

MISCELLANEOUS

World Peace Puzzle: www.thebigpuzzle.com

Playing for Keeps: www.playingforkeeps.org

Puzzle Museum (mostly mechanical puzzles, with a few jigsaws):
    www.puzzlemuseum.com

Puzzle World (mostly mechanical puzzles): www.johnrausch.com/PuzzleWorld

Lists of links: www.sculptor.org/wood/puzzles.htm
    www.yahoo.com/business_and_economy/shopping_and_services/games/
    puzzles/jigsaw_puzzles
    http://dmoz.org/Games/Puzzles/Jigsaw_Puzzles
    http://dmoz.org/shopping/toys_and_games/games/puzzles
    http://dmoz.org/shopping/crafts/woodcraft/puzzles/

Endnotes

PREFACE

1. Harry Manning, Salem, Massachusetts, Interviews 23 January 1992 and 11 September 1993; Helen Fiss Corson, Rosemont, Pennsylvania, Interview, 15 June 1989; Carroll A. Towne, Venice, Florida, Correspondence with author, 27 November 1986 and 7 January 1987; Mary-Lou Jones Palmer, Tucson, Arizona, Correspondence with author, 8 October 1992.

CHAPTER 1

1. Humorous approaches to puzzling include Tim Morris, "Puzzlement," *The American Scholar*, 67:4, Autumn 1998, pp. 113–123 and Francene and Louis Sabin, *The One, The Only, The Original Jigsaw Puzzle Book* (Chicago: Henry Regnery Co., 1977).
2. George H. Copeland, "The Country Is Off on a Jig-Saw Jag," *New York Times Magazine*, February 12, 1933, p. 8.
3. For an art historian's critical approach to the relationship between art and jigsaw puzzles, see James Elkins, *Why Are Our Pictures Puzzles?* (New York: Routledge, 1999).
4. Stave Puzzles, *Puzzle Catalog 1995–1996* (Norwich, Vermont: Stave Puzzles, 1995), p. 23.
5. For discussions of other types of puzzles see Marcel Danesi, *The Puzzle Instinct: The Meaning of Puzzles in Human Life* (Bloomington: Indiana University Press, 2002)

and Robert J. Sternberg and Janet E. Davidson, "The Mind of the Puzzler," *Psychology Today*, June 1982, pp. 37–44.

6. *New York Times*, "Jig-Saw Game Is Carrying On," December 13, 1936, Section XII, p. 18.

7. *Japan Economic Newswire*, "Jigsaw Puzzles Popular with Lima Hostages," April 10, 1997.

8. Ronda Tidrick, Warren Industries, Lafayette, Indiana, Telephone interview, 3 June 2003.

9. Erik H. Erikson, *Toys and Reasons* (New York: W. W. Norton & Co., 1977), pp. 139–140.

10. Thomas Sowell, *The Einstein Syndrome: Bright Children Who Talk Late* (New York: Basic Books, 2001).

11. Paul Recer, "Mind-Exercising Hobbies Can Help Protect the Brain Against Alzheimer's, Study Says," *St. Louis Post-Dispatch*, March 6, 2001, p. A7.

12. Laurence I. Barrett, "Alzheimer's and the Reagans," *New Choices* July/August 1996, quoted in *Washingtonian*, September 1996, p. 48.

13. "Male" and "female" parts and variations on this theme turn up too. One Navy captain, who took up puzzle cutting in his retirement years, favored particularly colorful language for the projecting parts. For a serious attempt at labels, see Bob Armstrong, "Jigsaw Puzzle Cutting Styles: A New Method of Classification," *Game Researchers' Notes* 25, February–May 1997, pp. 5581–5590.

14. Anne D. Williams, "Puzzle? or Game? or Both?" *Game Times*, No. 10, August 1988, pp. 190–192.

15. Betty A. Ford, Fayette City, Pennsylvania, Telephone interview, 23 June 2003.

16. Antoine Bello, *The Missing Piece*, translated from the French by Helen Stevenson (Orlando, Florida: Harcourt, Inc., 2003).

17. *Toys and Novelties*, "Jig-Saw Puzzles Make Safe Landing," August 1933, pp. 33–37; Associated Press, "Taiwanese Claim Biggest Jigsaw Puzzle Record," June 28, 1998.

18. *Guinness Book of Records 2004* (New York: Guinness World Records Ltd., 2003), p. 109; Associated Press, "Mexicans Piece Together Million Piece Jigsaw," July 30, 2003.

19. Oliver Burkeman, "Inside Story: Who Wants to Ruin a Millionaire?" *The Guardian*, October 30, 2000, p. 7; Christopher Monckton, "How I Bet the House on a Puzzle and Lost," *Sunday Times of London*, November 12, 2000.

20. Jerry Slocum, *The Tangram Book* (New York: Sterling Publishing, 2003), p. 11.

CHAPTER 2

Some portions of this chapter appeared earlier in Anne D. Williams, "Jigsaw Puzzles," *Early American Homes*, December 1997, pp. 28–31, 78.

1. Philippe Ariès, *Centuries of Childhood* (New York: Random House, 1962).
2. John Locke, *Some Thoughts Concerning Education*, edited by John W. and Jean S. Yolton (Oxford: Clarendon Press, 1989).
3. Linda Hannas, *The English Jigsaw Puzzle 1760–1890* (London: Wayland, 1972) and *The Jigsaw Book* (New York: Dial Press, 1981).
4. Jill Shefrin, *Such Constant Affectionate Care* (Los Angeles: Cotsen Occasional Press, 2003), p. 5.
5. Betsy and Geert Bekkering, *Piece by Piece: A History of Jigsaw Puzzles in the Netherlands*, translated from the Dutch by Geert Bekkering, Kay Curtis, and Felicity Whiteley (Amsterdam: Van Soeren & Co., 1988); Linda David (ed.), *The Lilly Library: Through the Eyes of Friends* (Bloomington, Indiana: Friends of the Lilly Library, 2001), p. 16.
6. Shefrin, *op. cit.*; Tyler, Tom, "1760s Jigsaw Puzzle Maps of Lady Charlotte Finch," *Game and Puzzle Collectors Quarterly* 1:3, September 2000, pp. 11–12.
7. Shefrin, *op. cit.* fully describes and illustrates the cabinet and its contents.
8. Linda Hannas, *The English Jigsaw Puzzle 1760–1890*, London: Wayland, 1972, p. 17.
9. Ibid., pp. 18–19.
10. Elizabeth W. Gilboy, *Wages in Eighteenth Century England* (Cambridge: Harvard University Press, 1934); Gregory, Clark, "Farm wages and living standards in the industrial revolution: England, 1670–1869," *Economic History Review* 54:3 (2001), pp. 477–505. (I am indebted to Michael Oliver for the latter reference.)
11. Hannas, *op. cit.*, p. 60.
12. Ibid., p. 93, plate 3.
13. Brown, Orlando, Letter to Mason Brown, 17 March 1811, www.libertyhall.org/Family%20Letter%20Writing1.htm (accessed on December 13, 2003). (I am indebted to Geert Bekkering for this reference.)
14. M. Newman, Advertisements in the *Daily Advertiser*, Boston: December 24, 1817, and December 23, 1818. (I am indebted to Jerry Slocum for this reference and the next two.)
15. A. T. Goodrich, Advertisement in the *New York Evening Post*, January 7, 1818.
16. A. T. Goodrich, Catalogs (New York: 1818, 1926).

17. J. P. McCaskey, Puzzle entitled "Lincoln Lessons in Graphic Geography" (Lancaster, Pennsylvania: 1903).

18. James J. Shea and Charles Mercer, *It's All in the Game* (New York: G. P. Putnam's Sons, 1960), pp. 52–56.

19. Edward Wiebé, *The Paradise of Childhood*, edited by Milton Bradley (Springfield, Massachusetts: Milton Bradley Co., 1869).

20. Michael Patrick Hearn, *McLoughlin Brothers Publishers* (New York: Justin G. Schiller, Ltd., 1980).

21. Paula Petrik, "The House That Parcheesi Built: Selchow & Righter Company," *Business History Review* 60, Autumn 1986, pp. 410–437.

22. Jerome Singer, Yale University, New Haven, Connecticut, Telephone interview, 18 June 2003.

23. Marlene Barron, "Three- and Four-Year-Olds Completing 150-piece Puzzles? Impossible!", *Young Children*, September 1999, pp. 10–11; Marlene Barron, West Side Montessori School, New York, New York, Telephone interview, 4 February 2004.

24. Evelyn Weber, "Play Materials in the Curriculum of Early Childhood," pp. 25–37 in *Educational Toys in America: 1800 to the Present*, edited by Karen Hewitt and Louise Roomet (Burlington, Vermont: University of Vermont, 1979).

25. Rita Kramer, *Maria Montessori* (New York: G. P. Putnam's Sons, 1976).

26. Maria Montessori, *Dr. Montessori's Own Handbook*, with introduction by Nancy McCormick Rambusch (New York: Schocken Books, 1965).

27. M. K. Gwyn, "The Healy Puzzle Picture and Defective Aliens," *Medical Record*, January 31, 1914, pp. 197–199.

28. Charlotte Gano Garrison, *Permanent Play Materials for Young Children* (New York: Charles Scribner's Sons, 1923).

29. Charlotte Gano Garrison and Thomas F. Hogan, *Reminiscences of Charlotte Garrison* (New York: Oral History Research Office, Columbia University, 1969), pp. 21–22.

30. Richard P. Kleeman, "Dad Said He Could Have Made Judy's Toy Better, and He Did," *Minneapolis Tribune*, September 30, 1956, pp. 1, 5.

31. Thomas Meehan, "Creative (and Mostly Upper-Middle-Class) Playthings," *Saturday Review*, December 16, 1972, pp. 42–47. See also Frank and Theresa Caplan, *The Power of Play* (Garden City: Anchor Press/Doubleday, 1973).

32. Nancy S. Maldonado, "Puzzles: A Pathetically Neglected, Commonly Available Resource," *Young Children*, May 1996, pp. 4–10.

33. *Playthings*, "Charting the Industry," January 1999, p. 24.

34. Rachel Carson, *Silent Spring* (Boston: Houghton Mifflin, 1962).

35. Donna C. Kaonis, "I Waz De One Who Started All Dis Funny Biznes!" *Collector's Showcase* 1:4, March/April 1982, p. 10.

36. Michele Himmelberg, "Mickey—The Modest Cartoon Character Grew into a Multibillion-Dollar Brand," *Orange County Register,* November 18, 2003.

37. Anne D. Williams, "Metamorphic Puzzles: Changeable Charlie's Genealogy," *Game and Puzzle Collectors Quarterly* 3:3, September 2002, pp. 8–11.

CHAPTER 3

1. *New York Times*, "New Puzzle Menaces the City's Sanity," May 24, 1908, Section 2, p. 7.

2. Betsy and Geert Bekkering, *Piece by Piece: A History of Jigsaw Puzzles in the Netherlands* (Amsterdam: Van Soeren & Co., 1988), p. 50. Translated from the Dutch by Geert Bekkering, Kay Curtis, and Felicity Whiteley.

3. Ellis A Davidson, *Pretty Arts for the Employment of Leisure Hours: A Book for Ladies* (London: Chapman and Hall, 1879).

4. R. S. T., *Sorrento Wood-Carving* (Boston: Loring, 1869); George A. Sawyer, *Fret-Sawing and Wood-Carving for Amateurs* (Boston: Lee and Shepard, 1875).

5. Julius Wilcox, "Fret-Sawing and Wood-Carving," *Harper's New Monthly Magazine*, Vol. 56, No. 334, March 1878, pp. 533–540.

6. Steven M. Gelber, *Hobbies* (New York: Columbia University Press, 1999), pp. 176–177.

7. Reverend Joseph Matthews (Uncle Joseph), *Harry Crawford: How He Learned to Make His Own Dissected Maps and Picture Puzzles* (London: Suter and Co., 1873).

8. Edward Williston Frentz, "Seizing the Chance, II: The Picture-Puzzle 'Craze,'" *Youth's Companion,* October 29, 1908, p. 543. Frentz wrote of the origins of the puzzle craze, but does not identify the woman. One clue comes from the November 19 and December 3, 1908, issues of *Life,* the nationally circulated weekly humor magazine. It ran advertisements for puzzles by Prudence Pride of Deerfield, Massachusetts, in which she claimed, "I made the original JIGSAW-PUZZLES that set Boston crazy." Although Deerfield is in central, not eastern, Massachusetts, it might be that Pride had recently moved there from the Boston area.

9. Ibid.

10. *Boston Sunday Herald*, "Merely to Rest the Tired Business Man," June 22, 1919, p. 7.

11. Parker Brothers Inc., *90 Years of Fun*, (Salem, Massachusetts: Parker Brothers, 1973), p. 26.

12. *Boston Sunday Herald, op. cit.*

13. *The Outlook,* "The Spectator," May 2, 1908, p. 17.

14. *New York Times,* "Stick to It, and You May Solve a Puzzle Picture," July 26, 1908, Section 5, p. 11.

15. *Playthings,* "Fifth Avenue Toy Shop Mystery Puzzle Solved," March 1909, p. 54.

16. *The Outlook, op. cit.*; Fitch, George, "Picture Puzzles," *Collier's National Weekly,* November 20, 1909, p. 23.

17. *New York Times,* "Boston's Latest Contribution to Cultured Fads—Puzzle Pictures," November 8, 1908, p. SM 8. (I am indebted to Jerry Slocum for this reference).

18. Mary A. Houghton, "Raised Puzzle for the Blind," patent no. 941,680 (Washington, D.C.: U.S. Patent and Trademark Office, November 30, 1909); Nellie Olinger, "Puzzle Postal Card," patent no. 939,074 (Washington, D.C.: U.S. Patent and Trademark Office, November 2, 1909); Theodore G. Strater, "Adjustable Frame for Assembling Picture Puzzles," patent no. 932,512 (Washington, D.C.: U.S. Patent and Trademark Office, August 31, 1909).

19. W. Lacey Amy, "The Picture Puzzle," *Canadian Magazine,* March 1910, pp. 436–441; Elizabeth Louise Haskell, "The Revolt of Jepson," *Harper's Bazar,* July 1909, pp. 658–663.

20. L. Frank Baum, *The Emerald City of Oz* (Chicago: Reilly & Britton, 1910), pp. 127–140.

21. *Playthings,* "Countess Festetics a Picture Puzzle Maker," May 1909, p. 65.

22. Dorothy G. Wayman, "Pens and Puzzles Make Her Living," *Boston Evening Globe,* May 24, 1938.

23. Margaret H. Richardson, *The Sign of the Motor Car* (Dennis, Massachusetts: privately printed, 1926), p. 4. (I am indebted to the Pauline Wixon Derick Library of Dennis, Massachusetts for this reference.)

24. Ibid, p. 6.

25. *The Outlook, op. cit.*

26. Theodore Pyle, unpublished letter to Gertrude Brinckle, November 16, 1943 (in the Pyle Collection at the Historical Society of Delaware, Wilmington). (I am indebted to Paul Davis for this reference.)

27. Helen Fiss Corson, Rosemont, Pennsylvania, Interview, 15 June 1989.

28. Ruth Clapp, Newington, Connecticut, Telephone interview, 22 March 1997.

29. Parker Brothers Inc., *op. cit.*, p. 26.

30. Philip E. Orbanes, *The Game Makers: The Story of Parker Brothers from Tiddledy Winks to Trivial Pursuit* (Boston: Harvard Business School Publishing Corporation, 2004), p. 45. See also John J. Fox, "Parker Pride: Memories of Working Days at Parker Brothers," *Essex Institute Historical Collections* 123:2, April 1987, pp. 150–181.

31. Matthews, *op. cit.*, p. 36.

32. Anne D. Williams, *Cutting A Fine Figure: The Art of the Jigsaw Puzzle* (Lexington, Massachusetts: Museum of Our National Heritage, 1996), p. 25.

33. Eva Gagnon, Salem, Massachusetts, Interview, 12 September 1993.

34. Pete Martin, "Game Maker," *Saturday Evening Post,* October 6, 1945, p. 26.

35. For a detailed history of Madmar, see Anne D. Williams, "Madmar: The Quality Company," *Game and Puzzle Collectors Quarterly* 4:1, March 2003, pp. 6–11.

CHAPTER 4

1. George H. Copeland, "The Country is Off on a Jig-Saw Jag," *New York Times Magazine,* February 12, 1933, p. 16; *Time,* "Puzzle Profits," February 20, 1933, p. 41. Some portions of this chapter appeared earlier in Anne D. Williams, "Leisure in the Great Depression: The Many Pieces of the Jigsaw Puzzle Story," *Ephemera Journal* 6, 1993, pp. 99–115.

2. *Advertising Age,* "Jig-Saw Puzzle Use Increasing," February 25, 1933, p. 6; U.S. Bureau of the Census, *Historical Statistics of the United States: Volume I* (Washington, D.C.: U.S. Government Printing Office, 1975), Series A350.

3. *Playthings,* "Will It Last?" April 1933, p. 128; "Some Facts on Jigsawcracy," p. 170.

4. Anne D. Williams, "Leisure in the Great Depression: The Many Pieces of the Jigsaw Puzzle Story," *Ephemera Journal* 6, 1993, p. 100.

5. Ibid.; U.S. Bureau of the Census, *op. cit.,* Series D739–764, E135; Joseph S. Zeisel, "The Workweek in American Industry," *Monthly Labor Review,* January 1958, pp. 23–29.

6. *Toy World,* "Popularity of Adult Games Reaches New High," January 1932, p. 47.

7. *Playthings,* "More on Adult Games," December 1930, p. 55; *Playthings,* "Some Facts on Jigsawcracy," April 1933, p. 170; *Toy World,* "Jig-Saw Jag," March 1933, p. 16; *New York Times,* "Hoovers Ascend Peak Near Camp," August 4, 1930, p. 3.

8. Anne D. Williams, "Puzzles in Films," *Game and Puzzle Collectors Quarterly* 3:2, June 2002, p. 11; *Time, op. cit.*

9. *Screen Play Secrets,* "Sunday at the Lloyds," July 1930, as quoted in *Playthings,* October 1930, p. 4.

10. Alice E. Kern, Portland, Maine, Telephone interview, 24 April 1990.

11. The Milton Bradley Co., "You, Too, Can Make Big Profits with This Special Assortment for Rental Libraries," *Playthings,* December 1932, back cover.

12. *Playthings,* "Joseph K. Straus, 77, Dies," April 1957, p. 155; Amy Straus, Jamaica, New York, Telephone interview, 27 August 1989.

13. *Publishers' Weekly,* "Customer's Choice," January 28, 1933, p. 376.

14. F. N. Hollingsworth, "Boston Going Strong for Jig Saw Puzzles," *Toys and Novelties,* December 1932, p. 58.

15. James Aswell, "My New York," *Lewiston* (Maine) *Evening Journal,* January 19, 1933, p. 4.

16. Williams, "Leisure in the Great Depression," p. 4.

17. L. Day Perry and T. K. Webster Jr. *Jigsaw Puzzles—And How to Make 'Em* (Chicago: Mack Publications, 1933); Towner K. Webster Jr., "Jig Saw Puzzles—How to Make 'Em," *Popular Homecraft,* September–October 1932, pp. 211–215; Towner K. Webster Jr., "Advanced Jigsaw Puzzle Making," *Popular Homecraft,* January–February 1933, pp. 423–426; Morton C. Walling, "Jig-Saw Puzzles Are Easy to Make," *Popular Science Monthly,* March 1932, pp. 80, 115; Anne D. Williams, "Depression Jigsaw Mania: The 'Webster School' of Puzzle Cutting," *Game Times,* No. 17, April 1992, pp. 352–353.

18. *Lewiston* (Maine) *Evening Journal,* "Tax Blight Hits Local Jig-Saw Puzzle Makers," March 4, 1933, p. 5.

19. Carroll A. Towne, Venice, Florida, Correspondence with author, 27 November 1986 and 7 January 1987.

20. Nadine N. Russell, "Auburn Cutup," *Worcester* (Massachusetts) *Sunday Telegram,* December 27, 1970, Feature Parade section, cover, pp. 6–7.

21. Anne D. Williams, *Jigsaw Puzzles: An Illustrated History and Price Guide* (Radnor, Pennsylvania: Wallace-Homestead/Chilton, 1990), pp. 27–28; Lora Willey, Hampden, Massachusetts, Correspondence with author, 13 October 1987.

22. Delta Specialty Co., *What Others Have Done with "Delta" Tools in Hobby, Spare Time and Production Work* (Milwaukee: Delta, circa 1931) p. 21; see also Anne D. Williams, "Jigsaw Bits: Phyllis McLellan," *Game Researchers' Notes* 28 (1998), pp. 5653, 5656–57.

23. Lorraine Riley, Joplin, Missouri, Telephone interview, 9 September 1990; Nancy Prater, "Topsy Turvy Craze Makes Comeback," *Carthage Press*, August 9, 1988, p. 5.

24. Edward Brewer, Skaneateles, New York, Telephone interview, 27 August 1994; William Brewer, Cortland, New York, Telephone interview, 27 August 1994. (I am indebted to Chris McCann for these contacts.)

25. Delta Specialty Co., *op. cit.*, p. 19; Anne D. Williams, "Bernard J. Roemer: Puzzle Entrepreneur," *Game Researchers' Notes* 29 (1999), pp. 5676–5683.

26. Anne D. Williams, "Falling for a . . . Falls," *Game Times*, No. 21, August 1993, pp. 458–459; Mary-Lou Jones Palmer, Tucson, Arizona, Correspondence with author, 8 October 1992; *Cleveland Plain Dealer*, "Her Royal Puzzle Will Fit Mrs. S. In," December 3, 1936, p. 9.

27. James L. Browning, Montague, New Jersey, Telephone interview, 8 September 1996.

28. Henry A. Martin Jr., Rochester, New York, Correspondence with author, 24 September 1994.

29. For hundreds of pictures of Great Depression era cardboard puzzles, see Chris McCann, *Master Pieces: The Art History of Jigsaw Puzzles* (Portland, Oregon: Collectors Press, 1998).

30. Copeland, *op. cit.*, p. 8; *Fortune*, "The Mechanics of a Craze," April 1933, p. 76.

31. Anne D. Williams, "Einson-Freeman: Depression 'House of Fads,'" *Game Times*, No. 32, April 1997, pp. 4–16.

32. *Business Week*, "Jig-Saw Jag," January 18, 1933, p. 8.

33. Chris McCann, "Building Your Own Miniature Art Gallery with Depression Jigsaw Puzzles," *Antique Trader*, January 3, 1990, p. 50.

34. *Advertising Age, op. cit.*

35. *Playthings*, "Selling Young and Old," April 1933, pp. 122–123.

36. *Toys and Novelties*, "Jig-Saw Puzzles Make Safe Landing," August 1933, p. 37.

37. Ibid., p. 36; Richard Brophy, "America, the Beautiful Jigsaw Puzzle," *American Heritage* 41:8, December 1990, p. 107.

38. *Tide*, "Jigsaw Jag," February 1933, p. 8; Copeland, *op. cit.*, p. 16; Williams, Anne D., "Hollywood Goes to Pieces," *Game Researchers' Notes* 14 (June 1993), pp. 5317–5320.

39. *New York Times*, "Uses Jig-Saw Puzzles for Nerves," March 4, 1933, p. 15; *Lewiston* (Maine) *Evening Journal*, "Would Puzzle Prisoners," February 16, 1933, p. 5.

40. Anne D. Williams, "Personalized du Pont Gifts," *Game and Puzzle Collectors*

Quarterly 3:1, March 2002, pp. 14–15; Irénée du Pont Jr., Montchanin, Delaware, Telephone interview, 13 December 1999.

41. *Playthings*, "Jig Saws," February 1933, p. 40.

42. Taylor Atkinson, "Adult Games and Puzzles," *Geyer's Stationer*, March 1933, p. 20.

43. *The Upson Circle*, "Upson Sells Tuco Puzzle and Chemical Subsidiaries," January–March 1971; *New York Times*, "Cut-Out Puzzles Keep Plant Busy," January 15, 1933, p. 12; Roger Slattery, Amherst, New York, Interview, 13 June 1991.

44. Chris McCann, "Vintage Jigsaw Puzzles," *Warman's Today's Collector*, January 1999, pp. 33–34.

45. *Toys and Novelties, op. cit.*, p. 33.

46. *Toy World*, "Puzzles Still Strong in Denver," April 1933, p. 62.

47. *New York Times*, "Tax Jig Saws as Sporting Goods," February 14, 1933, p. 17.

48. *Lewiston* (Maine) *Evening Journal*, "Tax Blight Hits Local Jig-Saw Puzzle Makers," March 4, 1933, p. 5.

49. Manufacturers' Liquidating Corp., "Jig Saw Puzzles as Your Fall Premium," *Premium Practice*, September 1933, p. 54.

50. *Playthings*, "Jig Saw Puzzles Are Back Again," March 1934, p. 79; "Puzzles Proving Popular," January 1937, p. 78.

CHAPTER 5

1. For extensive illustrated histories of toys and games during World War II, see Jack Matthews, *Toys Go to War*, Missoula (Montana: Pictorial Histories Publishing Company, 1994) and Gejus Van Diggele, "Games and Puzzles that Survived World War II," *Het Spel* No. 1, 1993, pp. 4–22 (translated from the Dutch by Iris Maher). Portions of this section come from Anne D. Williams, "War and Pieces," *Collector*, November 2001, pp. 23–28.

2. *Playthings*, "Jig Saws: They Were a Craze Ten Years Ago—Is Another in the Making?" April 1943, p. 34.

3. *Life*, "Troops on the Move," December 29, 1941, pp. 22–23.

4. Janet Jones, "One Woman's War Contribution: Her Jig-Saw Puzzles Entertain Men Sailing America's Submarines," *Boston Evening Globe*, June 27, 1942.

5. *New York Times*, "Jigsaw Puzzles Popular," June 18, 1945.

6. *Business Week*, "Jigsaw Puzzles Go Full Circle," July 10, 1965, p. 70; see also *Time*, "New Jag in Jigsaws," March 26, 1965, p. 67.

7. Katherine and Robert Lewin, Old Greenwich, Connecticut, Interview, 16 May 2003.

8. *Business Week, op. cit.*

9. Rachel Carson, *Silent Spring* (Boston: Houghton Mifflin, 1962).

10. Marla A. Baker, et al. "Save our Springboks!" www.petitiononline.com/bokunite/petition.html, 2002–03 (accessed on September 23, 2003).

11. Herbert Kavet, Waltham, Massachusetts, Telephone interview, 16 September 2003.

12. Ibid.

13. Connie Singer, "Front or Back, Prof. Sam Savage's Laser-Cut Schmuzzles Make Jigsaw Puzzlers Go to Pieces," *People*, June 2, 1980, p. 71.

14. Sara L. Wykes, "Stanford Professor to Market His Brain Teaser on TV," *San Jose Mercury News*, December 4, 2003.

15. *New England Business*, "A Perfect Fit," April 1989, pp. 33–39; Mary Ann Lombard, West Hartford, Connecticut, Telephone interview, 22 September 2003.

16. Carol Hall, "Puzzled Folks Can't Seem to Win Warren Holland's $100,000 Prize," *Wall Street Journal*, March 7, 1984, p. 1; Kiley Armstrong, "Diabolical Clues Puzzle Even Some Puzzle-Solvers," *Associated Press*, April 16, 1985.

17. *New York Times*, "The Jigsaw Puzzle Goes Vertical," October 22, 1992, p. C3.

18. Paul Delean, "Success Is Puzzling," *Montreal Gazette*, November 30, 1998, p. E1; Katherine Wilton, "3-D Puzzle Master," *Montreal Gazette*, September 27, 1993, p. F3; Jean Benoît Nadeau, "Puzzle Palaces," *Report on Business Magazine*, December 1995, pp. 92–98.

19. Paul Delean, "Wrebbit Picks Up Pieces After Losing Partners," *Montreal Gazette*, October 29, 2003, p. B1.

20. Carol Glazer, Watertown, Massachusetts, Telephone interview, 29 September 2003.

21. Don Scott, Buffalo, New York, Interview, 14 June 1991; Jerry Sullivan, "Jigsaw Junkies," *Buffalo News Magazine*, May 31, 1992, pp. 6–9.

CHAPTER 6

1. The sections on Par draw extensively from interviews with these people who graciously shared their memories of Par Company Ltd.: Francis Q. Ware, New York, Interview, 14 January 1981; Elizabeth Carlhian, Concord, Massachusetts, Interview, 18 June 2001; Jack Donahue, Bayside, New York, Telephone interview, 6 April 1996; Margaret Gallagher, Lindenhurst, New York, Telephone interviews, 12 July 2002 and 29 October 2002; and John Madden, Wantagh, New York, Telephone interview,

5 July 2002. They also rely on several comprehensive articles: Meyer Berger, "Jig Saw," *Good Housekeeping*, August 1944, pp. 24, 161–163; Sonny Kleinfield, "A Par Puzzle Isn't Easy to Assemble—Or Easy to Pay For," *Wall Street Journal*, July 27, 1972, p. 1; *Life*, "Speaking of Pictures . . . These Have Been Cut into Unusual Jigsaw Puzzles," July 10, 1944, pp. 12–14; *Sales Management*, "Jigsawmania," Vol. 47, No. 4, August 15, 1940, pp. 2–4. Finally, dozens of owners of Par puzzles have generously supplied information about their puzzles and their interactions with Par, with special help coming from Bob Armstrong, the late Anna Boardman, Pinney Deupree, Pagey Elliott, Robert L. Fisher, Peggy Mithoefer, Jim Phelan, and Annabelle Thompson. These sections first appeared in Anne D. Williams, "Making Par: Puzzles for the Rich and Famous," *Game and Puzzle Collectors Quarterly* 3:4, December 2002, pp. 6–15.

2. Par Company Ltd. Brochure, "Par Presents" (New York, circa 1935).

3. Sidney Fields, "Cheaper Than Doctors," *New York Daily News*, September 26, 1967.

4. George Ortman, "Artists' Games," *Art in America*, November–December 1969, pp. 69–77.

5. Robert L. Fisher, Sharon, Connecticut, Telephone interview, 18 September 1994.

6. *New Yorker*, "The Talk of the Town," December 28, 1946, pp. 15–16.

7. Anna Boardman, Amherst, New Hampshire, Correspondence with author, 27 July 1991.

8. *Life, op. cit.*; *Sports Illustrated*, "Shopwalk," August 16, 1971, p. M2; Pamela Knight, "Gamy Days Ahead," *Sports Illustrated*, November 22, 1965, pp. 72–77.

9. *New Yorker, op. cit.*

10. Par Company Ltd., *op. cit.*

11. Enid Nemy, "Boom in Jigsaw Puzzles: Three Pieces or Enough to Fill a Billiard Table," *New York Times*, December 24, 1966.

12. Fields, *op. cit.*

13. Information about Arthur Gallagher comes from Margaret Gallagher, Lindenhurst, New York, Telephone interviews, 12 July 2002 and 29 October 2002; John Madden, Wantagh, New York, Telephone interview, 5 July 2002; and Anna Quindlen, "The Jigsaw to End All Puzzles," *New York Times*, January 19, 1978, pp. 19, 22.

14. Kleinfield, *op. cit.*

15. The section on Stave is based on these sources: Steve Richardson, Stave Puzzles, Norwich, Vermont, Telephone interviews, 29 January 2001, 7 February 2001, and 11

November 2003; numerous Stave Puzzles Inc. catalogs; Ann Reynolds, "A Former Fat Man Puzzles Over Losing Weight," *Rutland* (Vermont) *Daily Herald*, January 15, 1981; Richard Wolkomir, "The 'Rolls-Royce of Puzzles' Drives Its Fans Round the Bend," *Smithsonian*, May 1990, pp. 103–112; John Grossmann, "Bits and Pieces," *USAir Magazine*, May 1992, pp. 64–71, 110. Portions of this section appeared earlier in Anne D. Williams, "Pieces of History: Steve Richardson and Stave Puzzles," *Game and Puzzle Collectors Quarterly* 2:1, March 2001, pp. 8–11.

16. Philip W. Shenon, "So You Must Have a Spiffy Hand-Sewn Ostrich-Skin Jacket?" *Wall Street Journal*, August 21, 1980, p. 1.

17. Sources for Elms Puzzles include Betsy Stuart, Elms Puzzles, Harrison, Maine, Interviews, 3 July 1988 and 26 May 2001; Nancy Bullet, "The Cutting Edge: Puzzle Maker Puts Together Business Savvy, Love of Jigsaw," *Lewiston* (Maine) *Sunday*, August 25, 1991, pp. 1F, 10F; *People*, "No Easy Pieces," December 11, 1995, pp. 137–139; Wayne Curtis, "Going to Pieces," *House Beautiful*, December 1998, p. 56.

18. Sources for J. C. Ayer puzzles include James C. Ayer, Salem, Massachusetts, Interviews 21 October 1987 and 25 July 1995; *Salem* (Massachusetts) *Evening News*, "Fitting Pieces of a Puzzle," November 3, 1989; Mac Daniel, "He's Got It Figured Out," *Boston Sunday Globe*, July 11, 1999, North Weekly section, p. 9.

19. Mark G. Cappitella, "The History of how MGC's Custom Made Jigsaw Puzzles Became Established," www.mgcpuzzles.com/mgcpuzzles/history.html (accessed on November 14, 2003).

20. *Print*, "Mini-Portfolios," September–October 1991, pp. 124–126.

21. Steve Richardson, Stave Puzzles, Norwich, Vermont, Telephone interview, 11 November 2003.

CHAPTER 7

1. For a general discussion of advertising, see Roland Marchand, *Advertising the American Dream* (Berkeley: University of California Press, 1985). W. B. Edwards, "That Little Extra Something that Clinches the Order," *Printers' Ink Monthly*, October 1932, pp. 35, 70, covers advertising premiums. Many advertising jigsaw puzzles are illustrated in Don Friedman, "Advertising Jigsaw Puzzles," *Past Times* 11:3, 2002, pp. 1, 3–20, and Harry L. Rinker, "Advertising Puzzles of the Depression Era," *Collectors' Showcase* 10:4, June 1990, pp. 18, 20–23, 26–29.

2. *Novelty News*, "Jig-Saw Puzzles as Premiums," April 1933, p. 47.

3. Frank Gonda, "How 'Picture-Puzzles' Stopped 'Price-Panic,' " *Display World*, January 1933, pp. 14–15. Gonda was a vice-president at Einson-Freeman, the largest producer of advertising puzzles in the 1930s.

4. Herbert Brean, "The Box-Top Business," *Life*, March 14, 1949, pp. 127–132; Stanley M. Ulanoff, *Advertising in America* (New York: Hastings House, 1977).

5. Donna C. Kaonis, "Hood's Sahr-sa-pa-ril'-a," *Collector's Showcase* 9:4, June 1989, p. 46.

6. Peckham, Richard T. "Picture-Puzzle," patent no. 950,951 (Washington, D.C.: U.S. Patent and Trademark Office, March 1, 1910).

7. *Voice of the Victor*, "A New Game in Town! Victor Puzzles," July 1922, p. 124.

8. The other three ideas submitted by Einson-Freeman vice-president N. Joseph Leigh were: a leatherette kit with samples of other Lambert products; a nail brush; and a disk chart of state capitals, populations, and facts. For more information see *Business Week*, "Jig-Saw Jag," January 18, 1933, p. 8, and Anne D. Williams, "Einson-Freeman: Depression 'House of Fads,' " *Game Times*, No. 32, April 1997, pp. 4–16.

9. *Advertising Age*, "Jig-Saw Puzzle Use Increasing," February 25, 1933, p. 6.

10. *Premium Practice*, "After the Jig-Saw, What?" July 1933, p. 34.

11. For more information on radio premiums and their designers, see Tom Tumbusch, *Illustrated Radio Premium Catalog and Price Guide* (Dayton, Ohio: Tomart Publications, 1989).

12. Darryl and Roxana Marie Matter, "McKesson's Puzzle Contests . . . 1933," *Antique Trader Weekly*, September 9, 1987, pp. 84–85.

13. *New York Times*, "An Absolut Puzzle: Jigsaw Ad for Vodka," February 12, 1991, p. D-17.

CHAPTER 8

1. *People*, "The Decorations All Go Together in Charley Lang's House of Puzzles, Where Each Piece Is One in a Million," November 28, 1988, p. 117.

2. For analyses of these questions, see Werner Muensterberger, *Collecting: An Unruly Passion* (Princeton, New Jersey: Princeton University Press, 1994); Russell W. Belk, *Collecting in a Consumer Society* (New York: Routledge, 1995); Douglas and Elizabeth Rigby, *Lock, Stock and Barrel* (Philadelphia: J. B. Lippincott, 1944); and Susan Cornell Poskanzer and Paul Harvey, *The Superduper Collector* (Mahwah, New Jersey: Troll Associates, 1986).

3. Armstrong, Bob, "Impact of eBay," *Game and Puzzle Collectors Quarterly* 1:4, December 2000, pp. 25–27.

4. Joel Steinfeldt, "Piecing It Back Together," *Pekin* (Illinois) *Daily Times*, July 15, 1995, p. C1.

5. For a good handbook of oral history techniques, see Willa K. Baum, *Oral History for the Local Historical Society*, third edition (Nashville, Tennessee: American Association for State and Local History, 1987).

6. Quoted in Karen K. Marshall, " 'Twas a Puzzlement in Athens, Ohio," *St. Louis Globe Democrat Magazine*, October 8–9, 1983, p. 6

CHAPTER 9

1. Michael Mandato, NPD Group, Port Washington, New York, Telephone interview, 6 June 2002.

2. Bill Van Siclen, "Pieces of the Fashion Puzzle," *Providence Journal*, May 22, 2003, p. L-25

3. "De Zichtbare Dood," *Ooit* 1, 1995, p. 9 (translated from the Dutch by Geert Bekkering).

4. Anne D. Williams, "Puzzles in Films," *Game and Puzzle Collectors Quarterly* 3:2, June 2002, pp. 10–13.

5. "Last Piece of Jigsaw in Place," *Science* 256, 24 April 1992, p. 439.

6. Adam Pertman, "Prosecution Starts with a Swipe at Fuhrman," *Boston Globe*, September 27, 1995, p. 3.

7. Georges Perec, *Life: A User's Manual*, translated from the French by David Bellos (Boston: David R. Godine, 1987); Shel Silverstein, *The Missing Piece* (New York: Harper & Row, 1976). See also Shel Silverstein, *The Missing Piece Meets the Big O* (New York, Harper & Row, 1981); David F. Birchman, *Jigsaw Jackson*, illustrated by Daniel San Souci (New York: Lothrop, Lee & Shepard, 1996).

8. Reverend Joseph Matthews, *Harry Crawford: How He Learned to Make His Own Dissected Maps and Picture Puzzles* (London: Suter and Co., 1873), p. 53.

9. John Stokes, "The Puzzle Tree," http://www.custompuzzlecraft.com/PuzzleTree/puzzletree.html (accessed on March 15, 2004).

10. Michael Auping, "Songs of Innocence," *Art in America*, January 1987, pp. 118–126, 147; Patricia C. Johnson, "Souza a Master of Composed Chaos," *Houston Chronicle*, March 29, 2003, p. 9; Alfred Hicking, "Mappin Open," *The Guardian*, August 28, 2002, p. 21.

11. Peter Meyer, "Jigsaw Management," *Canadian Business Review* 22:4, Winter 1995; Mark Henricks, "Pièce De Résistance," *Entrepreneur*, February 1994, pp. 44–47; John Mariotti, "Jigsaw-Puzzle Lessons," *Industry Week* 246:1, January 6, 1997, p. 29; Dick Shaw, "A Few Minutes in the Life of a Gracious Yoko Ono," *Bangor* (Maine) *Daily News*, May 20, 2003, p. C1.

12. Roger Boyes, "Swift Solution to Stasi's Jigsaw Puzzle of Secrets," *The Times of London*, June 17, 2003.

13. The latest techniques and a summary of earlier articles appear in Feng-Hui Yao and Gui-Feng Shao, "A Shape and Image Merging Technique to Solve Jigsaw Puzzles," *Pattern Recognition Letters* 24 (2003), pp. 1819–1835.

14. Catherine Zandonella, "Giotto's Giant Jigsaw," *New Scientist*, June 30, 2001, p. 24.

15. Anne Ross, Lauri Puzzles, Phillips-Avon, Maine, Telephone interview, 19 March 2004.

16. Ken Auletta, *World War 3.0: Microsoft and Its Enemies* (New York: Random House, 2001), p. 153.

APPENDIX A

1. Examples can be found in most woodworking magazines as well as in books such as Patrick and Patricia Spielman, *Scroll Saw Puzzle Patterns* (New York: Sterling, 1988) and Tony and June Burns, *Scroll Saw Art Puzzles* (East Petersburg, Pennsylvania: Fox Chapel Publishing, 1999).

2. These instructions are adapted from Anne D. Williams, "Puzzling Pursuits," *Country Home*, December 1994, pp. 34, 36. See also Anne D. Williams, "Jigsaw Puzzles," *Fine Woodworking*, No. 88, May/June 1991, pp. 52–55; Evan Kern, *Making Wooden Jigsaw Puzzles* (Mechanicsburg, Pennsylvania: Stackpole Books, 1996); and R. J. De Cristoforo, *The Jigsaw / Scroll Saw Book* (Blue Ridge Summit, Pennsylvania: Tab Books, 1990).

3. For example, Carol Belanger Grafton, *Silhouettes: A Pictorial Archive of Varied Illustrations* (New York: Dover Publications, 1979).

4. George Ciesek, Graffiti Graphics, Victoria, British Columbia, Telephone interview, 9 June 2003.

5. James Leith, The Wentworth Wooden Jigsaw Company, Malmesbury, England, Correspondence with author, 19 January 2004.

6. Toy Industry Association, *The Official American International Toy Fair Directory* (New York: Toy Industry Association, 2004).

7. Michael Mandato, NPD Group, Port Washington, New York, Telephone interviews, 6 June 2002 and 11 June 2003.

8. Ibid.; *Playthings*, "Charting the Industry," January 1999, p. 24.

9. Ronda Tidrick, Warren Industries, Lafayette, Indiana, Telephone interview, 3 June 2003.

10. *Playthings, op. cit.*; Tidrick, *op. cit.*

11. Tidrick, *op. cit.*

12. Ibid.

13. Some useful references include: Brian Tinsman, *The Game Inventor's Guidebook* (Iola, Wisconsin: Krause Publications, 2002); Stephen Peek, *Game Plan: The Game Inventor's Handbook* (Whitehall, Virginia: Betterway Publications, 1987); Richard C. Levy and Ronald O. Weingartner, *The Toy and Game Inventor's Handbook* (Indianapolis: Alpha Books, 2003).

Selected Bibliography

Advertising Age. "Jig-Saw Puzzle Use Increasing." February 25, 1933, p. 6.

Amy, W. Lacey. "The Picture Puzzle." *Canadian Magazine*, March 1910, pp. 436–441.

Ariès, Philippe. *Centuries of Childhood.* New York: Random House, 1962.

Armstrong, Bob. "Jigsaw Puzzle Cutting Styles: A New Method of Classification." *Game Researchers' Notes* 25, February–May 1997, pp. 5581–5590.

———. "Impact of eBay." *Game and Puzzle Collectors Quarterly* 1:4, December 2000, pp. 25–27.

Armstrong, Kiley. "Diabolical Clues Puzzle Even Some Puzzle-Solvers." Associated Press, April 16, 1985.

Associated Press. "Taiwanese Claim Biggest Jigsaw Puzzle Record." June 28, 1998.

———. "Mexicans Piece Together Million Piece Jigsaw." July 30, 2003.

Aswell, James. "My New York." *Lewiston* (Maine) *Evening Journal*, January 19, 1933, p. 4.

Atkinson, Taylor. "Adult Games and Puzzles." *Geyer's Stationer*, March 1933, pp. 19–21.

Auletta, Ken. *World War 3.0: Microsoft and Its Enemies.* New York: Random House, 2001.

Auping, Michael. "Songs of Innocence." *Art in America*, January 1987, pp. 118–126, 147.

Ayer, James C. Salem, Massachusetts. Interviews, 21 October 1987 and 25 July 1995.

Baker, Marla A. et al. "Save our Springboks!" www.petitiononline.com/bokunite/petition.html, 2002–03. Accessed on September 23, 2003.

Barrett, Laurence I. "Alzheimer's and the Reagans." *NewChoices* July/August 1996, quoted in *Washingtonian*, September 1996, p. 48.

Barron, Marlene. "Three- and Four-Year-Olds Completing 150-piece Puzzles? Impossible!" *Young Children*, September 1999, pp. 10–11.

———. West Side Montessori School, New York, New York. Telephone interview, 4 February 2004.

Baum, L. Frank. *The Emerald City of Oz*. Chicago: Reilly & Britton, 1910.

Baum, Willa K. *Oral History for the Local Historical Society*. Third edition. Nashville, Tennessee: American Association for State and Local History, 1987.

Bekkering, Betsy and Geert. *Piece by Piece: A History of Jigsaw Puzzles in the Netherlands*. Translated from the Dutch by Geert Bekkering, Kay Curtis, and Felicity Whiteley. Amsterdam: Van Soeren & Co., 1988.

Belk, Russell W. *Collecting in a Consumer Society*. New York: Routledge, 1995.

Bello, Antoine. *The Missing Piece*. Translated from the French by Helen Stevenson. Orlando, Florida: Harcourt, Inc., 2003.

Berger, Meyer. "Jig Saw." *Good Housekeeping*, August 1944, pp. 24, 161–163.

Birchman, David F. *Jigsaw Jackson*. Illustrated by Daniel San Souci. New York: Lothrop, Lee & Shepard, 1996.

Boardman, Anna. Amherst, New Hampshire. Correspondence with author, 27 July 1991.

Boston Sunday Herald. "Merely to Rest the Tired Business Man." June 22, 1919, p. 7.

Boyes, Roger. "Swift Solution to Stasi's Jigsaw Puzzle of Secrets," *The Times of London*, June 17, 2003.

Bradley Co., Milton. "You, Too, Can Make Big Profits with This Special Assortment for Rental Libraries." *Playthings*, December 1932, back cover.

Brean, Herbert. "The Box-Top Business." *Life*, March 14, 1949, pp. 127–132.

Brewer, Edward. Skaneateles, New York. Telephone interview, 27 August 1994.

Brewer, William. Cortland, New York. Telephone interview, 27 August 1994.

Brophy, Richard. "America, the Beautiful Jigsaw Puzzle." *American Heritage* 41:8, December 1990, pp. 102–107.

Brown, Orlando. Letter to Mason Brown, 17 March 1811. http://www.libertyhall.org/Family%20Letter%20Writing1.htm accessed on December 13, 2003.

Browning, James L. Montague, New Jersey. Telephone interview, 8 September 1996.

Bullet, Nancy. "Puzzle Maker Puts Together Business Savvy, Love of Jigsaw." *Lewiston* (Maine) *Sunday*, August 25, 1991, pp. 1F, 10F.

Burkeman, Oliver. "Inside Story: Who Wants to Ruin a Millionaire?" *The Guardian*, October 30, 2000, p. 7.

Burns, Tony and June. *Scroll Saw Art Puzzles*. East Petersburg, Pennsylvania: Fox Chapel Publishing, 1999.

Business Week. "Jig-Saw Jag." January 18, 1933, p. 8.

————. "Jigsaw Puzzles Go Full Circle." July 10, 1965, pp. 68–70.

Caplan, Frank and Theresa. *The Power of Play*. Garden City: Anchor Press/Doubleday, 1973.

Cappitella, Mark G. "The History of how MGC's Custom Made Jigsaw Puzzles Became Established," http://www.mgcpuzzles.com/mgcpuzzles/history.html. Accessed on November 14, 2003.

Carlhian, Elizabeth. Concord, Massachusetts. Interview, 18 June 2001.

Carson, Rachel. *Silent Spring*. Boston: Houghton Mifflin, 1962.

Ciesek, George. Graffiti Graphics, Victoria, British Columbia. Telephone interview, 9 June 2003.

Clapp, Ruth. Newington, Connecticut. Telephone interview, 22 March 1997.

Clark, Gregory. "Farm wages and living standards in the industrial revolution: England, 1670–1869." *Economic History Review* 54:3 (2001), pp. 477–505.

Cleveland Plain Dealer. "Her Royal Puzzle Will Fit Mrs. S. In." December 3, 1936, p. 9.

Copeland, George H. "The Country Is Off on a Jig-Saw Jag." *New York Times Magazine*, February 12, 1933, pp. 8, 16.

Corson, Helen Fiss. Rosemont, Pennsylvania. Interview, 15 June 1989.

Curtis, Wayne. "Going to Pieces." *House Beautiful*, December 1998, p. 56.

Danesi, Marcel. *The Puzzle Instinct: The Meaning of Puzzles in Human Life*. Bloomington: Indiana University Press, 2002.

Daniel, Mac. "He's Got It Figured Out." *Boston Sunday Globe*, July 11, 1999, North Weekly section, p. 9.

David, Linda (ed.). *The Lilly Library: Through the Eyes of Friends*. Bloomington, Indiana: Friends of the Lilly Library, 2001.

Davidson, Ellis A. *Pretty Arts for the Employment of Leisure Hours: A Book for Ladies*. London: Chapman and Hall, 1879.

De Cristoforo, R. J. *The Jigsaw / Scroll Saw Book*. Blue Ridge Summit, Pennsylvania: Tab Books, 1990.

Delean, Paul. "Success is Puzzling." *Montreal Gazette*, November 30, 1998, p. E1.

———. "Wrebbit Picks Up Pieces after Losing Partners," *Montreal Gazette*, October 29, 2003, p. B1.

Delta Specialty Co. *What Others Have Done with "Delta" Tools in Hobby, Spare Time and Production Work.* Milwaukee: Delta, circa 1931.

Donahue, Jack. Bayside, New York. Telephone interview, 6 April 1996.

du Pont, Irénée Jr. Montchanin, Delaware. Telephone interview, 13 December 1999.

Edwards, W. B. "That Little Extra Something that Clinches the Order." *Printers' Ink Monthly*, October 1932, pp. 35, 70.

Elkins, James. *Why Are Our Pictures Puzzles?* New York: Routledge, 1999.

Erikson, Erik H. *Toys and Reasons.* New York: W. W. Norton & Co., 1977.

Fields, Sidney. "Cheaper Than Doctors." *New York Daily News*, September 26, 1967.

Fisher, Robert L. Sharon, Connecticut. Telephone interview, 18 September 1994.

Fitch, George. "Picture Puzzles." *Collier's National Weekly*, November 20, 1909, p. 23.

Ford, Betty A. Fayette City, Pennsylvania. Telephone interview, 23 June 2003.

Fortune. "The Mechanics of a Craze." April 1933, p. 76.

Fox, John J. "Parker Pride: Memories of Working Days at Parker Brothers," *Essex Institute Historical Collections* 123:2, April 1987, pp. 150–181.

Frentz, Edward Williston. "Seizing the Chance, II: The Picture-Puzzle 'Craze.' " *Youth's Companion*, October 29, 1908, p. 543.

Friedman, Don. "Advertising Jigsaw Puzzles." *Past Times* 11:3, 2002, pp. 1, 3–20.

Gagnon, Eva. Salem, Massachusetts. Interviews, 7 June 1989; 10 March 1990; 15 March 1990; 12 September 1993.

Gallagher, Margaret. Lindenhurst, New York. Telephone interviews, 12 July 2002 and 29 October 2002.

Garrison, Charlotte Gano. *Permanent Play Materials for Young Children.* New York: Charles Scribner's Sons, 1923.

Garrison, Charlotte Gano and Thomas F. Hogan. *Reminiscences of Charlotte Garrison.* New York: Oral History Research Office, Columbia University, 1969.

Gelber, Steven M. *Hobbies.* New York: Columbia University Press, 1999.

Gilboy, Elizabeth W. *Wages in Eighteenth Century England.* Cambridge: Harvard University Press, 1934.

Glazer, Carol. Ceaco, Inc., Watertown, Massachusetts. Telephone interview, 29 September 2003.

Gonda, Frank. "How 'Picture-Puzzles' Stopped 'Price-Panic.'" *Display World*, January 1933, pp. 14–15.

Goodrich, A. T. Catalogs. New York: 1818, 1926.

———. Advertisement in the *Evening Post*, New York: January 7, 1818.

Grafton, Carol Belanger. *Silhouettes: A Pictorial Archive of Varied Illustrations*. New York: Dover Publications, 1979.

Grossmann, John. "Bits and Pieces." *USAir Magazine*, May 1992, pp. 64–71, 110.

Guinness World Records 2004. New York: Guinness World Records Ltd., 2003.

Gwyn, M. K. "The Healy Puzzle Picture and Defective Aliens." *Medical Record*, January 31, 1914, pp. 197–199.

Hall, Carol. "Puzzled Folks Can't Seem to Win Warren Holland's $100,000 Prize." *Wall Street Journal*, March 7, 1984, p. 1.

Hannas, Linda. *The English Jigsaw Puzzle 1760–1890*. London: Wayland, 1972.

———. *The Jigsaw Book*. New York: Dial Press, 1981.

Haskell, Elizabeth Louise. "The Revolt of Jepson." *Harper's Bazar*, July 1909, pp. 658–663.

Hearn, Michael Patrick. *McLoughlin Brothers Publishers*. New York: Justin G. Schiller, Ltd., 1980.

Henricks, Mark. "Pièce De Résistance." *Entrepreneur*, February 1994, pp. 44–47.

Hewitt, Karen and Louise Roomet (eds.). *Educational Toys in America: 1800 to the Present*. Burlington, Vermont: University of Vermont, 1979.

Hicking, Alfred. "Mappin Open." *The Guardian*, August 28, 2002, p. 21.

Himmelberg, Michele. "Mickey—The Modest Cartoon Character Grew into a Multibillion-Dollar Brand." *Orange County Register*, November 18, 2003.

Hollingsworth, F. N. "Boston Going Strong for Jig Saw Puzzles." *Toys and Novelties*, December 1932, p. 58.

Houghton, Mary A. "Raised Puzzle for the Blind," patent no. 941,680. Washington, D.C.: U.S. Patent and Trademark Office, November 30, 1909.

Japan Economic Newswire. "Jigsaw Puzzles Popular with Lima Hostages." April 10, 1997.

Johnson, Don. "Sniping: Love It or Hate It Everyone Has an Opinion." *Antique Week*, November 24, 2003, p. 6.

Johnson, Patricia C. "Souza a Master of Composed Chaos." *Houston Chronicle*, March 29, 2003, p. 9.

Jones, David. *Toy with the Idea*. Norfolk, England: Norfolk Museums Service, 1980.

Jones, Janet. "One Woman's War Contribution: Her Jig-Saw Puzzles Entertain Men Sailing America's Submarines." *Boston Evening Globe*, June 27, 1942.

Kaonis, Donna C. "Hood's Sahr-sa-pa-ril'-a," *Collector's Showcase* 9:4, June 1989, pp. 41–46.

———. "I Waz De One Who Started All Dis Funny Biznes!" *Collector's Showcase* 1:4, March/April 1982, pp. 9–13.

Kavet, Herbert. Waltham, Massachusetts. Telephone interview, 16 September 2003.

Kern, Alice E. Portland, Maine. Interview, 24 April 1990.

Kern, Evan. *Making Wooden Jigsaw Puzzles*. Mechanicsburg, Pennsylvania: Stackpole Books, 1996.

Kleeman, Richard P. "Dad Said He Could Have Made Judy's Toy Better, and He Did." *Minneapolis Tribune*, September 30, 1956, pp. 1, 5.

Kleinfield, Sonny. "A Par Puzzle Isn't Easy to Assemble—Or Easy to Pay For." *Wall Street Journal*, July 27, 1972, p. 1.

Knight, Pamela. "Gamy Days Ahead." *Sports Illustrated*, November 22, 1965, pp. 72–77.

Kramer, Rita. *Maria Montessori*. New York: G. P. Putnam's Sons, 1976.

Leith, James. The Wentworth Wooden Jigsaw Company, Malmesbury, England. Correspondence with author, 19 January 2004.

Levy, Richard C., and Ron Weingartner. *The Toy and Game Inventor's Handbook*. Indianapolis: Alpha Books, 2003.

Lewin, Katherine and Robert. Old Greenwich, Connecticut. Interview, 16 May 2003.

Lewiston (Maine) *Evening Journal*. "Would Puzzle Prisoners." February 16, 1933, p. 5.

———. "Tax Blight Hits Local Jig-Saw Puzzle Makers." March 4, 1933, p. 5.

Life. "Troops on the Move." December 29, 1941, pp. 22–23.

———. "Speaking of Pictures . . . These Have Been Cut into Unusual Jigsaw Puzzles." July 10, 1944, pp. 12–14.

Locke, John. *Some Thoughts Concerning Education*. Edited by John W. and Jean S. Yolton. Oxford: Clarendon Press, 1989.

Lombard, Mary Ann. West Hartford, Connecticut. Telephone interview, 22 September 2003.

Madden, John. Wantagh, New York. Telephone interview, 5 July 2002.

Maldonado, Nancy S. "Puzzles: A Pathetically Neglected, Commonly Available Resource." *Young Children*, May 1996, pp. 4–10.

Mandato, Michael. NPD Group, Port Washington, New York. Telephone interviews, 6 June 2002 and 11 June 2003.

Manning, Harry. Salem, Massachusetts. Interviews, 23 January 1992 and 11 September 1993.

Manufacturers' Liquidating Corp. "Jig Saw Puzzles as Your Fall Premium." *Premium Practice*, September 1933, p. 54.

Marchand, Roland. *Advertising the American Dream*. Berkeley: University of California Press, 1985.

Mariotti, John. "Jigsaw-Puzzle Lessons." *Industry Week* 246:1, January 6, 1997, p. 29.

Marshall, Karen K. " 'Twas a Puzzlement in Athens, Ohio." *St. Louis Globe-Democrat Magazine*, October 8–9, 1983, pp. 5–6, 12, 16.

Martin, Henry A. Jr. Rochester, New York. Correspondence with author, 24 September 1994.

Martin, Pete. "Game Maker." *Saturday Evening Post*, October 6, 1945, pp. 26–27, 48–54.

Matter, Darryl, and Roxana Marie. "McKesson's Puzzle Contests . . . 1933." *Antique Trader Weekly*, September 9, 1987, pp. 84–85.

Matthews, Jack. *Toys Go to War*. Missoula, Montana: Pictorial Histories Publishing Company, 1994.

Matthews, Reverend Joseph (Uncle Joseph). *Harry Crawford: How He Learned to Make His Own Dissected Maps and Picture Puzzles*. London: Suter and Co., 1873.

McCann, Chris. "Building Your Own Miniature Art Gallery with Depression Jigsaw Puzzles." *Antique Trader*, January 3, 1990, pp. 50–53.

———. *Master Pieces: The Art History of Jigsaw Puzzles*. Portland, Oregon: Collectors Press, 1998.

———. "Vintage Jigsaw Puzzles," *Warman's Today's Collector*, January 1999, pp. 31–35.

McCaskey, J. P. Puzzle entitled "Lincoln Lessons in Graphic Geography." Lancaster, Pennsylvania: 1903.

Meehan, Thomas. "Creative (and Mostly Upper-Middle-Class) Playthings." *Saturday Review*, December 16, 1972, pp. 42–47.

Meyer, Peter. "Jigsaw Management," *Canadian Business Review* 22:4, Winter 1995.

Monckton, Christopher. "How I Bet the House on a Puzzle and Lost." *Sunday Times of London*, November 12, 2000.

Montessori, Maria. *Dr. Montessori's Own Handbook*. Introduction by Nancy McCormick Rambusch. New York: Schocken Books, 1965.

Morris, Tim. "Puzzlement." *The American Scholar*, 67:4, Autumn 1998, pp. 113–123.

Muensterberger, Werner. *Collecting: An Unruly Passion*. Princeton: Princeton University Press, 1994.

Nadeau, Jean Benoît. "Puzzle Palaces." *Report on Business Magazine*, December 1995, pp. 92–98.

Nemy, Enid. "Boom in Jigsaw Puzzles: Three Pieces or Enough to Fill a Billiard Table." *New York Times*, December 24, 1966.

New England Business. "A Perfect Fit." April 1989, pp. 33–39.

New York Times. "New Puzzle Menaces the City's Sanity." May 24, 1908, section 2, p. 7.

———. "Stick to It, and You May Solve a Puzzle Picture." July 26, 1908, section 5, p. 11.

———. "Boston's Latest Contribution to Cultured Fads—Puzzle Pictures," November 8, 1908, p. SM8.

———. "Hoovers Ascend Peak Near Camp," August 4, 1930, p. 3.

———. "Cut-Out Puzzles Keep Plant Busy." January 15, 1933, p. 12.

———. "Tax Jig Saws as Sporting Goods." February 14, 1933, p. 17.

———. "Uses Jig-Saw Puzzles for Nerves." March 4, 1933, p. 15.

———. "Jig-Saw Game Is Carrying On." December 13, 1936, Section XII, p. 18.

———. "Jigsaw Puzzles Popular." June 18, 1945.

———. "An Absolut Puzzle: Jigsaw Ad for Vodka." February 12, 1991, p. D-17.

———. "The Jigsaw Puzzle Goes Vertical." October 22, 1992, p. C3.

New Yorker. "The Talk of the Town." December 28, 1946, pp. 15–16.

Newman, M. Advertisements in the *Daily Advertiser*. Boston: December 24, 1817 and December 23, 1818.

Novelty News. "Jig-Saw Puzzles as Premiums." April 1933, pp. 17, 46–50.

Olinger, Nellie. "Puzzle Postal Card," patent no. 939,074. Washington, D.C.: U.S. Patent and Trademark Office, November 2, 1909.

Ooit, "De Zichtbare Dood," Vol. 1, 1995, p. 1 (translated from the Dutch by Geert Bekkering).

Orbanes, Philip E. *The Game Makers: The Story of Parker Brothers from Tiddledy Winks to Trivial Pursuit*. Boston: Harvard Business School Publishing Corporation, 2004.

Ortman, George. "Artists' Games." *Art in America*, November–December 1969, pp. 69–77.

The Outlook. "The Spectator." May 2, 1908, pp. 17–18.

Palmer, Kelvin. *The Collector's Guide to Cluster Puzzles of the 1960s and 1970s*. Riverwoods, Illinois: A. Z. Plerp Co., 2003.

Palmer, Mary-Lou Jones. Tucson, Arizona. Correspondence with author, 8 October 1992.

Par Company Ltd. brochure. "Par Presents." New York, circa 1935.

Parker Brothers Inc. *90 Years of Fun*. Salem, Massachusetts: Parker Brothers, 1973.

Peckham, Richard T. "Picture-Puzzle," patent no. 950,951. Washington, D.C.: U.S. Patent and Trademark Office, March 1, 1910.

Peek, Stephen. *Game Plan: The Game Inventor's Handbook*. Whitehall, Virginia: Betterway Publications, 1987.

People. "The Decorations All Go Together in Charley Lang's House of Puzzles, Where Each Piece is One in a Million." November 28, 1988, p. 117.

———. "No Easy Pieces." December 11, 1995, pp. 137–139.

Perec, Georges. *Life: A User's Manual*. Translated from the French by David Bellos. Boston: David R. Godine, 1987.

Perry, L. Day, and T. K. Webster Jr. *Jigsaw Puzzles—And How to Make 'Em*. Chicago: Mack Publications, 1933.

Pertman, Adam. "Prosecution Starts with a Swipe at Fuhrman." *Boston Globe*, September 27, 1995, p. 3.

Petrik, Paula. "The House That Parcheesi Built: Selchow & Righter Company." *Business History Review* 60, Autumn 1986, pp. 410–437.

Playthings. "Picture Puzzles." November 1908, p. 34.

———. "Fifth Avenue Toy Shop Mystery Puzzle Solved." March 1909, p. 54.

———. "Countess Festetics a Picture Puzzle Maker." May 1909, p. 65.

———. "Sunday at the Lloyds." October 1930, p. 4.

———. "More on Adult Games." December 1930, p. 55.

———. "Jig Saws." February 1933, pp. 39–40, 96–97.

———. "Selling Young and Old." April 1933, pp. 122–123.

———. "Will It Last?" April 1933, p. 128.

———. "Some Facts on Jigsawcracy." April 1933, p. 170.

———. "Jig Saw Puzzles are Back Again." March 1934, p. 79.

———. "Puzzles Proving Popular." January 1937, p. 78.

———. "Jig Saws: They Were a Craze Ten Years Ago—Is Another in the Making?" April 1943, pp. 34–35.

————. "Joseph K. Straus, 77, Dies." April 1957, p. 155.

————. "Charting the Industry." January 1999, p. 24.

Popular Mechanics. "The Lure of Puzzle Inventing." January 1935, pp. 20–23, 128A, 130A.

Popular Science Monthly. "How Jig-Saw Puzzles Are Made by the Million." April 1933, p. 29.

Poskanzer, Susan Cornell, and Paul Harvey. *The Superduper Collector.* Mahwah, New Jersey: Troll Associates, 1986.

Prater, Nancy. "Topsy Turvy Craze Makes Comeback." *Carthage Press,* August 9, 1988, p. 5.

Premium Practice. "After the Jig-Saw, What?" July 1933, pp. 15, 32–34.

Pride, Prudence. Advertisements. *Life,* November 19, 1908, p. 565 and December 3, 1908, p. 647.

Print. "Mini-Portfolios." September–October 1991, pp. 124–126.

Publishers' Weekly. "Customer's Choice." January 28, 1933, p. 376.

Pyle, Theodore. Unpublished letter to Gertrude Brinckle, November 16, 1943. In the Pyle Collection of the Historical Society of Delaware, Wilmington.

Quindlen, Anna. "The Jigsaw to End All Puzzles." *New York Times,* January 19, 1978, pp. 19, 22.

R. S. T. *Sorrento Wood-Carving.* Boston: Loring, 1869.

Recer, Paul. "Mind-Exercising Hobbies Can Help Protect the Brain Against Alzheimer's, Study Says." *St. Louis Post-Dispatch,* March 6, 2001, p. A7.

Reynolds, Ann. "A Former Fat Man Puzzles Over Losing Weight." *Rutland* (Vermont) *Daily Herald,* January 15, 1981.

Richardson, Margaret H. *The Sign of the Motor Car.* Dennis, Massachusetts: privately printed, 1926.

Richardson, Steve. Stave Puzzles, Norwich, Vermont. Telephone interviews, 29 January 2001; 7 February 2001; 11 November 2003.

Rigby, Douglas and Elizabeth. *Lock, Stock and Barrel.* Philadelphia: J. B. Lippincott, 1944.

Riley, Lorraine. Joplin, Missouri. Telephone interview, 9 September 1990.

Rinker, Harry L. "Advertising Puzzles of the Depression Era." *Collectors' Showcase* 10:4, June 1990, pp. 18, 20–23, 26–29.

Ross, Anne. Lauri Puzzles. Phillips-Avon, Maine. Telephone interview, 19 March 2004.

Russell, Nadine N. "Auburn Cutup." *Worcester* (Massachusetts) *Sunday Telegram,* December 27, 1970, Feature Parade section, cover, pp. 6–7.

Sabin, Francene and Louis. "An Irreverent History of Jigsaw Puzzles." *Lithopinion* 10:3, Fall 1975, pp. 14–19.

———. *The One, The Only, The Original Jigsaw Puzzle Book.* Chicago: Henry Regnery Co., 1977.

Salem (Massachusetts) *Evening News.* "Fitting Pieces of a Puzzle." November 3, 1989.

Sales Management. "Jigsawmania." Vol. 47, No. 4, August 15, 1940, pp. 2–4.

Sawyer, George A. *Fret-Sawing and Wood-Carving for Amateurs.* Boston: Lee and Shepard, 1875.

Science. "Last Piece of Jigsaw in Place." Vol. 256, 24 April 1992, p. 439.

Scott, Don. Buffalo, New York. Interview, 14 June 1991.

Screen Play Secrets. "Sunday at the Lloyds," July 1930. Quoted in *Playthings*, October 1930, p. 4.

Shaw, Dick. "A Few Minutes in the Life of a Gracious Yoko Ono." *Bangor* (Maine) *Daily News*, May 20, 2003, p. C1.

Shea, James J., and Charles Mercer. *It's All in the Game.* New York: G. P. Putnam's Sons, 1960.

Shefrin, Jill. *Neatly Dissected: John Spilsbury and Early Dissected Puzzles.* Los Angeles: Cotsen Occasional Press, 1999.

———. *Such Constant Affectionate Care.* Los Angeles: Cotsen Occasional Press, 2003.

Shenon, Philip W. "So You Must Have a Spiffy Hand-Sewn Ostrich-Skin Jacket?" *Wall Street Journal*, August 21, 1980, p. 1.

Sherwin, Mark, and Charles Lam Markmann. *One Week in March.* New York: G. P. Putnam's Sons, 1961.

Silverstein, Shel. *The Missing Piece.* New York: Harper & Row, 1976.

———. *The Missing Piece Meets the Big O.* New York: Harper & Row, 1981.

Singer, Connie. "Front or Back, Prof. Sam Savage's Laser-Cut Schmuzzles Make Jigsaw Puzzlers Go to Pieces."*People*, June 2, 1980, p. 71.

Singer, Jerome. Yale University, New Haven, Connecticut. Telephone interview, 18 June 2003.

Slattery, Roger. Amherst, New York. Interview. 13 June 1991.

Slocum, Jerry. *The Tangram Book.* New York: Sterling Publishing, 2003.

Sowell, Thomas. *The Einstein Syndrome: Bright Children Who Talk Late.* New York: Basic Books, 2001.

Spielman, Patrick and Patricia. *Scroll Saw Puzzle Patterns.* New York: Sterling, 1988.

Sports Illustrated. "Shopwalk." August 16, 1971, p. M2.

Stave Puzzles. *Puzzle Catalog 1995–1996.* Norwich, Vermont: Stave Puzzles, 1995.

Steinfeldt, Joel. "Piecing It Back Together." *Pekin* (Illinois) *Daily Times,* July 15, 1995, p. C1.

Sternberg, Robert J., and Janet E. Davidson. "The Mind of the Puzzler," *Psychology Today,* June 1982, pp. 37–44.

Stokes, John. "The Puzzle Tree." http://www.custompuzzlecraft.com/PuzzleTree/puzzletree.html (accessed on March 15, 2004).

Strater, Theodore G. "Adjustable Frame for Assembling Picture Puzzles," patent no. 932,512. Washington, D.C.: U.S. Patent and Trademark Office, August 31, 1909.

Straus, Amy. Jamaica, New York. Telephone interview, 27 August 1989.

Stuart, Betsy. Elms Puzzles, Harrison, Maine. Interviews, 3 July 1988 and 26 May 2001.

Sullivan, Jerry. "Jigsaw Junkies." *Buffalo News Magazine,* May 31, 1992, pp. 6–9.

Tide. "Jigsaw Jag," February 1933, pp. 7–9.

Tidrick, Ronda. Warren Industries, Lafayette, Indiana. Telephone interview, 3 June 2003.

Time. "Puzzle Profits," February 20, 1933, p. 41.

———. "New Jag in Jigsaws," March 26, 1965, p. 67.

Tinsman, Brian. *The Game Inventor's Guidebook.* Iola, Wisconsin: Krause Publications, 2002.

Town & Country. "Piece Work." December 1947, pp. 70–71.

Towne, Carroll A. Venice, Florida. Correspondence with author, 27 November 1986 and 7 January 1987.

Toy Industry Association. *The Official American International Toy Fair Directory.* New York: 2004.

Toy World. "Popularity of Adult Games Reaches New High." January 1932, p. 47.

———. "Reports Indicate Extent of Jigsaw Craze." April 1933, p. 60.

———. "Jig-Saw Jag." March 1933, p. 16.

———. "Puzzles Still Strong in Denver." April 1933, p. 62.

Toys and Novelties. "Jig-Saw Puzzles Make Safe Landing." August 1933, pp. 33–37.

Tumbusch, Tom. *Illustrated Radio Premium Catalog and Price Guide.* Dayton, Ohio: Tomart Publications, 1989.

Tyler, Tom. *British Jigsaw Puzzles of the Twentieth Century.* Shepton Beauchamp, England: Richard Dennis, 1997.

———. "1760s Jigsaw Puzzle Maps of Lady Charlotte Finch." *Game and Puzzle Collectors Quarterly* 1:3, September 2000, pp. 11–12.

Ulanoff, Stanley M. *Advertising in America*. New York: Hastings House, 1977.

U.S. Bureau of the Census. *Historical Statistics of the United States*. Washington, D.C.: U.S. Government Printing Office, 1975.

Upson Circle, The. "Upson Sells Tuco Puzzle and Chemical Subsidiaries." January–March 1971.

Van Diggele, Gejus. "Games and Puzzles that Survived World War II." *Het Spel* No. 1, 1993, pp. 4–22 (translated from the Dutch by Iris Maher).

VanDivert, William and Rita. "Past Teaching Aids in Jigsaw Puzzles." *Smithsonian*, August 1974, pp. 66–73.

Van Siclen, Bill. "Pieces of the Fashion Puzzle," *Providence Journal*, May 22, 2003, p. L-25.

Voice of the Victor. "A New Game in Town! Victor Puzzles." July 1922, pp. 123–124.

Walling, Morton C. "Jig-Saw Puzzles Are Easy to Make." *Popular Science Monthly*, March 1932, pp. 80, 115.

Ware, Francis Q. New York, New York. Interview, 14 January 1981.

Wayman, Dorothy G. "Pens and Puzzles Make Her Living." *Boston Evening Globe*, May 24, 1938.

Weber, Evelyn. "Play Materials in the Curriculum of Early Childhood." pp. 25–37 in *Educational Toys in America: 1800 to the Present*, edited by Karen Hewitt and Louise Roomet. Burlington, Vermont: University of Vermont, 1979.

Webster, Towner K. Jr. "Jig Saw Puzzles—How to Make 'Em." *Popular Homecraft*, September–October 1932, pp. 211–215.

———. "Advanced Jigsaw Puzzle Making." *Popular Homecraft*, January–February 1933, pp. 423–426.

Wiebé, Edward. *The Paradise of Childhood*. Milton Bradley (ed.). Springfield, Massachusetts: Milton Bradley Co., 1869.

Wilcox, Julius. "Fret-Sawing and Wood-Carving." *Harper's New Monthly Magazine*, Vol. 56, No. 334, March 1878, pp. 533–540.

Willey, Lora. Hampden, Massachusetts. Correspondence with author, 13 October 1987.

Williams, Anne D. "Puzzle? or Game? or Both?" *Game Times*, No. 10, August 1988, pp. 190–192.

———. *Jigsaw Puzzles: An Illustrated History and Price Guide*. Radnor, Pennsylvania: Wallace-Homestead (Chilton), 1990.

———. "Jigsaw Puzzles." *Fine Woodworking*, No. 88, May/June 1991, pp. 52–55.

———. "Depression Jigsaw Mania: The 'Webster School' of Puzzle Cutting." *Game Times*, No. 17, April 1992, pp. 352–353.

———. "Hollywood Goes to Pieces." *Game Researchers' Notes*, No. 14, June 1993, pp. 5317–5320.

———. "Falling for a . . . Falls." *Game Times*, No. 21, August 1993, pp. 458–459.

———. "Leisure in the Great Depression: The Many Pieces of the Jigsaw Puzzle Story." *Ephemera Journal 6*, 1993, pp. 99–115.

———. "All-Fair Games, Cards, and Puzzles." *Game Times*, No. 24, August 1994, pp. 514–519.

———. "Puzzling Pursuits." *Country Home*, December 1994, pp. 34, 36.

———. *Cutting A Fine Figure: The Art of the Jigsaw Puzzle*. Lexington, Massachusetts: Museum of Our National Heritage, 1996.

———. "Einson-Freeman: Depression 'House of Fads.'" *Game Times*, No. 32, April 1997, pp. 4–16.

———. "Jigsaw Puzzles." *Early American Homes*, December 1997, pp. 28–31, 78.

———. "Jigsaw Bits: Phyllis McLellan." *Game Researchers' Notes* 28, 1998, pp. 5653, 5656–5657.

———. "Bernard J. Roemer: Puzzle Entrepreneur." *Game Researchers' Notes* 29, 1999, pp. 5676–5683.

———. "Jigsaw Puzzles: Their Long Popular Reign." in *The Art of the Puzzle: Astounding and Confounding*. Katonah, New York: Katonah Museum of Art, 2000.

———. "Pieces of History: Steve Richardson and Stave Puzzles." *Game and Puzzle Collectors Quarterly* 2:1, March 2001, pp. 8–11.

———. "Tales of the Underside." *Game and Puzzle Collectors Quarterly* 2:3, September 2001, pp. 9–10.

———. "War and Pieces." *Collector*, November 2001, pp. 23–28.

———. "Personalized du Pont Gifts." *Game and Puzzle Collectors Quarterly* 3:1, March 2002, pp. 14–15.

———. "Puzzles in Films." *Game and Puzzle Collectors Quarterly* 3:2, June 2002, pp. 10–13.

———. "Metamorphic Puzzles: Changeable Charlie's Genealogy." *Game and Puzzle Collectors Quarterly* 3:3, September 2002, pp. 8–11.

———. "Making Par: Puzzles for the Rich and Famous." *Game and Puzzle Collectors Quarterly* 3:4, December 2002, pp. 6–15.

———. "Madmar: The Quality Company." *Game and Puzzle Collectors Quarterly* 4:1, March 2003, pp. 6–11.

———. *Index of Pre-1971 U.S. Jigsaw Puzzle Manufacturers*. Photocopied, May 2003.

Wilton, Katherine. "3-D Puzzle Master." *Montreal Gazette*, September 27, 1993, p. F3.

Wolkomir, Richard. "The 'Rolls-Royce of Puzzles' Drives Its Fans Round the Bend." *Smithsonian*, May 1990, pp. 103–112.

Wykes, Sara L. "Stanford Professor to Market His Brain Teaser on TV." *San Jose Mercury News*, December 4, 2003.

Yao, Feng-Hui, and Gui-Feng Shao, "A Shape and Image Merging Technique to Solve Jigsaw Puzzles." *Pattern Recognition Letters* 24 (2003), pp. 1819–1835.

Zandonella, Catherine. "Giotto's Giant Jigsaw." *New Scientist*, June 30, 2001, p. 24.

Zeisel, Joseph S. "The Workweek in American Industry." *Monthly Labor Review*, January 1958, pp. 23–29.

Index

The author is engaged in continuing research on the history of jigsaw puzzles, their makers, and their use. She welcomes comments from readers. Please send them to: Anne D. Williams, Department of Economics, Bates College, 4 Andrews Road, Lewiston, Maine 04240.